The Official Photo CD Handbook

The Official Photo CD Handbook

Michael Gosney
Bill Hurter/Amy Stone/Mark Kaproff
Ray Baggarley
Brian Lawler
Jackie Estrada

A VERBUM INTERACTIVE GUIDE

PEACHPIT PRESS

The Official Photo CD Handbook
Michael Gosney et al Verbum, Inc.

Peachpit Press
2414 Sixth Street
Berkeley, California 94710
510-548-4393
510-548-5991 (fax)

Peachpit Press is a division of Addison-Wesley Publishing Company.

For a free catalog of Verbum books and CD-ROMs on digital creativity, contact: Verbum, P.O. Box 189, Cardiff, CA 92007
tel 619-944-9977, fax 619-944-9995, net pubinfo@verbum.com

Bookmakers:
Orchestration: Michael Gosney
Editorial and project management: Jackie Estrada
Production coordination: Leslie Banach
Design: John Odam and Janet Ashford
Production: Richard Carter, Gale Spitzley
Proofreading: Cathy Riggs
Graphics: Ed Roxburgh
Photography: Craig McClain

Disc Crafters:
Orchestration: Michael Gosney
Production coordination: Leslie Banach
Sound production: Jack Lampl, Erik Thompson
Interface and disc design: Michael Gosney and John Odam
Screen graphics: John Odam and Janet Ashford
Music composition and performance: Janet Ashford
Integration and premastering: Ray Baggarley (Digital Quickcolor, Irvine, CA)
Disc mastering: Carol Whaley (Wayne's World, Eastman Kodak Company, Rochester, NY)
Case study section: Kathy Bauer (Advanced Digital Imaging, Fort Collins, CO)
Photo CD services: Kim Kapin (Zzyzx Visual Systems, Los Angeles)

The Official Photo CD Handbook is a Verbum, Inc. production.

ISBN: 1-56609-172-1

10 9 8 7 6 5 4 3 2 1

Printed on recycled paper

Printed and bound in the United States of America

Producer:
Michael Gosney

Managing/Developmental Editor:
Jackie Estrada

Chief Writers:
Bill Hurter/Amy Stone/Mark Kaproff
Ray Baggarley
Brian Lawler

Contributors:
Carla King
Daphne Aurness and Richard Carson
Rosanne Esposito
Paul Goethel
Ken Hornbeck
Kathy Bauer

Vital Input and Support:
Linnea Dayton
Bernice Glenn
Phil Heller
Jay Torrance
Tim Corman
Randy Baer
Greg Walker
Craig Aurness
Claire Donahue
Susan Scott
Sal Parascandolo
Jeff Brice
Jeanne Juneau

Eastman Kodak Company
Digital Quick Color
Zzyzx Visual Systems
Advanced Digital Imaging
AXS
Westlight
Digital Stock
Firehouse Imaging

Contents

Foreword

by Scott Brownstein

Looking back, it really hasn't been that long—just a heartbeat in the history of imaging—but at the pace of innovation in digital imaging, 1987 was really a very long time ago. At Kodak, we had spent years trying to improve the photographic process with new films, cameras, and even some significant electronics. We were spending considerable time developing ways to help people use their images, rather than working on the photographic process itself.

When my group started work on dry thermal printing in 1983, there were few ways of printing manipulated digital images, let alone viewing them. In those days, digital imaging was limited to wonderful images of the planets that had been beamed back from unmanned spacecraft. The low-cost, full-color video card that sells today for $600 was unavailable at any price, and the ability to freeze and view images was reserved for very special broadcast video applications. But by 1985, high-quality, nonphotographic digital image printing was not only commonly available, it had already outstripped the quality available from the electronic image-capture devices of the day.

In the latter half of the 80s, it was obvious to those of us in the field that no matter what use "electronic" photographs were to have, film digitization would be the first step in the electronic process. High-quality film scanners were expensive and hard to use. It was clear that if owning and operating a film scanner were a required first step in the hybrid imaging process, few people would even begin the journey.

Visionaries in the computer industry like John Sculley and Scott McNealy knew that color imaging was the future for desktop computing, but few could see where quality images would come from in the first place. Of course, someday "all-electronic" photography would solve the problem by supplying instantly digitized, high-quality images—but we all knew that day was at least a decade off. It seemed as though the desktop color revolution was bogged down for lack of a standard image input method, and none of us wanted to wait another decade or two for electronic cameras to catch up.

We had just finished perfecting thermal dye sublimation printing of digital images, which surprisingly eclipsed the quality of chemical-based systems in a mere four or five years. We were stuck—video images just wouldn't do, but quality film scanners cost more than the total capital that even the most well-to-do consumers were willing to invest.

From today's viewpoint, the answer is obvious, but back then you had to sort of ignore some major implementation details to see it. Film digitization had to become part of the photographic process, with scanning, image compression, and digital recording occurring in the film processing lab, not on the user's desktop. In effect, the consumer would "rent" a scanner for a few minutes rather than buy one. But even assuming sufficient scanner speed could be achieved, how would the data be delivered to the user? A single high-quality color scan would occupy at least a minimum of 5 million bytes, which meant that a whole 24-exposure roll of 35mm film would fill more than a hundred floppy discs! Storage would be a problem, and clearly the situation required some form of optical memory. Writable CD-ROM would be great—but it didn't exist in 1988.

Playback, too, would be a problem. Every user would need a new, hopefully low-cost device to read back the digital data either for video display or computer usage. These players would have to be relatively inexpensive and multipurpose, since dedicated playback equipment is generally anathema in the marketplace. In the end, the advantages of a writable CD were just too overwhelming and we eventually forced the definition of the "multisession" CD-recordable specification and got the CD-ROM drive vendors and CD standards owners to buy in. Although countless hours of product definition, problem solving, and translation to management would follow, the basic technical strategy for what was to become Photo CD was complete.

While I pushed the project forward, two "partners in crime" recognized the potential of the system in the developing desktop computer market and joined the effort. Georgia McCabe was attempting to formulate a product and partnership strategy for Kodak in the coming era of desktop color imaging. Leveraging her 15 years of experience at IBM, she was desperately trying to get the company to recognize not only what the future world of digital imaging would look like, but also the nature of partnerships that we would have to develop with other important industry players, such as Apple, Microsoft, Adobe, and Quark. She immediately saw Photo CD as Kodak's opportunity to leverage its imaging experience and market reach into the digital world.

The other key player was Surinder Dahiya, a fantastic systems architect and free spirit, who at the time was employed by Kodak's Interactive Systems Division in Boulder, Colorado. An avid skier recovering from a recent accident, Surinder was looking for a challenge to take his mind off the recuperation process. Luckily for us, he was excited by the opportunity of helping to develop Photo CD and moved to Rochester for a six-month stint—which eventually stretched into years. Georgia became the major marketing and partnership strategist, positioning us with important partners in the industry, while Surinder and his team developed the final specifications for Photo CD and its extensions like Pro and Portfolio, as well as negotiating multisession recording and writable CD features with Philips and Sony. His lab in Boulder integrated the first high-speed scanning and CD recording systems that now crank out Photo CD discs in numerous processing labs throughout the world.

Hundreds of dedicated people were involved in developing Photo CD technology, devoting long hours and lost weekends to the effort. Several pieces of the Photo CD system were in fact monumental development programs in themselves. When we started, writable CD was just a laboratory curiosity. Recorded discs were physically and environmentally unstable—hardly an ideal medium for storage of priceless images. Kodak's Mass Memory Division, faced with the inevitable corporate restructuring, dug deep and developed durable, manufacturable CD media, delivering inventions on schedule in time for the product introduction in 1992. There were many long nights, but that's what we signed on for.

Was Photo CD a consumer product or really a commercial system clothed in consumer disguise? I always believed that it was both, with commercial markets instantly able to recognize a cost-effective solution to existing problems. Patience and education are always required for any new consumer product category. Consumer Imaging "rules the roost" at Kodak, and, while the consumer machine went into motion with TV advertisements and press conferences, our team quietly continued forging important alliances in the computer world. Apple's John Sculley shared our vision and became not only a key supporter encouraging collaboration with Apple, but a personal friend as well. Others in the industry recognized the impact that high-quality imaging would have on the desktop. While partially compatible with existing CD-ROM drives, modifications to future designs would be necessary not only for full compatibility with Photo CD but with Writable CD as well. The specification was written so as to require minimal CD-ROM drive modifications and no operating system software modifications at all. Technical teams from drive manufacturers often visited Surinder's lab and left a few days later with fully Photo CD–compatible products.

The Photo CD team operated as a company within a company, and while senior Kodak management understood the basic strategy, they were after a quick hit and had a hard time understanding our real vision. The Kodak machine was content with its consumer approach to the product, and our team's quiet commercial strategy soon fell victim—just as commercial market interest and acceptance blossomed.

Photo CD was quickly accepted by computer industry visionaries, but for us, the situation at Kodak was fraught with conflict. Continual corporate restructuring brought new managers with little knowledge of our vision, history, or accomplishments. It became increasingly difficult to publicly represent Kodak and maintain our own reputations in the computer world. Eventually Georgia, Surinder, and I, along with 15 of our colleagues from Photo CD, decided to leave as a group to form a digital imaging division for Applied Graphics Technology, a leading prepress and printing company owned by Mortimer Zuckerman and Fred Drasner. Fred was the antithesis of Kodak management at that time, running not only AGT but also *The New York Daily News, US News & World Report,* and *The Atlantic Monthly.* Unlike many senior Kodak managers, he knew that another wave was about to hit the publishing industry and wanted to lead rather than follow the transition.

Photo CD is by now firmly entrenched in the world of digital imaging. Kodak management, changed from the top down in recent years, now has a realistic vision of Photo CD, and the commercial users of the new medium will keep management realistic. Although many misunderstandings clouded its early adoption, Photo CD is well on its way toward becoming a de facto standard. And, as is the case with any well-implemented idea, new market demands and an endless stream of developing technologies are still allowing us to extend it into virgin territory.

Introduction

by Michael Gosney

Welcome to *The Official Photo CD Handbook—A Verbum Interactive Guide*. This book/CD has as its subject the juncture of photographic film and digital media. Photo CD is an exciting new standard in digital imaging technology. It has a wide range of professional applications and offers consumers an inexpensive, convenient way to display pictures on their television or desktop computer.

Photo CD is a 21st-century gesture from Eastman Kodak Company, the celebrated icon of American ingenuity and world leader in photographic media products. The diversified marketing giant was not going to be left behind as the digital revolution kicked into gear at the beginning of this decade; Kodak launched Photo CD as a way to link emulsion-based imaging with the ever-expanding world of computer-based media.

As with most breakthrough high tech products, the vision and drive to develop Photo CD technology came from a small, inspired team within the company (Scott Brownstein, point man of the Photo CD group at Kodak, shares his perspectives in the Foreword). Although Kodak's mass market–minded management was disappointed when broad consumer adoption of Photo CD didn't materialize, it wasn't long before the professional markets responded to the potentially revolutionary benefits of the new medium. Today, publishers, designers, photographers, video and presentation producers, and multimedia developers are using Photo CD for economical and convenient image scanning, storage, display, and transport. And the consumer market is growing, along with the gradual acceptance of Photo CD–compatible multimedia for the home.

Photo CD is a family of products and services, combining the basic retail service model of the film business with the new paradigm of desktop-based digital media production. Photo CD is a medium offered for use by authorized service providers, photo labs, and digital service bureaus that have invested in Kodak's Photo Imaging Workstations, which scan slides or negatives into a proprietary digital format and store them on an optical disc. With several formats now available—for standard photography, professional photography, and multimedia presentations—Photo CD offers many applications, with very definite advantages over other media in economy, convenience, and cross-platform compatibility.

Who This Book Is For

Beyond the basic consumer service, Photo CD products and services are being used by professionals in such varied fields as photography, graphic design, desktop publishing, presentation production, and multimedia development. This book is for professional communicators in all of these areas as well as for photography and computer enthusiasts. *The Official Photo CD Handbook* is also meant as a reference work on Photo CD for anyone involved in these professional fields.

Digital media create a blurring of boundaries between specialized practices that were once distinct. Hence, photographers have become more involved with the craft and tools of graphic designers (and vice versa), designers are working with music, videographers with typography, and so on. Creative cross-fertilization between fields is also encouraged by these interoperable digital media systems. Photo CD, as a truly cross-platform, cross-disciplinary standard, is a powerful symbol of this pervasive digital media convergence.

How to Use This Book

Throughout the book, you will find sidebars on specialized subjects and on the three Photo CD formats, case studies of real-world uses of Photo CD, and supportive infographics and illustrations. The book also contains two companion CDs: a Photo CD Portfolio disc with multimedia presentations, and a CD-ROM with software and usable Photo CD images.

Part I, Photo CD: An Overview, covers the technology and its evolution, the range of Photo CD products, and the various professional applications. You will want to read this section to get the big picture of Photo CD.

To learn the hands-on basics of Photo CD, Part II, Working with Photo CD Images, offers the essential information. It explains in detail how to put photos on a disc and how to access, edit, manage, and disseminate images with Photo CD.

The next three sections focus on the primary fields in which Photo CD products are being used: print, presentations, and multimedia. If one of these is your field, you should find ample guidance in the appropriate section, and you may also find the other sections of interest.

For a glimpse of specialized uses of Photo CD in libraries and museums, and for medical applications, see the final section, Part VI, Other Photo CD Applications. Many custom uses of Photo CD are in development, and this section gives an idea of the possibilities.

Appendix I offers information about using the companion Portfolio disc and software CD-ROM. The other appendixes offer listings of Photo CD service bureaus, technical information, and software resources. Finally, a comprehensive Glossary and a selection of special-offer coupons from leading Photo CD vendors round out the book content. But wait, there's more . . .

ABOUT THE COMPANION PORTFOLIO AND CD-ROM DISCS

The Official Photo CD Handbook has two additional components: an informative and entertaining multimedia Portfolio disc, and a CD-ROM packed with software and Photo CD images. Both discs work on Mac or Windows systems.

Photo CD Portfolio is a relatively new format that offers a basic interactive multimedia presentation environment, allowing for not only photos but also graphics and sound. Portfolio discs will play on Macs and IBM-compatible PCs, as well as on Photo CD players connected to televisions.

The Official Photo CD Handbook disc offers an overview of Photo CD technology, Case Studies in the use of Portfolio, and "edutainment" in the form of narrated presentations in the Photography, Digital Art, and Presentation galleries. The design, custom music, on-line help, and sample content make for an instructional resource that we hope inspires use of this convenient format.

The "hybrid" Mac/Windows CD-ROM offers usable Photo CD files from leading stock publishers, sound files, and demo applications for working with Photo CD from Kodak, Adobe, Apple, and others. Simply copy them to your hard drive, but please be sure to read the accompanying notices.

HOW THIS "INTERACTIVE GUIDE" CAME TO BE

In 1992, we at Verbum were working with Kodak and several other companies on a compact four-color guide called *The Desktop Color Book* (second edition published in 1995 by MIS Press), which led to another book in the same format, *The Photo CD Book*

(Verbum Books). That book, published in winter 93/94, was the first comprehensive reference on Photo CD—quite a challenge since many of the Kodak products were still formative. At the same time, we were producing a major multimedia production guide, *Multimedia Power Tools—A Verbum Interactive Book* (Random House), a complex project involving many contributors and the development of an ambitious, instructional multimedia CD-ROM linked to the book. We realized that Photo CD was a similarly broad subject also in need of a comprehensive book/disc package. Peachpit Press expressed interest, as did Kodak and many other key players in the field, and the project was launched.

The diverse subject matter covered in *The Official Photo CD Handbook* required several writers with different areas of expertise. These experts in turn worked closely with various parties within Kodak and, equally important, with the numerous groups and individuals who are pioneering the wide variety of Photo CD applications in the field. Managing editor Jackie Estrada worked her magic in weaving a coherent text from all these different voices.

The Portfolio disc was produced by the Verbum team, with the help of several outside groups, including Ray Baggarley and the Digital QuickColor division of Sir Speedy in Irvine, California, who authored the disc; Joel White and the folks at Wayne's World in Rochester (the Photo CD laboratory at Kodak headed by Wayne Niskala), who mastered the disc; Kim Kapin of Zzyzx in Los Angeles, who handled the Photo CD processing; and Kathy Bauer at Advanced Digital Imaging in Fort Collins, Colorado, who produced the Case Studies section. The photographers, artists, and presentation producers who contributed to the Gallery sections gave valuable time and resources to the development of their material.

Regarding Verbum, we've been around since the mid-1980s, educating people in the use of creative digital tools with the original *Verbum* magazine, the Verbum *Interactive* CD-ROM, and many books and events. This project, like all the publications we've produced, involved many talented people, whose inspired, diligent work led to the book you are now holding.

Thanks for using *The Official Photo CD Handbook*. We hope you enjoy and benefit from it in many ways!

Part I

PHOTO CD: AN OVERVIEW

1
What Is Photo CD?

Photographic images permeate our lives. We see photos in abundance in newspapers and magazines, on TV news programs and commercials, in brochures and catalogs, on billboards and posters, in slide shows and annual reports. We take pictures for business, pleasure, and artistic purposes. Our homes and workplaces are filled with snapshots of kids, pets, weddings, and vacation spots, as well as our favorite "arty" photos.

We've all heard about the "digital revolution" in photography—about how computers are changing the face of the way photography is done. Digital cameras—which bypass film altogether—are beginning to make inroads into professional and amateur markets. What effect will these changes have on the role of photographs and photography in our professional and personal lives?

Photography is a pervasive part of our lives.

The fact is that film remains the best, cheapest, fastest, and most accurate way to capture an image in an instant. Where the digital revolution *has* made a major impact on the photographic industry is in converting photos to digital form so they can be retouched, enhanced, and manipulated using sophisticated image-editing software; incorporated into publications from brochures to complex textbooks; and prepared for print output, whether color or black and white. Further, digitized images can be incorporated into slide shows (using presentation software), digital video projects (such as TV commercials), and multimedia projects (such as interactive programs and games sold in various compact disc forms).

With all the demand for and applications of digitized photos, it was only natural for Kodak, the longtime giant in film and photographic processing, to devise a new technology for processing and storing images digitally. You can now have your film fed into state-of-the-art equipment and get back not only your usual prints or slides but a gold-coated disc that contains your images in a versatile and powerful digital format. That disc is a Photo CD.

From Film to Disc

Since desktop publishing took hold in the 1980s, photographers, designers, and others who want to work with images on their computers have usually sent their photos or slides out to a service bureau to have them scanned (digitized), or they have invested in their own scanning equipment. This scanning can be expensive and time consuming. Photo CD technology now offers an alternative means for bridging the gap between film and the electronic image displayed on a computer or video screen.

Photo CD starts with film and ends with a disc. Here's how it works: You take one or more rolls of 35mm slide or negative film to a photo processor or service bureau equipped with a Kodak Photo Imaging Workstation (PIW). Your film is processed as usual (you get back your negatives or slides), but it is also run through the Kodak PCD scanner, which converts all the images to a proprietary digital file format. These files are then written to a compact disc that now contains all your photos in digitized form. If you don't fill up the disc the first time around, you can put additional images on later. You receive your disc in a standard CD jewelcase, along with a small print containing thumbnails of all of the images on the disc.

Once you have a disc, you need to be able to view or acquire the images on it. They can be accessed for viewing on either a TV

A Kodak Photo CD disc can be ordered from a photofinisher at the same time a roll of film is dropped off for processing. The Photo CD is delivered along with processed film. It comes in the same kind of CD case used for most audio CDs and CD-ROM discs. Inside the cover of the case is one or more sheets of index prints—small thermal prints of the images on the disc. Both the disc and the index prints show the disc's identifying number. In addition, the sheet of index prints gives file access numbers for each image.

4

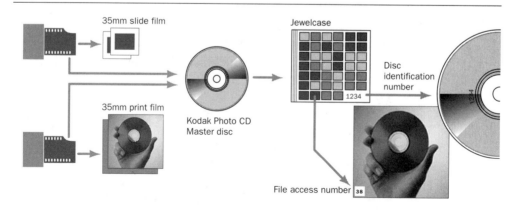

35mm slide film

Jewelcase

Disc identification number

1234

35mm print film

Kodak Photo CD Master disc

File access number 38

screen or a computer monitor. You can view the images on a television set by using a Kodak Photo CD player, a CD-I player, or a 3DO interactive multiplayer. Playback requires a remote control device that allows you to simply view the photos in order or to alter the sequence, zoom in, crop, rotate, and make other limited changes to photos and sequencing (depending on the player).

You can access Photo CD images on a personal computer by putting the disc into a compatible CD-ROM player and then using one of several applications to pull the image files from the disc into the computer's RAM or hard drive. Once imported into your computer, the digital files can be accessed for use in image editing, page layout, presentation, and other applications.

The Many Aspects of Photo CD

Put most simply, a Photo CD is a disc that contains digital images. Put a little less simply, it can be described as any of the following:

- *A CD-ROM.* CD-ROMs are discs that look like the audio CDs that you can play on any CD player, but they contain computer-readable data in one of a couple of special formats. The format that Photo CD uses is called ISO 9660.

Photo CD images can be played on a TV through a Kodak Photo CD player or other compatible multimedia player. They can also be loaded from a CD-ROM XA drive into a computer for image editing and for use with graphic design and presentation software.

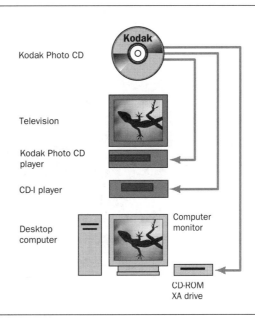

Kodak Photo CD

Television

Kodak Photo CD player

CD-I player

Desktop computer

Computer monitor

CD-ROM XA drive

- *A set of digitized images.* Each image on a Photo CD has been scanned on a special system (the Kodak PIW) and stored in a special format called an image pac. Each image pac represents a single scan, but the information is stored in such a way that you can retrieve that image in several resolutions from a single image pac. (*Resolution* refers to the amount of visual information stored in a file; the higher the resolution, the more detail and the greater the size of the file.)

- *An Eastman Kodak Company product.* Kodak developed the proprietary format, manufactures the systems that make the discs, releases new variations of Photo CD, writes software for computers, and makes consumer players to access the discs.

The basic Photo CD format, called Photo CD Master, is what most people mean when they talk about "Photo CD." A Photo CD Master disc can store about 100 images in image pac format.

Kodak has developed two other formats of Photo CD to serve particular purposes. The Pro Photo CD Master disc stores higher-resolution images than the Master disc and also allows for scanning 120 and 4 x 5 format transparencies and negatives. Photo CD Portfolio II fills multiple functions: for the purpose of the publishing industry, it can hold images and files for color prepress, while in multimedia production it serves as a storage medium, holding both images (in a variety of formats) and sound for playback on either computers or TVs equipped with an appropriate player.

Photo CD originally had five disc formats. The Photo CD Master disc and Pro Photo CD disc store digital versions of photos in "image pac" format. Photo CD Catalog was designed to hold thousands of thumbnail images. Print Photo CD (now part of Portfolio II) stored image files prepared for four-color printing. Photo CD Portfolio discs were used primarily for storing and playing multimedia presentations.

As you can see, Photo CD is actually a number of products that can be used for image digitizing, storage, and retrieval. The chapters that follow will tell more about these disc formats, how they're made, and how they can be used.

Why Photo CD?

Although we've briefly defined *what* Photo CD is, there's still the question of *why* it is. The answer lies in cost, quality, speed, storage, and portability.

- *Cost.* A high-quality scan at a service bureau can cost $50 to $200. Photo CD scans cost as little as $1 per image.

- *Quality.* The quality of Photo CD images is higher than that obtained from many desktop film scanners or flatbed scanners costing $15,000 to $20,000. The scans approach the quality of those from drum scanners, costing $25,000 to $1,000,000.

- *Speed.* Making a Photo CD is fast enough to meet the short turnaround time needed in newspaper and magazine publishing, as well as other fields with tight deadlines between when photographs are taken and when they must be reproduced.

- *Cross-platform compatibility.* Not only can Photo CD discs be accessed from any computer platform equipped with a CD-ROM XA drive, the Photo CD image pac format is a universal form of image file that is platform-independent.

Each Photo CD Master disc is packaged in a standard CD jewelcase and is accompanied by thumbnail versions of the images on the disc. Index numbers can be punched up on a Photo CD player remote control to view specific images on a TV screen.

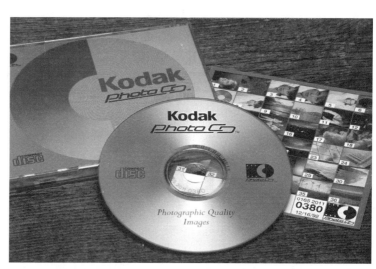

- *Storage.* A Photo CD Master disc can store about 600 MB or, on average, 100 images. The cost of the disc may be included in the scann ing, or it might be as much as an additional $15. Even with the surcharge, the cost is far below what it would cost in magneto-optical cartridges or other media to store the same data.

- *Portability.* Photo CD discs replace slides and prints for a variety of purposes that make images more easy to handle. A disc is easier to take to a meeting or presentation than a notebook or carousel full of slides. And the discs are easily sent through the mail.

Photo CD in Action

In its short time in the digital marketplace, Photo CD has already been adapted for a wide variety of uses. Here are just a few examples of how it's being put to work today.

BY PHOTOGRAPHERS

Putting both new and old photos on Photo CD discs helps photographers organize and manage their images. And Photo CD's low cost and high quality are enabling photographers to put more photos in a digital form for sending to clients, whether as a portfolio of the photographer's work or for immediate use. Some photographers are even offering "photo albums" of weddings and other events on Photo CD.

Photographers can also build "new" images on the desktop by combining parts of existing photos—without altering the original images stored on the Photo CD disc.

Issues of particular concern to photographers—putting images on Photo CD discs, retrieving the images, editing them, and managing them—are discussed in Part II of this book.

BY STOCK PHOTO AGENCIES

Many agencies are putting all their stock photos on Photo CD media for ease in cataloging and access. They can supply customers with discs full of thumbnail samples and then provide either physical photos or digital files of chosen images. Some agencies are also creating digital databases for online access to thumbnails or to the usable images themselves. The use of Photo CD for stock

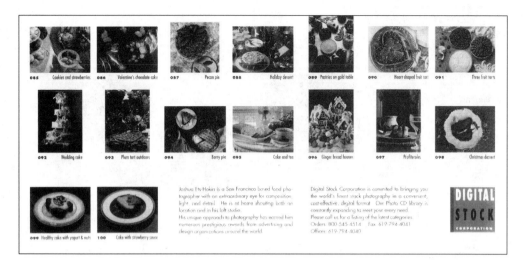

Some stock photo agencies are supplying images in Photo CD format.

photography is discussed in Chapter 9.

BY DESIGNERS AND ART DIRECTORS

Designers who work with desktop systems, whether preparing ads, brochures, posters, magazine layouts, or book designs, find Photo CD image files useful for a number of purposes. Because each image on a PCD disc comes in multiple resolutions, designers can use thumbnail versions for doing comps and layouts and later use the high-resolution versions for final editing and output. The PCD disc format was designed to be compatible with most desktop systems equipped with CD-ROM drives, so there's no worry about having the "right" version of a disc for your computer platform. And the Photo CD files are easily accessed with popular image-editing programs such as Adobe Photoshop, with page layout software, or with Kodak's own software. Chapters 6 and 7 provide detailed information on accessing and editing Photo CD images; Chapter 10 describes the use of Photo CD with page layout programs.

BY MAGAZINES AND NEWSPAPERS

Publications that use hundreds or even thousands of photos each year are always looking for more efficient ways to manage the flow of photographs, from selection to production to storage. Some of these high-volume photo users have turned to Photo CD in their streamlining efforts. They're asking assignment photographers to turn in film that goes directly to Photo CD processing. Photo CD images at low resolution are then used in page layouts, while the

One of Photo CD's advantages is that the same scan can be used for multiple purposes because it makes the image available in several resolutions.

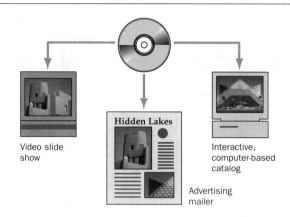

Video slide show

Hidden Lakes

Interactive, computer-based catalog

Advertising mailer

high-resolution versions are edited separately and used for final output. And even publications that use photos in smaller volume are finding that Photo CD technology is an economical way to obtain high-quality digital images. Part III examines print media applications, including desktop publishing processes, printing considerations, and high-end prepress issues.

BY AD AGENCIES AND MARKETERS

It didn't take long for innovative makers of TV commercials to discover that Photo CD offers an inexpensive way to incorporate large numbers of high-quality still photos into video productions. Producers like the cost savings at the scanning stage and the choice of resolutions for playback. And as with magazines and newspapers, print ad production can be enhanced by Photo CD technology. Of particular interest to advertisers is that the same image can be used for both print and electronic media, because it is available in multiple resolutions. Another economical advertising application of Photo CD is for product catalogs that require dozens or even hundreds of color photos.

BY CORPORATIONS

Corporations are finding a multitude of uses for Photo CD. Because of the archival quality of Photo CD discs, many companies are using them for long-term storage of data, and not just photos. Others are converting their photo archives to digital form, so that the images can be cataloged, stored, and retrieved for such purposes as company brochures, annual reports, and stock photo rental. Corporations are also incorporating PCD images into presentations produced with conventional presentation software or Kodak's own presentation authoring system, Portfolio CD. Presentation applications are described in Part IV.

BY MULTIMEDIA PRODUCERS

Producers using desktop multimedia authoring systems are incorporating Photo CD images into such products as CD-ROM magazines, games, marketing/promotional projects, and training programs. They are also taking advantage of Kodak's own authoring system, Portfolio, to produce discs that combine images, sound, and interactivity. You'll find a detailed discussion of multimedia uses for Photo CD, including how to publish and duplicate discs, in Part V.

BY INSTITUTIONS

Universities, libraries, and museums are among the institutions that have developed Photo CD–related projects. Many are using Photo CD to archive valuable documents, artwork, and scientific collections. Researchers and students can study the images on the Photo CD discs while the original materials remain safely stored. These institutions are also cataloging and organizing their digitized collections and making them available on national and international database networks.

Some schools are developing teaching materials that incorporate PCD images, from creating Photo CD Master discs of great works for an art history course to authoring an interactive program containing images of eye diseases to prepare ophthalmology students for exams. Part VI describes a number of institutional and medical uses for Photo CD.

Throughout this book you will find case studies highlighting some of the exciting ways in which individuals and organizations are using Photo CD to meet their own particular needs. You will learn about both the advantages and limitations of Photo CD for each of these applications. In addition, the Portfolio disc included with this book provides many examples of Photo CD in action. See the Appendix for an overview of the disc and instructions on how to use it.

2

How Photo CD Technology Evolved

Photo CD has been heralded as a revolutionary new approach that will change the whole way we use photos. Although that remains to be seen, at the very least, Photo CD promises to be a milestone along the path of technology that began in the middle of the nineteenth century, when photographers first began recording images on emulsion-coated copper or glass plates.

While the artistic or documentary aim of photography—to capture and preserve visual images—has remained much the same for over a hundred years, photographic technology has seen monumental changes, with a continuing general trend in making the photographic process easier, more precise and accurate, and more reliable. At the same time, the practice of photography has spread to a broader and broader population of participants and viewers.

A look back at some of the milestones along the road of photo technology provides a background that may help us see where Photo CD fits in:

- The development of the negative-to-positive process in the late 1800s made it easier to retouch and reproduce photos.

- The evolution of a film base (instead of glass or copper) to hold the emulsion that records the image made the photographic process easier and quicker.

- Eastman Kodak Company brought to market relatively small, easy-to-use, and inexpensive snapshot cameras for amateur photographers, from the first Kodak in 1888 to the fixed-focus Brownie in 1900 to the Instamatics of the 1960s and 1970s. These cameras used roll film, so that it was easy to take a series of pictures over time. And film processing was no longer a matter of maintaining a darkroom; rolls of film could be commercially processed into prints.

- Color photographic processes, in existence from the late 1800s, have become better and less expensive.

Over the course of nearly a century Kodak concentrated on improving ways of capturing images. Now the focus has shifted to ways of using the captured image.

- The development of the 35mm still camera, originally designed to use leftover movie film, was first applied in photojournalism and then for a segment of the consumer market ready for a higher-quality photographic system and the possibility of viewing images not only as prints collected in albums but also by projection on screens.

- Most recently, electronic scanning technology has made it possible to turn film images into digital copies that can be retouched, montaged, or manipulated outside the darkroom environment, inside the computer.

- As part of the revolution in publishing and printing, desktop technology has made it relatively easy and inexpensive to include photos in all kinds of printed pages and video screens.

Now, little more than a century after George Eastman introduced his first Kodak camera, the company he founded has launched what it proclaims is "the first new photographic medium in more than 100 years" and "a turning point in the history of photography": the Photo CD system, which combines both analog (film) and digital (computer) technologies.

Kodak maintains that film will remain the premiere image-capture medium for decades to come; other industry insiders and observers predict an all-digital imaging world in the not too distant future. Regardless of who is proven right, there is no doubt that the Photo CD format will play a significant role.

The Arrival of Photo CD

Photo CD technology is an outgrowth of the CD-ROM technology that was introduced worldwide in the early 1980s and of the audio compact discs pioneered by Sony and Philips. And that technology can trace its roots to the optical disc research carried out by the consumer electronics industry in the 1960s and 1970s, as manufacturers sought to develop home video disc systems that could be sold as accessories to TV sets.

While CD-ROM and Photo CD technology may be relatively new, the concept of easily storing and retrieving vast amounts of data, either text or images, is not. Writing in the *Atlantic Monthly* in 1945, Vannevar Bush, the first director of the U.S. Office of Scientific Research and Development, described "a future device for individual use, which is sort of a mechanized private file and library . . . a device in which an individual stores his books, records, and communications, and which is mechanized so that it may be consulted with exceeding speed and flexibility. It is an enlarged supplement to his memory." CD-ROMS come close to fulfilling that vision.

By the mid-1980s, audio CDs, with their superior sound fidelity and ruggedness, had taken off. CD-ROMs, in a variety of formats, were not far behind. By 1993 approximately 100 million CD-ROM discs were being manufactured worldwide. And the appetite for CD-ROM titles is only expected to grow; in 1994, for instance, the number of households with CD-ROM–equipped computers is estimated to have doubled.

Kodak was quick to recognize the potential of CD-ROM as a vehicle for electronically storing photos that had originally been captured on film. CD-ROM was inexpensive, could easily be incorporated into equipment for scanning film images, and was a rela-

The number of CD-ROM titles being produced has exploded in the past few years.

15

tively mature product. More important, Kodak saw this hybrid technology as a way to regain business lost to its rivals in electronic imaging. Camcorders, for example, had all but replaced home movie cameras. And the threat of electronic still cameras, notably the introduction of the Sony Mavica, gave greater impetus to Kodak to address what it perceived as a threat to its film business.

Those early electronic still cameras proved not to be such a threat after all. Their resolution was limited by the CCD, or sensor, that captured the images. And there was the problem of where to store the low-resolution images once they were recorded.

Instead of competing head-on with electronic still cameras, Kodak took the approach that film is still the best capture and source medium. And with millions upon millions of 35mm cameras already out in the marketplace, there would be a ready market for the proposed Photo CD technology.

The Photo CD idea not only maintained film sales—the heart of Kodak's imaging business—but allowed the company to move into the digital arena with a new and unique product.

Realizing that CD-ROM would hold the key as a new storage medium for photos, Kodak set out in 1989 to test the waters. It conducted surveys and focus groups with more than 2,000 people worldwide, asking them what they most wanted to see in a 35mm film system. (Respondents didn't know the survey was being conducted by Kodak.) The results showed that people wanted an easy, convenient way to share their "memories" with large groups of people. Prints, while still highly desirable, weren't particularly well suited for that purpose. Nor was having to drag out a slide projector and screen and darkening the room. Showing images on a TV set, in ambient light, was a popular choice. So that's what Kodak set out to do with Photo CD.

The Photo CD concept also answered another need: to help the so-called "back end" of the photographic process catch up with the advancements in the front end. Although automatic 35mm cameras and new films combined in the 1980s to enable photographers to take better pictures more easily, the process of storing and retrieving the resulting photos remained much as it had for decades. Now, instead of tossing pictures into a shoebox or drawer with the idea of one day putting them into an album— which most people never get around to—people could have that "album" chore essentially handled by the photofinisher. One or several rolls could be placed on a Photo CD disc at the time of processing, or certain images could be selected for placement on a disc.

In the spring of 1989, Kodak put together a team of people from various disciplines—research, marketing, manufacturing—to develop this new technology. Working outside the Kodak "mainstream," the group was able to avoid getting bogged down in the corporate bureaucracy. That may explain how Kodak was able to bring to market an entirely new product line in only 18 months.

From the outset, the Photo CD system had been designed as a consumer product. The idea was that when John Q. Public brought in rolls of 35mm film to his local photofinisher, he would get back not only prints or slides but a gold-colored Photo CD Master disc. Once back home, he could pop the disc into a Photo CD player and voilà—bright, beautiful high-resolution photos on his TV monitor.

By the time the Photo CD system hit the market in 1992—two years after it had been announced—all the pieces were in place. Kodak supplied Photo CD Imaging Workstations (PIWs) for photofinishers, retail photo stores, and commercial photo labs to scan 35mm negatives or transparencies to disc. Photo CD players (which could be hooked up to any TV set) had been developed jointly by Philips and Kodak. And the discs could also be used with

17

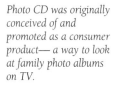

Photo CD was originally conceived of and promoted as a consumer product— a way to look at family photo albums on TV.

CD-ROM XA and CD-I drives (the latter developed by Philips in conjunction with Sony) to allow them to be viewed on a computer.

But despite Photo CD's arrival with much PR hoopla, consumers—who worldwide shoot some 60 billion photographs every year—didn't exactly beat down the doors to jump on the Photo CD bandwagon. Commercial users, on the other hand, quickly saw the potential of the system.

The Commercial Explosion

Among the first to recognize the value of the technology were people involved with desktop publishing. Photo CD technology gave them, for the first time, inexpensive and easy desktop access to high-quality photographic images. It didn't take long before commercial applications of Photo CD technology literally exploded. Any and all imaging applications, from archiving museum art collections to distributing stock photos to business and multimedia presentations, began to incorporate Photo CD scans or discs.

Photofinishers, for the most part, encouraged the growth of the commercial markets. Given the choice of handling high-volume, low-margin consumer business or low-volume, high-margin commercial accounts, most photofinishers opted for the latter. The higher price generally charged for those commercial applications has, up to now, been one of the greatest barriers to widespread consumer acceptance in the United States. In Europe, consumers have more readily embraced the Photo CD system.

PHOTO CD DISC FORMATS

With each new application, more demands have been placed on the technology. Kodak has responded with new formats, products, and applications. Even today, the technology continues to evolve at a rapid pace.

Here's a summary of the various Photo CD disc formats that Kodak already has available or that will soon be out:

- *Photo CD Master disc.* This is the disc that started it all. Designed for 35mm consumer photography, it can hold about 100 images. The disc stores each picture at five levels of resolution, in files called image pacs. The resolutions range from a low end of 128 x 192 pixels to a high of 2048 x 3072 pixels. The images are stored using the Photo YCC color encoding metric developed by Kodak. Also included on the disc is software that allows users of popular word-processing software to access the images on the disc. The technical details of YCC and image pacs are described in Chapter 3.

- *Pro Photo CD Master disc.* Pro Photo CD was developed for larger format films, including 120 and 4 x 5, favored by many professional photographers. Each disc can hold 25 to 50 images, depending on the film format. In addition to the same five levels of resolution as in the image pacs on Master discs, Pro Photo CD discs add an optional higher level of resolution: 4096 x 6144 pixels. Service bureaus set up with a Pro Photo CD PIW offer individual attention to each scan, so prices per scan are higher, as is the level of quality. You'll learn more about Pro Photo CD in Chapter 5.

- *Photo CD Portfolio II disc.* The Portfolio II disc is multipurpose. It can hold other file types in addition to image pac files. Portfolio was originally developed as a medium for storing and playing multimedia presentations. Thus, with a Portfolio disc and Kodak's Portfolio software, you combine photos, audio, graphics, text, and programmed access to create your own interactive sound-and-picture presentations. The discs can hold up to 700 TV-resolution images, making them ideal for business presentations, informational kiosks, trade show displays, and educational programs. This use of Portfolio II is covered in detail in Chapters 13 (for presentations) and 15 (for multimedia).

  In addition, Portfolio II can be used in printers as a prepress medium. The key feature is the disc's ability to store images in CMYK (cyan, magenta, yellow, and black), the color system used throughout the printing industry. It stores not only photographic images but complete page layouts and can also be used as a data storage medium. Chapter 11 offers further information on prepress uses of Portfolio II.

These disc formats have evolved as Photo CD technology has developed. A few other original formats' features have been folded into these three discs or are still being explored for future products. The discontinued products are Print Photo CD, whose features have been merged into Portfolio II, and Photo CD Catalog, which was intended for cataloging and storing thousands of low-resolution images. See Chapter 8 for more details.

Kodak Photo CD Master
"Digital negative"
Written by photofinishers
Full photographic resolution
images

Kodak Photo CD Portfolio
Multimedia/slide show
Written by photofinisher or on
a computer
Full- or display-resolution
images
Up to 700 images or 1 hour of
sound, or some combination
Optional text, graphics, audio,
and branching

Kodak Photo CD Catalog
Photo library
Written by photofinisher
on a computer
4,000 or more low-resolution images
Optional text, graphics, audio, and
branching

Kodak Pro Photo CD Master
Professional "digital negative"
Written by Professional Photo
CD Imaging Workstation
Supports larger film formats in
addition to 35mm
Supports higher-resolution film scans

Kodak Print Photo CD
Prepress "job jacket"
Written by Print Photo CD authoring
workstations
Compatible with CEPS prepress standards
Up to 100 images
Can store any type of digital file

Kodak originally announced five separate disc formats to meet a variety of needs. It has since announced a revised version of Portfolio, called Portfolio II, that incorporates the features of Print Photo CD in addition to its original multimedia features. Photo CD Catalog has been discontinued.

All of the Photo CD discs are 120mm platters; smaller 80mm discs, designed for laptops, notebooks, and personal digital assistants (PDAs), are in the works. The smaller discs will be compatible with the larger drives.

In addition to those disc formats, Kodak also offers *Writable CD,* which allows users to master CD-ROM discs from their desktop computers. This system is designed for low-volume commercial production of *data* CDs, with each disc holding the equivalent of 240,000 pages of text, or 550 high-density floppy discs. The authored writable CDs can be read by all standard hardware devices, including CD-ROMs, CD-ROM XA, CD-I, and CD audio players. For more on Writable CD, see Chapter 16.

KODAK'S PHOTO CD–RELATED SOFTWARE AND SUPPORT PRODUCTS

Kodak has developed a number of specialized software and support products to enable all the Photo CD technology to work. Some of these products are still in development and may not see the market place anytime soon. These packages range from image access software to presentation and multimedia authoring tools. Following is a brief overview of these products; each is covered in greater detail in appropriate chapters in the book:

- Photo CD *Access* is a package for casual users of Photo CD images. It's designed to import Photo CD images to current applications. It allows you to read and display the scanned images as well as crop, zoom, and rotate them.

- Photo CD *Access Plus,* also aimed at the casual user, supports all Photo CD formats and includes Photo CD Player software, which allows users to play Portfolio discs on any compatible CD-ROM drive.

- The Photo CD *Acquire Module* is a low-cost plug-in for Adobe Photoshop (the most popular image-editing software) that increases control over color when opening images from Photo CD Master and Pro Photo CD Master discs.

- *PhotoEdge* is an image-editing program that offers the ability to edit the overall appearance of images, including sharpening the focus and adjusting the color or contrast. It is available for both Windows-based and Macintosh platforms.

- Kodak *Shoebox* is for users who need to search through large numbers of stored images. It helps automate the storage and retrieval of images for anyone who maintains an image archive. Lower-resolution thumbnail images are stored in the database, which resides on a hard drive or similar media. Images can be

21

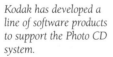
Kodak has developed a line of software products to support the Photo CD system.

Kodak's Family of Photo CD Software

Product	User	Description	Platform Supported
Photo CD Access	Casual users of PCD images	Low-cost tool designed to import Photo CD Master disc images to current applications; users can read and display PCD images and can crop, zoom, and rotate images	Windows, DOS, Macintosh
Photo CD Access Plus	Casual users of PCD images	Similar function to Access software; supports all PCD formats, including Pro Photo CD discs; includes Photo CD Player software, which allows users to play Portfolio discs on any compatible CD-ROM drive	Macintosh, Windows
Photo CD Acquire Module	Users of Adobe Photoshop wanting to import PCD images	Low-cost plug-in that increases control over color when opening images from PCD Master and Pro discs	Macintosh, Windows
PhotoEdge	Business presenters	Image enhancement and correction software that lets users do more advanced image correction and improvement	Macintosh, Windows

searched rapidly using key words on either a Windows-based or Macintosh computer.

- *Professional Photo CD Library* is an automated library, or "jukebox," that can hold up to 100 discs. To retrieve an image, you simply key in a request, and in seconds the image is located.

- *Kodak Picture Exchange* is a global on-line computer service linking more than a dozen stock photo agencies with photo buyers.

- *Create-It, Arrange-It,* and *Build-It* are software packages for authoring Photo CD Portfolio discs. Create-It is a presentation creation package, while Arrange-It and Build-It are components of a multimedia authoring and production system.

22

Kodak's Family of Photo CD Software			
Product	**User**	**Description**	**Platform Supported**
Shoebox	Users who need to search through large numbers of stored images	Helps automate storage and retrieval of images for anyone maintaining an image archive; users store lower-resolution thumbnail images on their hard drive or similar media; images can be searched rapidly, using key words	Macintosh, Windows
Create-It	Producers of presentations, slide shows	A presentation software package that lets users design slide shows; can output to slides, Portfolio discs, or computer screen	Macintosh
Arrange-It	Designers/ producers of multimedia projects for output to Portfolio discs	For designing advanced multimedia programs with sound and branching; can incorporate images and files from other applications	Macintosh, Windows
Build-It	Service bureaus and other producers of PCD Portfolio discs	Formats data for writing onto PCD Portfolio discs using the Kodak PCD Writer	Macintosh, Windows NT, Sun SPARCstation

23

Photo CD technology continues to evolve rapidly as users identify their needs for digital imaging. Throughout this book you will learn about many of the imaginative ways in which photographers, designers, educators, and others have taken the basics of this system and created their own unique applications.

3

How Photo CD Works

The advent of the Photo CD system does not make film obsolete; rather, it *enhances* film's usefulness. Photographers can continue taking photographs as they always have, on the film that they've always used, and receive the slides or prints to which they've always been accustomed. But, Photo CD technology maximizes the life and versatility of these images.

Photo CD is a remarkable process on many levels, and the technology is astounding, as you will see. This chapter deals with how the process works, taking you through the various stages, from capturing an image, through scanning and compression, to the many and varied ways the images on a Photo CD can be accessed.

The Storage Medium: Film Versus Photo CD

Film uses an analog, cause-and-effect system that has been in existence for over 150 years. When light reacts with the film's silver halide crystals, in the proper proportion and through a light-focusing lens system, a latent image of the scene is produced. Chemical processing is then necessary to "develop" the latent image and make it permanent.

Once processed, 35mm film, the most popular format by far, is a powerful image-storage medium. A 35mm slide is so densely packed with image information that it has no equivalent in the computer world—just approximations thereof. A 1 x 1½ 35mm color slide contains over 10 million bits of image information. Thus, film remains the most accurate way to record the maximum amount of visual data from a scene, especially when compared to other media, such as video and still-video. Furthermore, film images are extremely inexpensive to produce—only pennies per frame—which accounts for the fact that over 60 billion photographs are made each year.

But film images have some very definite limitations:

1. Film eventually ages and fades, making its survival over more

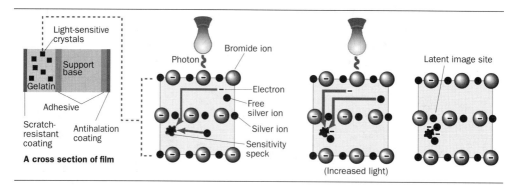

Light-sensitive crystals
Support base
Gelatin
Adhesive
Scratch-resistant coating
Antihalation coating

A cross section of film

Photon
Bromide ion
Electron
Free silver ion
Silver ion
Sensitivity speck

Latent image site

(Increased light)

In traditional photography, light (photons) strikes bromide ions in the light-sensitive crystals on the film. This releases electrons, which join free silver ions in migrating toward "sensitivity specks." As more light strikes the structure, more atoms of silver migrate to the speck until a "latent image" is formed. Developer magnifies the chemical charges and creates the visible image.

than a few decades questionable. Although great strides have been made to improve the manufacturing specifications and storage recommendations for film, the fact still remains that the dyes used in color film fade, and the image will eventually degrade significantly. While black-and-white negatives and prints are longer-lasting than color products, they, too, will eventually degrade; an "archivally treated" black-and-white image will last for about 100 years.

2. Film images degrade with every successive generation. A print, which is a second-generation image made from a negative, does not include all of the fine detail and image information contained in the original negative. A slide is a first-generation original, with all of the original data intact, but once a print or subsequent-generation image is made from a slide, much of its pristine detail is lost. And a printed reproduction, made with the four-color process, does not have anywhere near the data contained in the original image. The pictures you see printed in books and magazines are simply close approximations of the originals.

3. By its very nature, film is a limited medium. Processed film is basically a stand-alone system, incapable of being directly integrated into any system other than its own. You can make prints or slides, or duplicates of original negatives, but for more varied or sophisticated uses, film must be transferred to another medium, such as video. And in that process, image data are lost.

A Photo CD, on the other hand, manages to retain the best aspects of film—clarity, brilliance, and affordability of images—while circumventing all of film's inherent shortcomings. Photo CD

26

Images recorded on film cannot help but visually degrade over successive generations and enlargements. In the color section (page C4), you can see how the same image, duplicated as second- and third-generation slides, not only loses sharpness and gains contrast but shows a significant color shift from the original. Digitized images don't suffer these afflictions, because digital "dupes" are identical to the original in every way.

is able to achieve these advantages because of the way the images are recorded. For starters, unlike film, which is physically handled at all stages of its existence (from camera to chemistry to storage), the information stored on a Photo CD never comes into physical contact with any device. While the disc itself is handled during various stages of production and playback, the photographic image is written to Photo CD *optically,* with a high-intensity laser, and the image information is stored between two protective polymer layers. Consequently, the image data contained on the disc cannot be affected by such things as thumbprints, spills, or pollutants.

Unlike film, which degrades over each successive generation, an image reproduced from a Photo CD is, for all intents and purposes, a brand-new original. When copies are made from Photo CD images (and this is true of all digital files), the copy contains identical image data to the original. Photo CD, therefore, facilitates an accountable means of preserving valuable, original film images in a decidedly more stable medium than the original film emulsion, or duplicates thereof. Moreover, because all photographic materials are susceptible to the aging and fading effects of light and humidity, the medium of Photo CD provides an inexpensive and safe storage environment.

What's more, the cost of having images written to a Photo CD is relatively low. While slightly more expensive than film and film processing, writing images to Photo CD, especially when it is done at the same time the film is processed, is quite affordable.

Finally, once an image is recorded to a Photo CD, it is not limited to producing only slides and prints—it can be brought into the digital environment, where you can interact with it, alter it, and apply it in an almost infinite number of ways.

The Underlying Basis of Photo CD: The YCC System

To achieve the quality necessary to appease the most demanding professionals and consumers, the Photo CD system had to be able to do three things:

1. Create a standardization process, so that images photographed on different film stocks, under varying light sources, and with

significant exposure variations could be introduced into the digital environment quickly, consistently, accurately, and inexpensively.

2. Create a method of compressing the enormous digital files without sacrificing access speed or image quality.

3. Create a means of making the digital images "device independent," such that the images could be displayed on any TV or computer monitor or could be output from any printing device, regardless of make or model, and even be compatible with those systems destined to emerge in the future.

Kodak's solution to these challenges is the Photo YCC color-encoding and compression scheme (which we'll describe in detail later in this chapter). Every image storage system *must* have a color-encoding scheme in order to do its job, which consists of storing and conveying the color and tone information for each pixel contained in an image. Kodak's Photo YCC scheme is able to do this quickly, accurately, and consistently. Just as important, the image data produced are in the same language as television broadcast signals, so that no further color translation is necessary to accurately display Photo CD images on a TV monitor, or even on an HDTV monitor. In fact, the Photo YCC color-encoding scheme was specifically designed to be faithfully translated by virtually any display or output device, including those yet to be developed.

Combine the Photo YCC compression scheme with the hardware and software contained in Kodak's Photo Imaging Workstation, and you've got an imaging system that:

1. Can provide across-the-board standardization for introducing photographic images into the digital environment without any visible reduction in image quality.

2. Is simple enough to be operated by a single worker, with a minimum of training, and affordable enough to be purchased and operated economically by small, independent businesses.

3. Produces an image file that can be universally accessed by any and all input and output devices.

The Kodak Photo Imaging Workstation (PIW)

Creation of a Photo CD takes place at a Photo Imaging Workstation (PIW), which consists of the following elements:

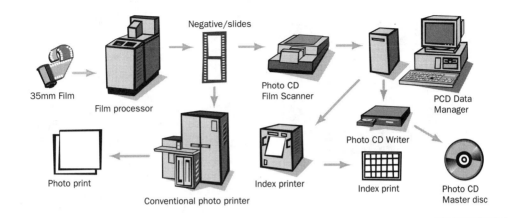

Negative/slides

35mm Film

Film processor

Photo CD Film Scanner

PCD Data Manager

Photo print

Conventional photo printer

Index printer

Photo CD Writer

Index print

Photo CD Master disc

Components of the Photo Imaging Workstation

Along with the Data Manager, Photo CD Writer, and index printer, the Kodak PCD Scanner is part of the basic Photo Imaging Workstation (PIW). Film is processed normally, then scanned. Color data from the light transmitted through the film is recorded by a fixed array of charge-coupled devices (CCDs). The PCD scanner can record over 2,000 color samples per linear inch of film.

- The Kodak PCD scanner, which scans negatives and slides to be written to Photo CD.

- The Kodak PCD Data Manager, which adjusts and compresses scanned images and prepares them to be written to Photo CD.

- The Kodak PCD Writer, which encodes the blank Photo CD disc with the image data.

- The Kodak PCD Printer, which creates index prints and high-quality thermal enlargements from Photo CD images.

- The Kodak PCD CD-ROM drive, which reads Photo CDs and downloads the image data to the printer, or to another PCD Writer, for copying images from one disc to another.

Let's take a closer look at what happens to images as they are processed at each stage.

SCANNING

Once the 35mm film image has been cleaned and prepped, it is ready for the Kodak PCD Film Scanner. Here, the photographic images are electronically sampled by a halogen light source that shines through the film emulsion. Each frame is sampled and translated into an RGB (red, green, and blue) digital image.

A film scanner is much like a slide projector, in that it shines a beam of light through the film emulsion, by means of a high-quality optical system, onto the scanning stage of the unit. On the other side of the scanning stage is an array of light sensors that probe the transmitted light and convert it into electrical signals in

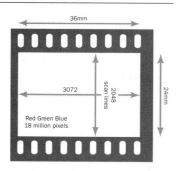

36mm

3072

2048 scan lines

24mm

Red Green Blue
18 million pixels

The 35mm frame has a 3:2 image-size ratio. A Photo CD scan of a 35mm frame maintains that ratio to produce a 16XBase digital image that is 3072 pixels x 2048 scan lines (where each of the 2048 scans across the length of the 35mm frame records 3072 pixels of information).

three different channels—you guessed it: red, green, and blue (RGB), the components of visible light.

The quality and resolution of the scan depend on the number of samples taken of the image during the scanning process. The most effective scanner takes a huge number of samples in a short period of time. Such is the case with the Kodak PCD 2000 scanner, a highly efficient, quick-operating digital scanner that takes about 6 seconds to fully scan a 35mm negative or slide. A scan's resolution is measured in pixels. The scan produced by the PCD scanner is a high-resolution scan, 2048 x 3072 pixels. For each pixel, three samplings are made simultaneously—one each for the red, green, and blue components of the image. Because this is actually more information than is needed to successfully reconstruct the image in full detail, another aspect of the scanner's job is to eliminate the excess signal data. The scanner then reduces this information to 3 *bytes* (a byte being the smallest *usable* unit of digital data), one byte per color component.

The scanning process also provides the opportunity to correct for errors made in the original image, either in the exposure or the processing stage. Much like an automatic exposure (AE) camera, which can automatically correct for scene brightness differentials, the PCD scanner—and, more specifically, its *scene-balance algorithm*—can automatically correct for under- or overexposure problems and certain processing errors affecting color balance, density, or both. In addition, the scanner operator can perform further adjustments of color balance, based on the appearance of the image on the scanner's on-screen preview.

The PCD scanner also makes allowances for film types and

For a comparison of scene space color versus universal film terms, see color section page C4.

permits the operator to adjust the image either (1) to value the distinctive qualities of the film by choosing the *universal film term* option, or (2) to choose the *scene-space* option, which produces a common rendition of the image, with adherence to certain memory colors (green grass, gray cement, or blue sky, for example). The universal film term is often used for scanning slide film,

30

which has distinctive color qualities—the fierce reds of Kodachrome, for instance. The scene-space option is much like the program used to print color negatives—it's a series of compromises resulting in an overall acceptable image.

IMAGE COMPRESSION

Without an image-compression scheme, each image would occupy 18 MB of disc storage, making it impossible to fit more than 30 images on a single Photo CD Master disc. Furthermore, it would take several minutes to access such an image, whether via a Photo CD player or a CD-ROM drive. Thanks to the Photo YCC color-encoding and compression scheme, each image can be reduced to 2–6 MB, enabling up to 100 images to be stored on a single disc and reducing access time to mere seconds.

The PCD Data Manager works in tandem with the Photo YCC scheme both to compress an image as much as possible and to make it easily accessible by a variety of media, each with its own display or output parameters. To this end, each image is bundled on the Photo CD as an *image pac*, a file that contains five resolution levels, from low to high, that can be retrieved individually as needed by the display or output device. Here's a closer look at the process that creates the final, compressed image.

First, the Data Manager converts the RGB image data to Photo YCC data (one luminance [Y] and two chrominance [C^1 and C^2] channels), taking advantage of a phenomenon found in human color vision. Because the human eye is more sensitive to brightness (luminance) than to color (chrominance), we are more acutely aware of slight changes in the brightness of minute details than we are to small differences in hue. Therefore, when files are compressed to form the image pac, much of the chrominance information is removed by averaging the colors of adjacent pixels, and the smaller bundles of information are repacked as efficiently as possible.

Once the scan is in the Photo YCC mode, the system uses a technique called *chrominance averaging and subsampling* to significantly reduce an image's file size without reducing its overall quality. Here, three quarters of the chrominance data in the file is removed—half of the total amount of file data—initially reducing file size from 18 MB to 9 MB. A second color averaging and subsampling routine is then performed, which further reduces the image's file size.

After each subsampling phase, the data from the new file are

Once the initial Photo CD scan is made, the RGB values for each pixel in the scanned image are converted to new luminance and chroma values in the Photo YCC color system (see color section, page C5).

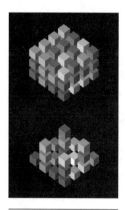

(left) In chroma decimation, the first step in image pac compression, the chroma values for three-fourths of the pixels in the image are removed (see color section, page C6). This process retains all of the original luminance information but reduces the amount of data in the file to half.

(right) A sophisticated averaging and subsampling program averages the color values in the 9 MB file to produce a Base version (see color section, page C6). At each of the two stages, the residual information (the difference between the averaged and the original data) is saved in a compressed format so that it can later be added to the Base data to reconstitute two higher-resolution versions of the image (4XBase and 16XBase).

compared to the original data, and the differences, called *residuals,* are stored in a separate file. These residuals are saved in a compressed format, so that they can later be recombined with the subsampled data to rebuild the two high-resolution versions of the image.

Once compression is complete, the PCD Data Manager organizes the information so that it may be stored in five separate resolutions in one file—the image pac. The Base image contains the data that have been averaged and subsampled twice. There are two low-resolution versions smaller than Base (Base/4 and Base/16), and two high-resolution versions larger than Base (4XBase and 16XBase). 4XBase is composed of the Base version *plus* the residuals of the second subsampling. 16XBase is the Base version with the first and second set of residuals added.

Once in image pac format, images can be accessed by various media. The Base image, with a resolution of 512 lines by 768 pixels, is used for TV presentation on PAL (European) and NTSC (North American) television formats. 4XBase (1024 lines by 1536 pixels) supports HDTV (high-definition TV), which uses 960 or more scan lines. 16XBase resolution (2048 lines by 3072 pixels) is for thermal printing and photomechanical reproduction. The lower resolution components, Base/4 (256 lines by 384 pixels) and Base/16 (128 lines by 192 pixels), are for rapid access of the scanned image. Base/16 is basically an index resolution, which is used in the overview pac; Base/4 is a fast-access resolution, useful when multiple images are displayed simultaneously or for bringing images into graphic-design layouts, for position only (FPO).

The higher resolutions of 4XBase and 16XBase are used in layout and design and can be output as prints or converted to the CMYK color mode for color separation and subsequent printing on an offset printing press (we will say more about the various resolutions in the image pac in Chapter 4).

If you've been wondering why Kodak chose such an esoteric system of labeling resolution components in the image pac, rest assured that the system actually makes more sense than you might think. A Base/16 image, for example, contains $\frac{1}{16}$ the number of pixels contained in the Base image; a 16XBase image contains 16 times as many pixels as the Base image. Therefore, at a glance, you

32

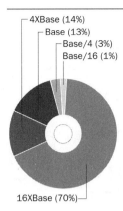

4XBase (14%)
Base (13%)
Base/4 (3%)
Base/16 (1%)

16XBase (70%)

On a Photo CD Master disc, the Base/4 and Base/16 files, designed to produce images at very small sizes, require very little of the data storage space in an image pac. The base file occupies about 13% of the total. To "reconstitute" the 4XBase version of the image, the 4X residuals (occupying about 14 percent of the image pac storage space) are recombined with the Base data. For the 16XBase version, additional residual data that occupy about 70% of the storage space are recombined with the Base and 4XBase data.

The Image Pac

Format	Primary Use	Resolution	
Base/16	Photo CD Index print, "thumbnail" sketches	128 x 192 pixels	
Base/4	For position only in graphic design	256 x 384 pixels	
Base	TV, multimedia, Desktop presentations	512 x 768 pixels	Mutimedia
4XBase	HDTV (high-definition TV), printing at small sizes	1024 x 1536 pixels	Pocket Book Cover
16XBase	Enlargement in print	2048 x 3072 pixels	MAGAZINE COVER

can tell if an image is less than or more than Base resolution and by how much.

WRITING

As images are being scanned, and subsequently compressed and stuffed for storage by the PCD Data Manager, they are also being prepared to be written to the Photo CD Master disc. This is a job for the PCD Writer.

Compact discs, whether audio or visual, carry their information between two polymer coatings. With "read-only" discs, the digital information is literally "stamped" onto the surface in the manufacturing process. Both audio CDs and CD-ROMs exhibit a distinctive silver sheen, the result of a thin layer of aluminum, indicative of mass production. A Kodak Photo CD, on the other hand, has a thin layer of gold. Every CD requires some type of metallized surface coating in order to reflect the low-intensity laser beam that reads the disc's encoded data in CD players and CD-ROM drives. However, the higher the quality of the metal coating, the more stable and protected the information will be over time. This is why Photo CDs use gold instead of aluminum.

Beneath the layer of gold is an organic, light-sensitive dye layer that changes properties when affected by a high-intensity laser. Wherever dye properties are altered, the light reflected from the disc to the disc reader is different from the light reflected by

33

The disc medium used for Photo CD consists of a polymer coating, a reflective layer, a data layer, and a second polymer coating. The polymer coatings protect the photographic data and the reflective layer. The top coating also provides a surface for the printed label, while the bottom layer must remain clear so that the image data sandwiched between can be read. The reflective layer is a thin, uniform, highly durable coating of gold that reflects the low-intensity laser beam used in reading the images from the disc. The data layer consists of a light-activated dye whose properties are changed by the high-intensity laser used to record digital image data on the disc. Wherever the dye properties are changed, the light reflected from the disc to the disc reader is different than the light reflected from the unaltered dye. It is this pattern of altered and unaltered spots that stores the color information in the image files.

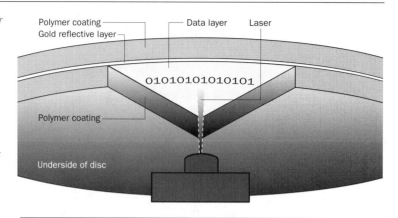

unchanged dye. The resulting pattern of changed and unchanged organic dye areas is what forms the encoded data that contain the image. Kodak Photo CDs utilize "WORM" (write once, read many times) technology. The PCD Writer uses an intense laser (more intense than those used to *read* CDs) to encrypt—or record—digital image information.

Also encoded on the disc is the location of each photo, otherwise known as the "directory," so that Photo CD players and CD-ROM drives can locate an individual image quickly, without having to scan the entire disc from first image to last.

INDEXING

At the same time the image pac is being created, an overview pac, which shows the lowest-resolution version of each photo (128 by 192 pixels), is also generated by the PCD Data Manager. The overview pac acts like a digital table of contents for the Photo CD. When the job is complete, the PCD Printer can print the contents of the overview pac to create an index print showing all of the images contained on the disc. The index print, which fits inside the Photo CD's jewelcase, will show images previously written to the Photo CD as well.

THERMAL PRINTING

The thermal printing component of the PIW can print high-quality thermal prints up to 11 x 11 inches, as well as the index print, which contains 40 images on a 4.75 inch-square sheet. Four index prints per single sheet of Thermacolor paper can be printed simultaneously.

34

The Photo CD player uses a laser beam to read the pattern of altered and unaltered dye information stored on a Photo CD. A prism package is used to divert the laser light to an electronics processing bundle, which then decodes the information to produce the image realistically on a TV monitor.

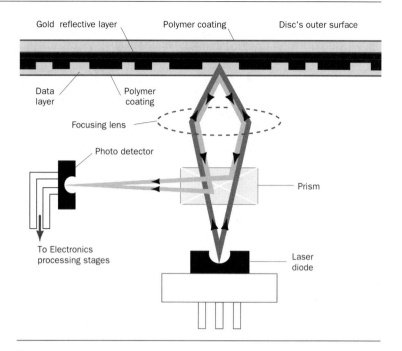

PLAYBACK

Photo CD players and CD-ROM drives use a laser pickup device to read the data on the disc. A low-intensity laser light is focused through a prism system, through the disc's clear polymer coating, onto the data layer of the disc. The disc's reflective coating maximizes the laser's output and focuses the information back onto another surface of the prism, where the coded light is redirected into a photo-detector array. The information travels from there to an electronics processing web that decodes the information, and translates it, per the parameters of the output device—whether a computer monitor, TV display monitor, telecommunications device, or printer.

The Final Product: The Disc

Images stored on a Kodak Photo CD are well protected, thanks to (1) the gold reflector surface, which, as a result of its highly stable characteristics protects the stored information against temperature fluctuations and radiation; (2) a polymer coating that protects against moisture, solvents, and airborne pollutants; (3) the laser-sensitive dye, which was specifically selected by Kodak for its stable and durable qualities that further protect the image data from extreme heat, humidity, and light; and (4) the Kodak Info-Guard Protection System, a manufacturing process that strengthens the polymer coatings on either side of the disc's surfaces, thus protecting the information from excess handling and abrasion.

SESSIONS

Whether you take in a 36-exposure roll of film, 100 hand-picked slides, or two individual negatives to be written to a Photo CD, the PIW operator must open up a "session" on the disc. Each time new images are written to a disc, a new session must be added. While this feature is advantageous, in that you needn't fill a disc all at once, the drawback is that for each session a directory is written to the disc that eats up a certain amount of storage space. Consequently, the number of images that can be written to the disc will vary, depending on how many sessions are contained on the disc.

A disc that contains more than one session is called a "multi-session" disc and requires a playback device or drive that's capable of reading multisession discs. If a CD-ROM drive, for instance, is capable of reading only the first session on the disc, you will have no way of accessing any subsequently added images with that drive. The multisession feature in Photo CD greatly expands the usefulness of CD technology. Picture researchers, for example, can combine images from various sources on a single disc. Companies can put training programs on a PCD disc and have the option of updating their programs from time to time.

RESOLUTIONS

Up to this point, we've been discussing Photo CD Master discs, with their five-resolution image pacs. There is, however, another disc, the Pro Photo CD Master, which contains one more resolution level, not previously mentioned. This is the 64XBase resolution that extends the Photo CD Master's highest resolution of 16XBase by a factor of 4, allowing the introduction of medium- and large-format (up to 4 x 5, currently) images into the Photo CD environment. The 64XBase resolution produces a resolution of 4096 lines x 6144 pixels. To produce Pro Photo CD Master discs, a different authoring system (specifically, the Kodak Professional PCD Imaging Workstation 4200) is required.

The Photo Imaging Workstation (PIW) 4200 is used to produce Pro Photo CD Master discs. It has a more sophisticated scanner that can handle larger film formats, up to 4 x 5.

This new workstation is not limited to medium- to large-format images, however. A 35mm negative or transparency at 64XBase is a very high-resolution digital image capable of withstanding extreme enlargements and scrutiny at the highest levels of the printing medium.

Accessing Photo CD Discs: A Brief Overview

Photo CD images can be accessed via:

- Dedicated Photo CD players

- Interactive CD players, including 3DO and various CD-I players (the "I" stands for "interactive")

- CD-ROM XA drives for computers ("XA" stands for "extended architecture")

All of these playback devices will also play audio CDs, so Photo CDs containing audio files can be heard with their full-stereo sound. Photo CD is a universal format, meaning that discs can be played on any player that features the Photo CD logo. Furthermore, Photo CDs can be played in the PAL, NTSC, SECAM, and HDTV television formats on appropriate players.

TV PLAYBACK

Most Photo CD players are similar in size to VCR units, making them a natural extension of the home-entertainment system. In fact, the new breed of Photo CD player is the portable Kodak PCD 970, which connects to any TV, comes with headphones, and is small enough to fit in a briefcase. Multidisc players, such as Kodak's

37

Kodak offers a line of Photo CD players, from the compact portable player to a multidisc player that holds up to five discs. All players can be used for playing traditional audio CDs as well as Photo CDs.

PCD 5870 player, accept up to five discs in a carousel, so that you can create a sophisticated image presentation that includes pictures from multiple Photo CDs.

Photo CD players offer many viewing features, all accessible by remote control. You can select specific images while suppressing others from playback and can program those favorite images to appear in any desired order. Images can be rotated or zoomed in on for a closer look. You can even program your "picture edits" into memory so that when the image is recalled, it comes up in its new cropped or rotated view. You can also see the image in full frame, or watch the series of selected images in reverse. Some models of PCD players feature on-screen display of the image number for easier programming.

COMPUTER PLAYBACK

To be able to download Photo CD images to your computer, you need a CD-ROM drive that's capable of reading Mode 2, Form 1 data (the CD-ROM format in which Photo CD images are recorded). It's important to note that not all CD-ROM drives can access Photo CD files—you must have a CD-ROM *XA* drive. From there, you need the appropriate software in order to access the Photo CD images. Kodak Photo CD Access and Access Plus Software (available for Macintosh and Windows 3.x) are such

*To play Photo CD discs
and access Photo CD
images on a computer
you need a CD-ROM XA
drive.*

39

examples. Macintosh computers equipped with Apple QuickTime
(version 1.5 or later) enable you to access Photo CD images in
many applications.

Once a Photo CD image is brought into an image-editing application, it can be saved in PICT, TIFF, and EPS Macintosh formats,
and in BMP, EPS, PCX, RIFF, TIFF, and WMF Windows formats.

The latest generation of CD-ROM XA drives feature multiple
drive speeds (either double speed or quadruple speed, at this
writing) that speed up the time it takes to access Photo CD images
and other data.

Be aware that some CD-ROM XA drives can read only the first
recording session on a multisession Photo CD disc. These drives,
called single-session drives, are acceptable if you want to play
prerecorded discs or if you want to acquire and process all your
images in a single session. Multisession CD-ROM drives are preferable to single-session drives because they can access all the
images on a Photo CD, regardless of how many sessions were
required to produce them. The Photo CD logo implies that a drive
is a multisession drive. If you have a question about a drive's
multisession capability, contact the drive manufacturer. Otherwise,
you can call Kodak's product support number (800-CD-KODAK,
extension 53) for further information.

4

Professional Applications of Photo CD

Today, with the digital environment becoming as integral a part of photography as lens optics and film emulsions, photographers no longer shoot, edit, catalog, and distribute their photographs in the same manner as before. For the first time, photographers needn't be limited only to the craft of photography—they can be image re-touchers, designers, graphic artists, publishers, and business managers. Other lines are blurring as well, as Photo CD helps stock photo agencies become part of the "information superhighway" via on-line delivery, as art directors and designers become prepress experts, and as educators become multimedia developers.

The Desktop Darkroom

Photo CD, and related products, have brought the traditional darkroom into a whole new light—literally! In place of chemistry, timers, and safelights, the photographer now has a computer, a CD-ROM drive, and an arsenal of digital images on Photo CD. Instead of wasting costly enlarging paper to zero in on the perfect exposure and experimenting with burning and dodging times, the photographer can work cleanly and safely in a comfortable, well-lit room, performing all the same tasks that would be required in the darkroom. But here's the real kicker: Photographers no longer have to manually duplicate each process exactly in order to create identical "perfect" prints. This laborious procedure is completely unnecessary in the digital darkroom.

THE USER-FRIENDLY NEGATIVE

When you've got an image on a Photo CD that you want to work with in your desktop darkroom, here's what you *don't* have to do: locate the glassine sleeve that contains the desired frame; gently remove it and carefully insert it in a negative carrier, then dust it off with compressed air and a camel's hair brush; adjust the enlarger to the desired height; verify focus with a grain magnifier; and make a stabbing, albeit educated, guess at the necessary filtration and a starting exposure time.

Thanks to Photo CD, here's what you do instead: You download the image of your choosing, in the resolution of your choosing, into the image-enhancement application of your choosing (such as Adobe Photoshop or Aldus PhotoStyler). You can then crop and size the image and perform any necessary enhancements (burning, dodging, retouching, contrast balancing, sharpening). If, at any point during these operations, you take a wrong turn, you have a number of convenient ways to restore the original image—or parts thereof—to regain your footing and try again.

Once your image is finalized to your satisfaction, you can save it in the mode (RGB, CMYK, grayscale) and format (TIFF, EPS, PICT, etc.) to suit your specifications. The result is a brand-new *original* image that can be duplicated *exactly* as is, ad infinitum, and even written back to the Photo CD format (via Portfolio Photo CD or Writable CD), depending on your needs.

SYSTEM REQUIREMENTS

The ideal components of a typical "desktop darkroom" vary widely, but two basic platforms are the most widely used: Macintosh computers and IBM or IBM-compatible PCs running Microsoft Windows software. To run the types of software needed to work with Photo CD images, and to work on these images at higher resolutions, your computer system will have to meet some specific criteria.

When you load a Photo CD disc into a CD-ROM drive, you are giving yourself access to a file cabinet of images. Via your image-enhancement or page layout software, you can access Photo CD images and work with them in the digital environment. However, when you want to save your edited image, you cannot save it back to the Photo CD. This is because a Photo CD is ROM (read-only memory) only—the information contained on a CD-ROM disc can only be read and accessed. ROM is a one-way medium!

Images stored on Photo CD are compressed in the medium's Photo YCC format (see Chapter 3) and occupy relatively little disc space. However, when a Photo CD image is brought into an image-editing program (thereby decompressing it), worked on, and then saved, the image file becomes extremely large—approximately four to five times larger than its compressed form. There-

Working with Photo CD on the desktop requires at minimum a CD-ROM XA drive and lots of storage space.

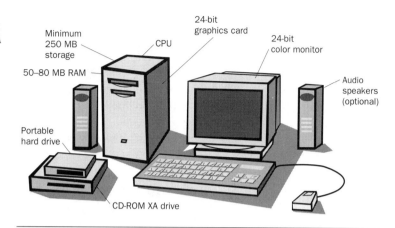

fore, your system's first requirement is lots of storage space. It is not unusual for high-resolution image files to be 20–30 MB each; and, 64XBase images from Pro Photo CD, when brought onto the desktop, can be 72 MB! A minimum of 250 MB of storage capacity is therefore recommended. Realistic storage capacity, if you are going to work on high-resolution images frequently, should range from 500 MB to 1 GB. Additional internal or external hard drives can be integrated into your computer system to expand its current storage capacity.

The second, and perhaps even more important, system requirement is RAM—and lots of it! Random access memory is the computer's internal, working memory, where data are processed. Your computer uses RAM for every operation it undertakes. Basic operating systems, such as the desktop and the Finder, require only small amounts of RAM. However, powerful image-enhancement programs such as Photoshop require huge amounts of RAM— a minimum of two to three times the size of the image is recommended. Introduce Photo CD images, even at Base resolution, and the most basic tasks performed in an image-editing program will immediately expend the remaining, unused RAM. To work on Photo CD images at Base, you need a minimum of 8– 15 MB; to work on images at 16XBase, the highest Photo CD Master resolution, you're looking at 50–80 MB of RAM if you want quick, painless operation. You can expand your computer's RAM by purchasing the appropriate SIMMs (single in-line memory modules).

You'll also need a CD-ROM XA drive for accessing Photo CD

43

discs. In particular, you need a multisession drive, so that all of the images written to the disc will be accessible, not just those written in the first session (for a discussion of single-session versus multisession CD-ROM drives and discs, see Chapter 3; for more information on available CD-ROM drives, see Chapter 6).

For transporting files—from the desktop to the service bureau for image output, for instance—portable hard drives, which use high-capacity, removable media, are a must. The most popular portable hard drive is the SyQuest, which uses removable 44 MB, 88 MB, 105 MB, 200 MB, or 270 MB cartridges. Another popular portable hard drive is the Bernoulli, which uses 40, 90, or 150 MB disks. Even greater storage capacity can be obtained with a magneto-optical drive and disks that have a capacity ranging from 125 MB to 1.3 GB. When selecting a removable storage system, be careful to choose one that is also used by your imagesetter or color separation house.

As Writable CDs gain acceptance, it will be possible to write modified images back to Photo CD in their new form, making Photo CD even more practical (see Chapter 16 for a discussion of Writable CD).

To see photographic image quality on screen, and particularly the full range of colors produced in a photographic image, your system should have a 24-bit graphics card, with a compatible color monitor. Having 24-bit color allows you to display millions of colors on screen. You could also make do with 16-bit color, which will display thousands of colors and is acceptable for working with Photo CD images for some applications. However, 8-bit color, which will only effectively reproduce 256 colors, will not adequately represent the full color components of a digital photograph; it can nevertheless be used for comps, rough layouts, and other, less stringent applications.

APPLICATIONS OF THE PHOTO CD DESKTOP DARKROOM

Photo CD provides a wide range of solutions—some artistic, some pragmatic, and some economic—to the difficulties of integrating photographic images into complex applications. Photo CD is also spawning a new family of applications unique to CD technology, such as interactive CDs for education and entertainment. Photo CD is giving new life and security to once-perilous tasks, such as portfolio presentations, photo submissions, and stock photography, which often require the use of irreplaceable original photographs. Let's take a closer look at some of the ways Photo CD is being used. We will expand on all these areas in later chapters.

Archiving: Image Storage and Retrieval

Corporations, museums, libraries, and other organizations are now converting large collections of historical or otherwise valuable photographs and documents to Photo CD for preservation, access, and display. Extremely old, fragile, or valuable photographs, regardless of format (black-and-white prints, color prints, glass plates, negatives, slides) can be converted to Photo CD by first rephotographing the images on either 35mm, 120, or 4 x 5 negative or transparency film. (Only Pro Photo CD can accommodate formats larger than 35mm; however, organizations concerned with obtaining the highest quality will choose only the larger formats.). The copy film is then converted to Photo CD in the traditional manner (as described in Chapter 3).

Because images written to Photo CD are accessible in five or six different resolutions, the system represents the ultimate convenience and versatility in image storage and retrieval. Low-resolution versions can be used for cataloging and databasing; Base resolutions can be used for display or for a wide variety of presentation formats; high-resolution versions can be brought into the computer environment and manipulated, and they can be incorporated into publications for reproduction and dissemination.

The beauty of the Photo CD system of archiving and retrieval is

This is one of thousands of photos being transferred to Photo CD at Caterpillar Corporation. The digital versions not only serve the purpose of archival storage but can be accessed for use in company publications and are available on-line (through Kodak Picture Exchange) as stock photos.

that once the images are written to Photo CD, the valuable originals can be safely stored, while stable, high-quality facsimiles of the images are available for a wide spectrum of applications. Some of these applications in academic settings are discussed in Chapters 17 and 18.

For organizations and institutions that need to maintain and manage vast numbers of Photo CD discs and images, the Kodak Professional Photo CD Image Library, a storage and retrieval system, is capable of previewing over 30,000 thumbnail views of the images on up to 300 Photo CDs. Individual images can be accessed at any resolution in seconds.

Photo Illustration

Photo CD and high-powered image-manipulation software are changing the way photographers plan, edit, and shoot photo assignments. Photographers can now have the option of assembling individual image elements to later be combined using such applications as Adobe Photoshop (a topic we cover in detail in Chapter 7). Images that aren't that impressive on their own may actually prove to be ideal composite elements for the digital environment. Many photographers routinely shoot such diverse elements as textures, patterns, and assorted objects in order to combine them later in an image-editing program.

Photographers can use photo manipulation software to jazz up some of their "duller" images.

One reason that Photo CD is the ideal medium for digital photo illustration is the relatively low cost of digitizing. High-

quality drum scans can cost anywhere from $50 to $200—each. Images scanned and written to a Photo CD Master cost as little as $1 to $3 apiece. Of course it is preferable for scans to be done on Pro Photo CD if you want them to be of the highest quality (see Chapter 5 for a discussion of Photo CD Master versus Pro Photo

FOCUS ON LANDMINE PRODUCTIONS

LandMine Productions, a small Los Angeles company that specializes in design and advertising on a national level, has been using Photo CD since its inception. By being able to amass a large selection of photographic images on disc, the company can explore a wide range of visual possibilities for a client, without costly scanning expenses and time delays.

LandMine's most recent project, a national advertising campaign for Lowepro camera bags, could not have been accomplished as smoothly and cost effectively without Photo CD. Further, Photo CD has proven a cost-effective means of storing the final product, an ad in several different configurations,

Final texture   Original texture

without eating up a lot of valuable storage space on the hard drive. Once completed, the page layout, graphics, and Photo CD images for each ad are written to a writable CD disc, where the files can remain safely stored and easily accessible.

The ad shown here is a composite of three separate Photo CD images. The company logo was scanned conventionally and brought into Quark XPress, where text was added. The two Photo CD images consist of the background, a 35mm black-and-white shot of rock texture, and the two shots of the product, also shot in 35mm black-and-white.

It's worth noting that none of the images were "proofed" conventionally prior to their being written to disc. The background texture was acquired in Photoshop at the 16XBase resolution, where it was made into a positive, then flopped and enhanced, in the form of lowering its contrast and darkening specific areas for overall continuity. The shot of the waterfall and bag, also acquired at 16XBase, was reversed, and then adjusted for its highlights, so that the image would reproduce with detail throughout. The company logo was added to the front of the bag using a combination of Photoshop's opacity control and perspective adjustment (to match the perspective of the bag). Finally, Unsharp Mask was applied to both product shots, for heightened clarity; the effect was not applied to the background, in order to retain its subtlety.

47

CD), but even these scans ($15 to $25 each) cost considerably less than conventional drum scanning. Photo CD is also an ideal storage medium for image files, since the permanent digital "negatives" remain intact on the disc.

Photographers working on design projects can access Base-resolution images from a Photo CD and bring them into a page layout program, such as QuarkXpress or Aldus PageMaker (both of which allow users to import Photo CD images directly into page layouts, converting the images from the Photo YCC mode to RGB mode for desktop computer use or to CMYK mode for direct color separation and printing) to show the exact positioning of photos, illustrations, and type. The resulting layout is a professional, finished design comp, which can be either printed or modemed to clients for approval.

Stock Photography

Photo CD has become fully integrated into the world of stock photography as a storage, distribution, and delivery medium, allowing for the economical creation of huge picture libraries on disc that can be organized by topic, photographer, location, or any other parameter of your choosing. With the introduction of Pro Photo CD, which accommodates multiple film formats, high-quality image libraries can be economically created and quickly distributed to a wide range of clients for immediate use.

Stock photo agencies no longer have to retain millions of dollars worth of valuable originals in order to license the work of top photographers. Once an image is written to Photo CD, the original may be returned to the photographer for safekeeping. And because Photo CD is an internationally accepted format, stock photo agencies may conveniently license their photographs anywhere in the world. Photo CD has also become a popular medium for disseminating "clip photos," which can include picture elements (skies, planets, trees), textures (walls, fabrics), or backgrounds (scenics, cityscapes, etc.).

Photo CD Portfolio II, which can store some 4400 images at thumbnail resolution, is an economical means for stock photo agencies to stuff large numbers of images onto a single disc for review. Kodak's Browser software can be added to the discs to facilitate easy search and retrieval of the images. Higher resolution versions must be ordered from the photo agency.

Individual photographers benefit from Photo CD as an archiving and image-management system as well. Personal portfolios, photographic submissions, and stock photo libraries can be stored on Photo CD and accessed quickly and conveniently. A number of software programs are available to help photographers organize and access their Photo CD images. Kodak Shoebox, Aldus Fetch, and Kudo Image Browser will help retrieve not only Photo CD images but other graphics files, as well. (See Chapter 8 for a detailed discussion of image management and available software.)

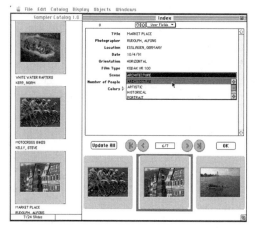

Kodak Shoebox is one of several software packages designed to help you catalog and sort your collection of Photo CD images.

An exciting development in the evolution of stock photography is the advent of on-line stock photos available for browsing and downloading. Kodak's own Picture Exchange is an on-line image library that allows subscribers to search through its huge database, select thumbnail images for downloading and inspection, and choose particular images. After making a selection, the subscriber can download a design proof for layout or other purposes; a handy order form then comes on screen so the subscriber can arrange to receive the image in digital or traditional form. (For more on Kodak Picture Exchange, see Chapter 9.)

Desktop Publishing and Prepress

Virtually all magazines, most books, and a large number of newspapers are now desktop published. Editors and layout personnel, using networked computers, produce page layout files that incorporate scanned images, text, graphics, and even advertisements, so that the final layout is exactly as it will appear in the printed publication. Finished files are sent to commercial imagesetters and color separators for proofing and film (which is used to make the printing plates).

The cost savings of desktop publishing is staggering when compared to former publishing methods, which required large numbers of skilled personnel, particularly in the prepress and on-press phases. Now, the majority of the prepress work is completed by the publisher's staff before the publication reaches the printer.

Photo CD has become an integral part of desktop publishing,

primarily because the cost of scanning images conventionally (either by drum or by flatbed scanner) is anywhere from 5 to 25 times higher than having images scanned to Photo CD. Even small desktop publications can use anywhere from 50 to 200 scanned images per issue. The cost savings of using Photo CD images is thus quite substantial. And because the images are already archived in their original state on Photo CD, they can be easily retrieved at any time for other publication uses. The same photo can be used, for example, in a magazine, an ad, a poster, or a brochure, without having to be rescanned at different sizes.

Four basic types of software are used to modify or utilize Photo CD images for prepress purposes:

- *Page layout software* is used to assemble text, artwork, photos, and any other page elements. Programs such as QuarkXPress and Aldus PageMaker provide design and typesetting functions and can produce finished, multiple-page documents from which film can be furnished for printing. QuarkXPress is now being bundled with the Eficolor Xtension, a utility that allows you to match your image and page layout files' color profiles with virtually any output device.

Photo CD images can be imported directly into your page layout program, for combining with type and graphics. The application will permit you to access the Base or lower resolutions, for "position only" quality. The appropriate higher-resolution version will be accessed by the color separator, for reproduction purposes.

CASE STUDY

FOCUS ON MILLER IMAGING

A new company that has emerged as a result of the explosion of Photo CD technology is Miller Imaging, an offshoot of Miller Pro Lab, in Santa Monica, California. Steven F. Miller, the president of Miller Imaging, saw the potential of Photo CD and has expanded the company from a single PIW, in a room not much larger than a broom closet, to a rapidly expanding full-service imaging facility that specializes in all the PCD formats and platforms, including Pro, Portfolio, and Writable Photo CDs with both Macintosh and IBM PC-compatible systems.

Among Miller Imaging's clients are Mattel, the Los Angeles Dodgers and the San Francisco Giants, the Image Bank, UCLA Medical School, and numerous international clients. Much of the work for these clients includes the archiving of images produced by in-house advertising and graphic-design departments onto Photo CD. One of Miller's more popular services is restoring modified Photo CD images. This involves rebuilding the image pac of an image that has been written to a CD as a compressed PICT or TIFF file; the rebuilt version can then be written to a Portfolio disc as a new Photo CD image in the Photo YCC format, enabling the customer to access all five image resolutions. Miller has even taken Photo CD to billboard size from a Pro Photo CD image.

A presentation shouldn't remind people of their 11th grade science teacher.

Presenting Portfolio Photo CD at Miller Imaging.
It'll get your ideas across a lot more creatively than she will.

- Data transfer for storage on CD
- Image pack builder – Stores, tiff and pict files back on CD
- Image transfer – Storing at specified resolution from Photo CD
- Arrange and link materials into exciting interactive structures ideal for multimedia presentations.

2718 WILSHIRE BOULEVARD, SANTA MONICA, CALIFORNIA 90403, USA
310.264.4711 • FAX 310.264.4717

Realizing the very real gap between technology and hands-on knowledge of it, Miller's newest service is education. At the Miller Digital Learning Center, customers are taught everything from how best to acquire Photo CD images into their software applications, to advanced courses in the applications themselves, to the fine points of prepress production.

In Miller's experience, people seem to know the least about image acquisition. "You need more than just a computer, a CD-ROM drive, and Photoshop," he explains. "People think they can just pull their images into Photoshop and utilize them." He points out that an image intended only for display on a TV monitor is best acquired with Kodak Access or Access Plus software, which is optimized for TV's NTSC display standards. On the other hand, images intended for print publication require a completely different means of acquisition, such as Kodak's CMS Photo CD plug-in, which can convert a Photo CD image from Photo YCC directly to CMYK, completely bypassing RGB, if so desired. One of Miller Imaging's strengths, therefore, is in educating their customers as to the proper way to acquire a Photo CD image to best suit their specific needs.

Already, Miller Imaging has generated a number of helpful brochures and charts designed to demystify Photo CD, and put a wealth of useful information into the hands of the Photo CD user.

51

- *Image-enhancement software* is used to sharpen the image; adjust color, tone, contrast, and saturation; and manipulate the image in myriad creative ways. Programs such as Adobe Photoshop (for Mac and IBM) and Aldus PhotoStyler (for IBM only) are needed not only to modify the image creatively but also to prepare the image for photomechanical reproduction.

- *Illustration software* can be used with images to produce photo illustrations. However, their main purpose is to enable users to treat the computer as a drawing medium. Programs such as Adobe Illustrator and Aldus FreeHand can import photos and other graphics files as object-oriented images.

- *3D software* allows the user to build three-dimensional objects that can be assembled and photographed, in a manner of speaking, from different perspectives. Programs such as Adobe Dimensions and Stratavision 3D allow the user to use scanned images as backgrounds for 3D objects or as surface textures to to apply to 3D-modeled objects, or to create three-dimensional elements for integration into Photo CD images in Adobe Photoshop, for example.

Color separation for printing has long been the province of prepress experts, who are able to work magic with a photographic image. With current developments in desktop publishing, however, that aspect of production is expected to increasingly fall to the publisher's staff as well. We have a lot more to say about how Photo CD is affecting desktop publishing and prepress in Chapters 10 and 11.

Presentations and Multimedia

Photo CD was originally developed as a means for viewing "slide shows" of family snapshots on TV. You can still do that with images on your Photo CD Master disc, but the photos can be put to much more sophisticated use as well, in presentations and in multimedia productions.

PRESENTATIONS

There are two ways of producing presentations with Photo CD. The first is a linear slide show, in which you simply show slides in sequence with no embellishments. The second incorporates graphics,

52

Kodak's Create-It presentation software provides basic tools for designing individual screens and creating a sequence of screens. The program allows you to combine text, graphics, images, and audio and to edit and organize your files with drag-and-drop operations. You can also create hotspots for introducing interactive branches to your presentation program.

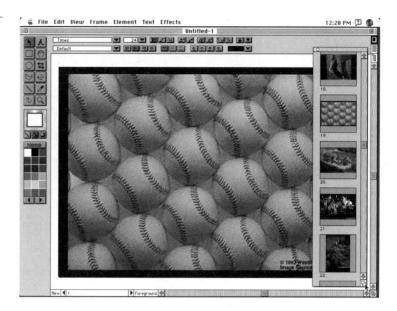

text, backgrounds, narration, music, and even some level of interaction with the viewer.

The most basic way to produce a linear presentation with Photo CD is to have up to 100 images written to a Kodak Photo CD Master disc. From there, with the added functionality of the Photo CD player and remote control, you can customize the presentation to suit your needs. This might mean changing the order in which the images appear, cropping them, rotating them, or enlarging them, as you see fit (see Chapter 6 for some of the programming features of Photo CD players). The final presentation can then be played over and over with all of your changes intact but you must use the same Photo CD player on which your presentation was programmed. When combined with live voice narration, this type of presentation can be a highly effective means of communication.

A more sophisticated means of producing a presentation is to incorporate such elements as backgrounds, graphics, and text using presentation software such as Aldus Persuasion or Microsoft PowerPoint. Such software lets you combine your own images, graphics, and text with preexisting background templates to create a final, integrated presentation. Once you've completed all the frames, you can take the elements you used to create them (the graphics, text, and image files) to a service bureau, where 35mm slides will be produced. You can then use the slides with a traditional projection system, or you can have them written onto a Kodak Photo CD Master disc.

If you want to add sound or a limited degree of interactivity to your presentation, you will need to use multimedia software, such as Kodak's Create-It. With Create-It, you can integrate narration or music and incorporate *branching* that allows users to choose from up to six *paths* for viewing the images. The most practical way of outputting such a presentation is to use Kodak Photo CD Portfolio discs, which can hold up to 700 Photo YCC images, an hour of sound, or a combination thereof. (For more on developing presentations, see Chapter 12; for more on using Create-It and Portfolio CD, see Chapter 13.)

Here are a few key things to remember about Photo CD as a presentation medium:

- Photo CD's YCC images at Base resolution are fully optimized for TV/CRT viewing, so they need minimal manipulation or preparation.

- Photo CD is essentially a random-access medium, whereby information can be accessed in a myriad ways, depending on the viewer's needs.

- The cost of scanning images to Photo CD makes such presentations affordable to even the most meager of budgets.

Kodak's Photo CD Portfolio discs are becoming widely used in interactive kiosks at shopping centers, trade shows, and museums. These kiosks consist of a Photo CD player, a color monitor, and keyboard access. A kiosk can be programmed to play only selected portions of a Photo CD, or the user can select the information manually.

MULTIMEDIA

In multimedia productions, graphics, photos, text, and backgrounds are combined with video, audio, animation, and a sophisticated degree of interactivity. Such programs are produced with special authoring software, such as Passport Producer or Macromedia Director, and are written to CD-ROM and played on any computer equipped with an interactive CD-ROM player or CD-ROM XA drive with player software.

If you plan to include video, animation, and a sophisticated interface, it's best to use high-end authoring software such as Director to produce your script (see Chapter 14). If you want to

Kodak's Arrange-It software allows you to import files from other formats besides Photo CD and to create interactive multimedia programs with as much branching as you desire. In this example, the images have been chosen, arranged in paths, and assembled in sequences. Sound files have been attached to individual images, so that narration or music will play while the image is on-screen.

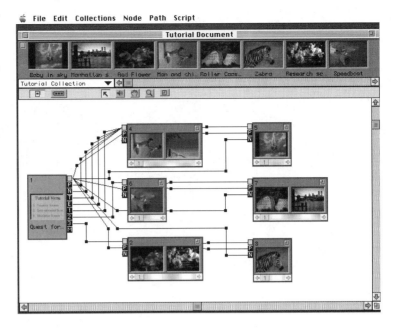

produce a multimedia program *without* video or animation, Kodak's Arrange-It software may fill the bill. With Arrange-It you can import screens created in other applications and even attach sound files to specific images. One of the advantages of this software is that it reduces the otherwise complex production process to a simple matter of clicking and dragging the elements of your choosing to the appropriate menu node or sequence node. (Menu nodes are the main building blocks of the presentation; sequence nodes are strings of elements built on a branch of the program.) Paths (connections between sequence and menu nodes) may then be used to interrelate sequences and branches with other sequences and branches by clicking on the color-coded path palette.

Once you've developed your script with Arrange-It, you need to take all of the files, including Photo CDs, sound files, and image files, to a service bureau, which will then assemble all the elements into a final presentation on a Portfolio CD using Kodak's Build-It software. (Producing multimedia with Arrange-It and Portfolio is described in detail in Chapter 15.)

USES

Large corporations are using Photo CD presentations for everything from tutorials for training new employees, to comprehensive catalogs that detail all of the company's products and services.

Small companies are using Photo CD to present their products in an entertaining and informative way—and because the cost of replicating Photo CDs is relatively inexpensive, the entire promotion can be realized at less cost than a modest advertising campaign.

Individuals, such as artists and photographers, are creating presentations on Photo CD or Portfolio discs that allow potential customers to select a purchase from their inventory or to simply get an idea of their work.

Other companies that are finding uses for Photo CD presentations include travel agencies, which produce travelogue discs that incorporate dramatic images and sounds of a particular locale. An offshoot of the travelogue is the Photo CD book, which combines text with interactivity, allowing the user to experience the material multidimensionally.

Interactive kiosks featuring Photo CD discs are finding new and varied applications in such unusual places as car dealerships, hotels, and even hardware stores. The more accepted places for kiosks, museums and libraries, which were among the first to embrace Photo CD Portfolio presentations, have found that their interactivity does, indeed, heighten the user's interest and responsiveness to new subject matter.

Education and Research

A wide variety of applications for Photo CD are emerging in the scientific, medical, and educational fields, running the gamut from archiving of images and data to classroom applications

The Kodak Library Image Consortium (KLIC) is studying Photo CD as a means by which libraries, museums, and universities can preserve rare, historical photographs and documents. Photo CD provides an inexpensive means of producing high-quality facsimiles or on-screen versions of originals, allowing researchers to examine the documents closely. The consortium is also studying ways in which vast image and document libraries can be compiled onto Photo CD and then networked for worldwide access. Some of the programs that have already been set up are described in Chapter 17.

In the area of medicine, Photo CD's high-resolution images are being incorporated into tutorials for students to learn about detailed features of the human anatomy, complex monitoring equipment, and intricate surgical procedures. All types of data can be introduced into such tutorials—X rays, pathology slides, photo-microscopy—as well as text, patient histories, and statistical data.

Because Photo CD is essentially a random-access display medium, educational Photo CDs can be used as a new form of interactive textbook, allowing students to access pertinent data in ways never before possible. Even "linear," slide show–type tutorials prepared on Photo CD can provide more detailed information than conventional textbooks, slides, or lectures. Educators, particularly at the university level, are experimenting with multimedia presentations on Photo CD to find more stimulating ways of conveying information. Interactivity involves the student in the learning process, making retention of the information more attainable and practical.

Other Uses

So far the applications of Photo CD have just begun to be explored. Individuals in specialized fields are finding new uses for the technology that fit their particular needs. For example, one architect has put her designs on Photo CD to show to clients. Filmmakers are using Photo CD in producing some of their special effects. Marketers are using Photo CD discs as product catalogs—one jeweler, for example, put a variety of his designs on disc (he was later able to use the same image files to create a brochure). Real estate agents are putting together informational flyers with four-color photos of each currently available property. With PCD scanning, the flyers are inexpensive to produce and impressive to potential buyers. Finally, movie studios are cataloging their costumes, props, and location shots on Photo CDs and are organizing publicity stills as well.

As you will discover in reading the rest of this book, Photo CD technology is simply a new tool that many are finding useful in whatever image-related desktop computer endeavor they've undertaken.

Part II

WORKING WITH PHOTO CD IMAGES

5

Putting Images on Photo CD

To put images on a Photo CD, you must have a motive. That motive is usually personal or professional. If it is personal, Photo CD offers a wonderful opportunity to indulge in technology and at the same time enjoy seeing your photographic handiwork on a television set. But if your motive is professional, your need for putting images on a Photo CD takes on a whole new meaning and entails a whole new way of thinking about those images. In this chapter, we attempt to demystify the differences between a consumer approach and a professional approach to Photo CD images, and the consequences of choosing each.

Two Methods, Two Costs, Two Quality Issues

The best way to begin is to look at the two methods for placing images on a Photo CD. Both methods consist of a hardware and software system supplied by Kodak. Both systems are called Photo Imaging Workstations (PIWs), but they differ in their usage and their evolution.

METHOD ONE—THE BEGINNING

As noted in Chapter 2, Kodak originally announced Photo CD as a consumer product. Ads showed a family grouped around the TV, viewing their own snapshots made big and beautiful on the screen. Consumers were encouraged to take their rolls of 35mm film to their photofinisher and get back not only prints but a shiny Photo CD disc ready to pop into the home player. Kodak suggested a consumer list price of around $24 for putting a roll of 24 exposures on Photo CD. The philosophy was to use the photofinisher channel to both process the film and scan it to Photo CD. The typical outlet might be a local drugstore or supermarket. Kodak's intention was to provide a high enough quality level for these Photo CD images that what people saw on their TV would closely resemble the scene they took with their camera. In other words, the Photo CD was to become a new type of color negative.

As a natural consequence of having images on Photo CD, consumers could

- View them on their TV.

- Have prints made from the Photo CD.

- Have a copy of the Photo CD, made at the time of processing, to send to relatives.

- Store photos in such a way that they would no longer deteriorate over time.

So, generally, the consumer's *expectations* of Photo CD and the images they had placed on the disc were about the same as they would have for the prints or slides from a roll of film they took on their vacation.

With this in mind, let's take a look at the consumer Photo CD workstation. The consumer PIW is designed for speed of processing and a level of quality that the consumer has come to expect. Most of the existing consumer PIWs are in photofinisher labs. The workstation consists of a 35mm scanner, a Sun SPARCstation computer with the Kodak proprietary software for processing the scanned images into the YCC Photo CD image pac format (see Chapter 3), and the Kodak PCD CD Writer 200. The only film types that can be scanned are limited to just-processed 35mm slide film, 35mm slides in mounts, and color or black-and-white negatives.

If necessary, the roll of exposed film is first processed. It is then placed in the scanner for scanning. The scanner automatically

Photo finishers are equipped with the consumer version of the Photo Imaging Workstation.

PCD FORMAT 1
PHOTO CD MASTER

Image source: 35mm color or black-and-white negative or slide film

Playback: Photo CD players, CD-I player, 3DO player, Photo CD compatible CD-ROM with Photo CD acquisition and/or player software

Authoring system: Kodak Photo CD Imaging Workstation (PIW) 2200, 2400, 4200, or 6600

Storage capacity: 100 images in image pac format

Optional features: Can add images in multiple sessions until capacity is reached

Description:
The Kodak Photo CD Master disc is the basic Photo CD disc. It was originally marketed as a storage medium for family photos, which could be played on a home TV screen using a Kodak Photo CD player. But photographers, desktop publishers, and other commercial users of photographs were quick to discover that Photo CD fit their needs for an inexpensive way to turn film and slides into digital form.

Photos, in the form of negative or transparency film, are placed on Photo CD Master discs at a Photo Imaging Workstation (PIW). The customer takes 35mm undeveloped film, negatives, or slides to a photofinisher or service bureau equipped with a PIW. The PIW operator scans the originals, converting them to digital files called *image pacs*. These files are then written to a Master disc. The customer is given the developed film or slides, prints if desired, and the Master disc. The disc is placed in a standard CD jewelcase and is accompanied by thumbnail prints of the images it contains. The Master disc holds about 100 image pacs. More images can be added to a disc in later sessions until this maximum is reached.

Images on Photo CD Master discs can be accessed for playing on television monitors or for viewing or editing on computers. Playing the disc on a television requires a Kodak Photo CD player, a CD-I player, or a 3DO player. Accessing Photo CD Master discs on a computer requires a CD-ROM XA drive, along with appropriate player or acquisition software.

63

scans each image on the film strip and stores the information on the workstation. Once all of the images are scanned, the Photo CD is "burned," and a dye sublimation print of all of the thumbnail images is printed to go into the front of the jewelcase package.

The key point is that the consumer PIW is designed for volume. The operator is typically not a skilled digital color technologist. The operator keys in the film type (Ektachrome, Kodachrome, and so on), places the film strip in the scanner, hits GO, and lets the PIW do the rest. Obviously, the operation is somewhat more detailed than this, but the idea is to reduce the amount of labor-intensive involvement in the overall process. Volume means profit. Remember, this Photo CD is a consumer product, and the price must be competitive with traditional methods of photofinishing for prints or slides. An unfortunate side effect of all of this is since photofinishers are very good at processing film and creating prints, their expertise does not always lie in the operation of digital-based scanning equipment and maintenance. The scanner used in this PIW needs to be calibrated often in order to be able to maintain a consistent quality level. Because the PIW operator may not be skilled at this, and because his or her primary goal is to push the film through the scanner, ensuring that consistent quality is maintained on a roll-to-roll or even day-to-day basis is not a primary focus. This is not to say that the quality of the finished image will not look good on the TV screen. Again, the consumer has a certain level of *expectation* for the finished product, and the consumer PIW and its operation, in most cases, delivers on that level of quality.

METHOD TWO—THE EVOLUTION

Unfortunately for Kodak, consumers didn't take to the Photo CD as quickly as the company had hoped. What happened was completely unexpected. Professional photographers and the graphic arts industry saw Photo CD as a terrific way to store digital images. They also saw the advertised consumer price for scanning 24 images and thought Photo CD would be an inexpensive way to get images into digital form for prepress processing on their desktop publishing equipment.

Because these professional groups were much more demanding, and their level of expectation for their images was very high, the problem of the quality of Photo CD images for printing pur-

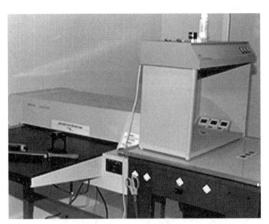

Professional photo labs are equipped to give individual attention to images that will be scanned to Pro discs.

poses quickly became an issue between Kodak and its newfound customers. As a result of these concerns, Kodak developed and introduced the Professional PIW.

This PIW consists of not only the 35mm scanner but a beefed up Sun SPARCstation computer, software that allows for color balancing and color correction, and a high-resolution transparency scanner that can scan a 4 x 5 transparency yielding a 72 MB file. The Professional PIW can accept black-and-white or color negatives and transparencies at sizes from 35mm to 4 x 5.

The Professional PIW with this high-resolution scanner can produce not only the standard "Master" image pac but also a sixth resolution called 64XBase. This sixth image in the image pac makes the disc a Pro Photo CD Master disc.

With the advent of this professional system, images produced on Photo CD became more accepted by professional photographers and the graphics arts industry. But, with the quality came the need for a highly skilled operator to work with images one at a time. Additionally, both scanners must be calibrated daily. The high-resolution scanner is calibrated after each change in transparency size scanned. Although this step slows down the production process, it guarantees consistent quality image to image.

A typical job flow for a Professional PIW consists of multiple quality-control steps. The images are first cleaned, and each image is individually inspected for dirt, smudges, fingerprints, and so on. One installation even uses tweezers to remove any loose hairlike cardboard pieces hanging into the image from slide mounts. The image is then scanned and brought up onto a color-calibrated monitor. The operator color corrects and color balances the image, using the original slide to check for matching if that has been

65

PCD FORMAT 2
PRO PHOTO CD MASTER

Image source: 35mm, 120, and 4 x 5 color or black-and-white negative or transparency film

Playback: Photo CD players, CD-I player, 3DO player, Photo CD–compatible CD-ROM (with Pro Photo CD acquisition software for the highest-resolution files)

Authoring system: Kodak Photo Imaging Workstation (PIW) 4200

Storage capacity: Approximately 25 to 40 image pacs, depending on the size of the originals

Optional features: Can add images in multiple sessions until capacity is reached; in the future images will be "watermarked" for security purposes and a password assigned so that only authorized access is permitted

Description: Pro Photo CD Master discs are identical to Photo CD Master discs; the difference is in what's written to them. The Photo Imaging Workstation for producing Pro Photo CD discs is able to accept film formats larger than 35mm, including 120, and 4 x 5 negatives or transparencies. In addition, the image pacs on Pro Photo CD discs include an optional sixth resolution, 64XBase (typically a 72 MB file). Because the larger files require more disc space than standard image pacs, the disc can hold only about 25 images from 4 by 5 originals.

Whereas photofinishers and service bureaus usually charge by the disc for processing film for Photo CD Master discs, they typically charge by the number of images for writing Pro Photo CD discs. That's because each original is individually cleaned, loaded into the scanner, and color adjusted, rather than automatically run through the PIW.

Pro Photo CD is necessary for digitizing larger-format images to Photo CD, but it is also recommended for those who want to ensure professional-quality scans for such uses as prepress, stock photography, and presentations or multimedia.

66

the source. Once the operator is satisfied with the corrections, he or she then saves the image on the workstation. After all of the images have undergone these steps, the Photo CD is "burned," and a dye sublimation print of the thumbnails is produced for insertion into the jewelcase package.

As you can see, the processes of doing a consumer Photo CD scan and doing a Professional Photo CD scan are quite different. And, as you might expect, the cost is also quite different. Having a 35mm slide written to Photo CD through a Professional PIW shop will cost you more than having it done at a consumer photo-finisher, but the quality will be heads above, and the scans will be guaranteed to be of prepress quality.

Before Placing Your Photo CD Order

If you are planning to have photos put on a Photo CD, you need to take into account what sorts of images scan best to Photo CD, which films work the best, and how you are most likely to use the photos once they are digitized.

Photos with a greater depth of field (bottom) tend to be sharper and thus better candidates for digitizing.

CHOOSING THE IDEAL IMAGE

If you have a Photo CD made at the time of film processing, all the images on the roll will be written to Photo CD, regardless of whether one frame is out of focus and another is an unintentional shot of your finger. If, however, you hand-pick certain images to have written to Photo CD, it's important to make sure they are of the best possible quality.

For a photograph to retain the optimum amount of data when it is transferred to the Photo CD format, it should have excellent image quality. Here are some things to look for in choosing images:

• *High degree of sharpness.* The sharper the image is, the better it will translate to the digital environment. Camera movement and subject movement will degrade an image, so you should examine your originals carefully with a *loupe* (a small magnifying lens) to inspect for optimum sharpness. Also, be aware of *depth of field* (the band of sharpness from the foreground to the background that can be in-

Photos with full tonal ranges are good candidates for Photo CD scanning.

creased by stopping down your camera's lens aperture). The greater the depth of field in an image, the greater the overall impression of image sharpness.

- *Detail in highlights and shadows.* A properly exposed image will contain detail in the brightest highlights and the deepest shadow areas. Using a loupe, you should inspect your negatives or slides for such high- and low-end image detail. The more detail in the original, the more detail will be transferred to the Photo CD. The notable exception to this rule of thumb is that certain slide films have a tonal range from dark to light that exceeds the range of Photo CD. In most imaging situations, this discrepancy will not be a problem; however, in certain scenes made in bright sunlight of subjects that are both exceedingly bright and dark, you may be forced to abandon detail in either the shadows or in the highlights in favor of a richer overall image.

- *Correct exposure.* In evaluating the exposure of your original images, you should analyze the image detail *in your main subject.* Don't be as concerned with the overall lightness or darkness of the image but rather with the highlight and shadow detail of your subject.

When evaluating color negative film, you will encounter the familiar orange mask—an integral part of any color negative. To analyze a color negative, evaluate the density *only*—ignore the color attributes completely. Furthermore, do not attempt to evaluate exposure and sharpness based on a *print* made from the negative, as it is only an approximation, with its own inherent color, exposure, and sharpness attributes.

Another factor to keep in mind when choosing film is that Kodak's original intent with Photo CD was to ensure that all photos looked the same when viewed on a TV no matter what type of film you shot the image on. Thus, Kodak created several filters, or *film terms,* to help ensure this balance. As we noted in Chapter 3, by using these film terms, such as the scene-balancing algorithm, the PIW "adjusts" the color to balance the image.

The problem with this type of adjustment is that you may have picked a certain type of film for its particular color characteristics when processed. If, for example, you've chosen a film because it gives a "warm" cast to images, that warmth will be lost when the scene balancing algorithm is used. Therefore, it is important to ask that the professional PIW shop use the *universal film term* if you do not want the scene balancing algorithm to be used.

NEGATIVES VERSUS TRANSPARENCIES:
WHICH IS BEST FOR PHOTO CD?

While any image can be transferred to a Photo CD with an acceptable level of accuracy, the more discriminating user will want to give some consideration to choosing the "right" film to achieve the best particular results. To this end, color negative film is much more friendly to the scanning and Photo CD process than is transparency film. There are several reasons for this:

- Color negative film's wide exposure latitude reduces the risk of exposure and color-balance errors made in creating the original film image.

- Color negative film has a relatively narrow density range (the difference between the image's deepest shadows and brightest highlights) that is more in keeping with the tonal range reproducible on Photo CD.

Should you shoot negatives or transparencies with Photo CD scanning in mind? It makes a difference—see color section page C7.

69

- Transparency film is finicky, even for professionals. The film has very little exposure latitude, making accurate exposure critical, and minor mistakes can make a significant difference in how well the image transfers to Photo CD.

- Transparency film has a very broad density range, sometimes beyond the range of tones the PCD scanner can faithfully capture.

In the days before electronic prepress, photographers used transparency film exclusively when they knew their images would be color-separated for printing. The theory was that a slide contains much more data than a negative and that this added information would make for the best possible separation. This theory has changed now that images are scanned and brought into the prepress environment digitally. More and more professional photographers are shooting color negative film, for the same reasons that color negative films are the more desirable capture medium for Photo CD.

Black-and-white film, once the staple of the photojournalist, has now been replaced, to some extent, by color negative film, which can be processed as speedily as black-and-white and can be used effectively in either black-and-white or color display.

OUTPUT CONSIDERATIONS

It can't be overemphasized that the quality of the scan for multiple use is probably the most important aspect in considering which method to use to get your images onto Photo CD. In today's digital output world, original image quality is everything. The images on your Photo CD can be used for:

- Digital prepress and print—need 4XBase to 64XBase resolution

- Presentations—need Base resolution

- Multimedia—need at least Base resolution

- Posters—need 4XBase to 64XBase resolution, depending on output size

- Color documents on desktop color printers or on color copiers—need 4XBase or higher

All of these output methods will show fingerprints, smudges, and dirt. Even though a software product like Adobe Photoshop is terrific at removing these unsightly blemishes, it's a good idea to consider your time to do these alterations to the image. Is the price difference between a consumer PIW scan and a professional PIW scan worth the 15 minutes to an hour you might spend cleaning up an image or two for print?

Considerations When Selecting the Consumer Processor

If cost is your only consideration when putting images onto a Photo CD, your best bet is to use a consumer PIW. To find a consumer PIW dropoff point, you need normally look no further than where you already take your film to be processed. Most such locations are set up to take the film and give you Photo CDs back. (Check your Yellow Pages for photofinishers that do PCD processing.)

Keep in mind that these places typically will take only unprocessed 35mm film, color print negatives, and 35mm slides. Be sure you clean your film prior to sending it out, as the processor won't do it for you. Also, remember that using a consumer PIW will be somewhat of a turkey shoot. If you send your Photo CD back with new film for adding the new images to it (making it a multisession disc), chances are your images will vary from one session to the next because of calibration, or the lack of it.

71

Considerations When Selecting the Professional Processor

If you want high quality and expect to use your Photo CD images for more than one purpose, you should go with a Professional PIW shop. Finding one of these shops is much more difficult than finding a consumer Photo CD dropoff point because there aren't as many of them. Consult the Appendix for a listing of some of the major Pro Photo CD service bureaus. Once you've located a shop or two, call and ask for a brochure, a copy of the guarantee of the quality provided, and a few references of customers you could call to verify their quality. A professional organization committed to quality will be happy to supply you with this information.

An important consideration when choosing a Professional PIW shop is the price charged for a standard Master disc image pac, especially compared to the cost of the traditional method for getting 35mm slides scanned. The typical price for a traditional high-quality scan can run from $30 to $200, depending where you go and what equipment is used. Compared to that even the highest cost for a 72 MB (64XBase) image on Pro Photo CD of

FOCUS ON FIREHOUSE

Indianapolis, like other major urban centers, is a hub of commerce, industry, and culture. It is home to both an NBA and an NFL franchise, and for many Americans is the model of a midwestern capital. Mention the name to countless millions world-wide, however, and Indianapolis is immediately associated with the number 500.

Critical for journalists attending the Indianapolis 500 is the ability to get the story out quickly, which in sports includes the images that depict the action before and during the race. The challenge of getting high-quality images to the picture editors is especially difficult for America's premiere weekly sports magazine *Sports Illustrated,* whose publication schedule dictates that copies be on newsstands just days after an event. The magazine's staff had to work out a system for getting racing images shot, processed, and into production under a horrendous deadline. They turned to Firehouse Image Center and Color Lab in Indianapolis and to Photo CD technology.

Days before the crowds began arriving for the big race, a special dedicated data phone line was installed at Firehouse to link the lab with the editorial offices of *Sports Illustrated.* As a legion of photographers began producing the huge volume of film from the event, the staff shifted into high gear, developing the rolls as soon as they hit the door. Film went directly from drying to a Kodak Photo Imaging Workstation 2200, where the images were digitized and and written to PCD Master discs. These discs were then loaded into SI's own Macintosh workstations installed at Firehouse, where operators were able to do preliminary editing of the images before sending the digital information to the magazine's offices via modem.

Firehouse (named for the fact that the company is located in a turn-of-the-century firehouse) is a full-service photo lab that has come to specialize in Photo CD scanning. In addition to the PIW 2200, the facility includes a PIW 4045, four Macintosh workstations, a Solitaire 8 film recorder, a Dianet raster image processor, and a Scitex Dolev 2000.

The Indianapolis Motor Speedway is another of Firehouse's clients. Firehouse has archived thousands of Speedway images onto Photo CD discs. These include not only the popular portraits of the drivers and crews posing with their cars, but photo montages, past winners, and historic images of the "Brickyard" in earlier times. Via a Photo CD player hooked to the Speedway's closed-circuit TV system, fans are able to view these images, which are available for purchase in print form at a shop on the Speedway grounds. Firehouse produces the prints.

As Firehouse co-owner Tim Corman explained, archiving and retrieving of image data is an area that corporate clients are especially interested in. The twin factors that make Photo CD so unique in this capability are the long-term durability of the discs and the search and cataloging power provided with digital storage. For example, when Valvoline Motor Oil needed to reproduce some images from a brochure that had been printed months before, Firehouse was able to use Kodak's Shoebox image-management software to search through its Photo CD jukebox and deliver the images on time.

Firehouse also offers prepress services, including image retouching, page layout, and film output. Corman believes that Photo CD has helped bring down the costs of prepress film production considerably.

Comparison Price List for Photo CD Services			
Service	**Bureau A**	**Bureau B**	**Bureau C**
Master discs			
Individual scans	$3–$3.95 each + $8 for disc	$3 each + $10 for disc	$2.79–$2.99 each + $9.95 for disc
Scans when film developed	$1.45 each + $8 for disc	$3 each + $10 for disc	$2.59 each + $9.95 for disc
Pro discs			
Individual scans			
35mm	$20 each + $20 for disc	$25 each + $20 for disc	$20–$25 each + $18 for disc
2 ¼ or 4 x 5	$20 each	$20 each	$16–$20 each

about $20 is still a bargain. And most 18 MB equivalent scans probably will run from $4 to $6 each.

Photo CD to Print Issues

All images taken from a Photo CD must be converted to the printing colors of **C**yan, **M**agenta, **Y**ellow, and **B**lack in order to print on a press (a topic we explore in depth in Chapter 10). Naturally, the images on a Photo CD are in Photo YCC format, not CMYK. The first question to ask yourself is, how good are you as a color separator? Using Photoshop, could you correctly and successfully convert the image from the Photo YCC format to the RGB format to the CMYK format and color correct it if necessary? If the answer is no to any of these questions, you will need to use a service bureau that specializes in converting Photo YCC to RGB to CMYK.

When using a service bureau, be sure to insist on a color proofing method that will allow you to see what the image is going to look like when printed. Most service bureaus will work with you to complete your overall project, from incorporating your separated images into the digital layout to the actual production of the composite film output for your printer.

If you are involved in high-end printing using Photo CD images, you will want to consult Chapter 11, which provides greater detail in Pro Photo CD processing and the handling of very high-resolution images.

6

Accessing Photo CD Images

Once you've had your images put on a Photo CD Master or Pro disc, you need to be able to access them for viewing on your TV or your computer or for placing into various desktop applications. In this chapter we take a look at how you can view Photo CD images on various players and at the various means available for importing Photo CD images onto your computer desktop.

Kodak Photo CD Players

If you want to see your Photo CD images on your television screen, you need a special player, whether one of Kodak's Photo CD player models or a multimedia player that also accepts Photo CDs.

Kodak originally offered three Photo CD players, available in different models that support NTSC, SECAM, or PAL TV standards:

- The PCD 870 player has a full range of viewing and picture-editing options, including zooming, cropping, and rotation. Users can program a sequence of images for a particular disc, which the player then stores for future playback (a feature described in detail below). (This player has been discontinued.)

- The PCD 5870 offers all of the features of the PCD 870 with the addition of a five-disc carousel, so that you can assemble a picture program that includes images from more than one Photo CD. This player also provides on-screen display of each photo's ID number, as well as other information, for easy indexing and programming. Suggested retail price is around $440.

- The PCD 970 is a portable player that is roughly the same size and weight as a videocassette. This player has most of the viewing features of the Kodak console players, including full remote control. The advantage of this portable version is that you can take it on location for "mobile" presentations. The

PCD 970 can store up to nine individual programs in active RAM, which is preserved by battery power when the unit is used portably. The unit comes with stereo headphones and a full range of video connections; it can be powered from a standard wall outlet or four AA-size batteries. Suggested retail price is around $440.

The console units for North America are fitted with composite RGB video-out and SVHS plugs and stereo RCA receptacles, while overseas models have Europlugs that carry video and stereo sound signals through the same cable to amplifiers, tuners, televisions, and other audio and video devices. Europlug systems reduce the rat's nest of wires so commonly found behind audio and video systems in North America. Unfortunately, there is no similar standard for cabling in North America.

All of the Kodak players come with a full-featured remote control that allows you to create custom playback programs that not only control the *order* in which the images appear on screen but the *way* in which the images appear. You can also use the remote for accessing the various multimedia "branches" contained on a Photo CD Portfolio disc (see Chapter 13).

The Photo CD player's remote control allows you to play your Photo CDs in a variety of ways.

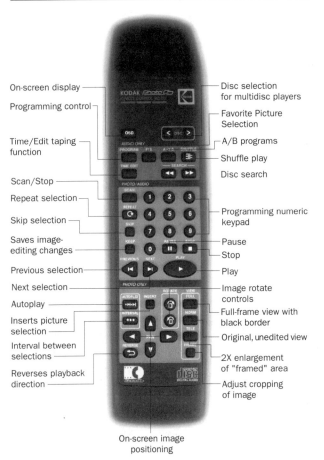

On-screen display
Programming control
Time/Edit taping function
Scan/Stop
Repeat selection
Skip selection
Saves image-editing changes
Previous selection
Next selection
Autoplay
Inserts picture selection
Interval between selections
Reverses playback direction

Disc selection for multidisc players
Favorite Picture Selection
A/B programs
Shuffle play
Disc search
Programming numeric keypad
Pause
Stop
Play
Image rotate controls
Full-frame view with black border
Original, unedited view
2X enlargement of "framed" area
Adjust cropping of image

On-screen image positioning

PLAYBACK FEATURES

All Kodak Photo CD players offer sophisticated picture-viewing features. Using the player's FPS ("Favorite Picture Selection") option, you can program custom slide shows, controlling not only the order in which the Photo CD images are displayed but also how they are displayed. The player stores the program so that it can be replayed at any time.

Since each Photo CD image has an ID number (which is included on the index print that comes with the Photo CD), whenever you enter the image number with the remote control, that photo instantly appears on screen. Using the ID numbers, you can select the sequence of images that will then play back in your chosen order, either manually or in Autoplay mode. At the time you are programming your show, you can also input the amount of time each image will remain on screen or leave that option to the player's default setting. You can also reverse the order of the show, return to one or more images, or repeat individual picture selections. A particularly nice feature of the Kodak players is the video wipe, which provides smooth, professional-looking transitions between images.

The playback programs you create can be keyed to a Photo CD disc's serial number, or they can be universal, allowing any disc to be played according to the same program. Furthermore, a slide show can be programmed to run in a continuous loop, making it self-running for kiosks, window displays, trade shows, and other situations that require independent operation.

It is important to realize that your custom programming is stored in the *player* and *not* on the Photo CD. Consequently, a Photo CD loaded into a different player will not carry your personal playback preferences.

EDITING FEATURES

In addition to the Kodak player's playback options, you also have a number of image-editing functions at your fingertips. For example, you don't have to settle for the composition you captured in-camera. Using the Frame control on the remote causes a reticle (a small, rectangular area over the photo) to appear on screen. When you position the frame (with the direction controls on the remote) anywhere within the main photo and punch TELE, the selected area enlarges to fill the screen. If you want to fine-tune the composition of the enlarged image, you can use the PAN buttons to achieve the proper cropping. Press Keep, and the image will be stored as edited. You can revert to the image's original appearance at any time by pressing the Normal button on the remote control.

The Kodak Photo CD player's TELE function allows you to crop a small area of the image and enlarge it to fill the screen.

The TELE function gives 2x blow-ups

77

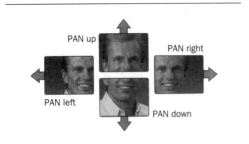

The PAN arrows on the remote control allow you to fine-tune the positioning of the enlarged image.

Another useful editing feature is Full View, which displays the full 35mm frame on screen, surrounded by a black border. Normal View crops the image so that it fills the entire TV screen. Furthermore, you can rotate images clockwise or counterclockwise, a quarter turn at a time. Press Keep, and the rotation becomes permanent.

AUDIO FEATURES

Each Kodak Photo CD player comes complete with a full range of audio playback features, such as the ability to program which CD tracks are played and which tracks are skipped. Other accoutrements include FTS (Favorite Track Selection), which enables you to store your edited program; a Shuffle feature, which randomizes the playback order; Scan, which lets you play the first 10 seconds of each track; and Forward and Reverse Search, for locating a favorite passage. Time Edit halts the taping of an audio CD after a specified length of time. If a CD track exceeds the tape length specified, the recording is stopped before that track (instead of stopping in the middle of it). All Kodak Photo CD players use bitstream-conversion technology for enhanced audio performance.

Keep in mind that you cannot play an audio CD at the same time that you are playing a Photo CD. The only sound accompaniment you can access for Photo CD playback is with the Portfolio format discs.

Other Players

Kodak Photo CD players aren't the only devices that can access Photo CD images. Some players, while designed for interactive, multimedia CD-ROMs, will also accept the Photo CD format, allowing you to access your images on a TV screen and even enjoy some of the display and editing functions of the Kodak players. Both Philips CD-I and Panasonic 3DO players are capable of playing Photo CD and Photo CD Portfolio discs on television monitors and even allow you to perform such operations as cropping, enlarging, panning, and rotating Photo CD images; however, your custom alterations cannot be saved and repeated. All of the players and drives that support Photo CD also support Red Book

Photo CD discs can be played on both the Philips CD-I (top) and Panasonic 3DO (bottom) players.

audio standards, for optimum audio performance, on par with dedicated, audio CD players.

As we noted in earlier chapters, you need a CD-ROM XA drive for displaying Photo CD images on your computer monitor. Only an "XA" drive (short for eXtended Architecture) is capable of reading the Mode 2, Form 1 data in which Photo CD images are recorded. The newest CD-ROM XA drives provide multiple-speed access that reduce the time it takes to access the data from Portfolio, Catalog, and Writable CDs. However, it's important to realize that the amount of time required to "read," or decompress, Photo CD images from a Photo CD Master is based *not* on the XA drive's speed but rather on your *CPU's* processor speed.

While the first CD-ROM drives produced could only read the first recording session on a multisession Photo CD, this is no longer the case. Today, multisession drives are commonplace and are certainly preferable to single-session drives. If you're unsure of whether a CD-ROM drive is multisession, look for the Photo CD logo, which signifies a multisession drive.

Stand-Alone Software

While Photo CD images can be accessed from image-editing and page layout applications, as we will discuss shortly, it is also possible to access images using various stand-alone software packages that are not application-dependent. Such applications as Kodak Photo CD Access and Photo CD Access Plus (which includes Photo CD Player software for accessing Photo CD Portfolio discs) can run on both IBM-compatible and Macintosh computers and are much smaller than complex applications. They allow you to preview a disc's images, open a single image, and save it to your computer's hard drive in the format required by your image-editing or page-layout application. Some of these mini-applications even let you perform several image-correcting operations that can save both time and energy.

Kodak Photo CD Access is primarily designed for displaying Photo CD Master and Pro images (up to 64XBase resolution) on a computer monitor and is generally not considered appropriate for opening images that are intended for reproduction, since the software translates Photo YCC color information to RGB in a manner optimized for monitor display. Consequently, much of the highlight information contained in the Photo YCC image, which is necessary for obtaining good results in print, is eliminated.

Other stand-alone products include Apple PhotoFlash, Purup PhotoImpress, and Human Software's Color Extreme. These applications, which are described in detail in Chapter 10, vary primarily in the number of file-format options they provide for saving your images and in their image-enhancement capabilities.

Plug-Ins

Both Adobe Photoshop (available for both Macintosh and Windows) and Aldus PhotoStyler (for Windows) have the ability to open or acquire Photo CD images, converting them to the RGB mode for use on the computer or CMYK mode for process print-

80

ing. Such applications are capable of directly accessing Photo CD images as a result of a *plug-in*, a program extension that adds to an application's functionality when dropped into the application's Plug-in folder.

The Photo CD-specific plug-ins currently available all aim to do the following:

• Retain as much of the Photo CD images' original color information as possible.

• Make the conversion from Photo YCC to RGB as quickly as possible.

• Provide some basic image-editing capabilities.

Three plug-ins are specifically designed for accessing Photo CD images: the Photoshop Photo CD plug-in (from Kodak's original Developer's Toolkit), the Kodak Photo CD Acquire Module (designed as a plug-in for Photoshop versions 2.0 and later), and the Kodak CMS Photo CD plug-in (supplied with Photoshop versions 2.5.1 and 3.0). Each has its own unique characteristics and advantages.

These are the options presented by the basic Photoshop plug-in used to access Photo CD images. It's worth noting that when you acquire an image in the Grayscale mode, the image actually enters Photoshop in the Index color mode, even though the image "appears" in grayscale.

81

TIP: *Bear in mind that most Photo CD acquisition software brings images in at 72 dpi, regardless of the resolution you've selected— only the dimensions will vary. Therefore, be sure to convert the image (using the Image Size command under the Image menu) to the desired resolution (which will proportionally decrease the dimensions of the image) prior to output. Note: Newer versions of acquisition software, such as the Acquire Module 2.2, automatically acquires images at 300 dpi; other high-end software requires you to specify the input resolution.*

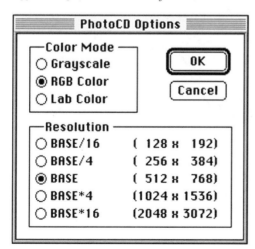

PHOTOSHOP PHOTO CD PLUG-IN

The most basic—and limited—of the three plug-ins is the Photo CD plug-in. It was the first Photo CD access plug-in available to Photoshop users, permitting direct acquisition of Photo CD images with minimal interaction. When you select "Open" from Photoshop's File menu and choose a Photo CD image, the Photo CD plug-in automatically opens a dialog box request-

SIDEBAR:
What's on a Photo CD?

When you open a Photo CD on a Macintosh by double-clicking on its desktop icon, you will be greeted by a window containing four elements: a "Photos" folder, a "Photo CD"

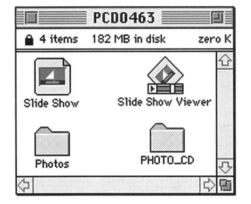

folder, a "Slide Show Viewer," and a "Slide Show" document.

The "Slide Show Viewer" lets you examine the "Slide Show" document, in which the

images contained on the Photo CD can be accessed in sequence and by image number. It also gives you various options, including copying, opening a selected image in the image-enhancement application of your choosing, and saving a copy of the slide show to your hard drive.

The "Photos" folder contains *aliases* of each Photo CD image, at each of the five resolutions contained in the image pac. Double-clicking on an image icon converts the corresponding Photo CD file into a PICT file that can then be accessed by software capable of reading this format, such as presentation software.

The "Photo CD" folder contains the actual Photo CD image pac files, which can be opened in any image-editing program equipped with the appropriate acquisition plug-in or software module. Newer Photo CD discs also contain software that allows access to images by word-processing programs.

ing you to choose the resolution and color mode for that image. The other two plug-ins have pretty much replaced this version.

Kodak Photo CD Acquire Module

A more sophisticated plug-in, the Kodak Photo CD Acquire Module 2.2, will open a Photo CD Master or Pro Photo CD file in Photoshop and perform such image-editing operations as sharpening, cropping, color-balance corrections, and saturation and brightness adjustments. The advantage of being able to crop an image prior to opening it in Photoshop is that you can drastically reduce the amount of RAM otherwise required to open the full-size image. You will particularly appreciate this feature when you want to use only a small portion of a 16XBase or 64XBase image, which would ordinarily tax your computer's memory to capacity.

You can open the Acquire module by going to the File menu in Photoshop and selecting the Acquire submenu, then Photo CD. A dialog box will appear displaying a list of all the images stored on the Photo CD loaded in your CD-ROM drive; an image preview

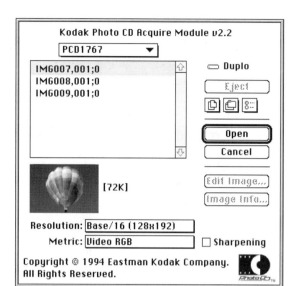

The Kodak Photo CD Acquire Module features sophisticated color-adjustment controls, as well as brightness and saturation controls. The Metric menu allows access to various Gamma and White Point options, as well as Monitor Setup options, which establish precise control over the color profile of the image. Making these adjustments with the Acquire Module uses all the color and luma information of the Photo YCC format, which RGB and CMYK files lack.

box, in which you can view any color or density alterations; a Resolution menu, for selecting among the six resolutions from the image pac; a Metric menu, for choosing the color transformation curve you desire; and image-editing controls, for adjusting color balance and density. An additional benefit of making such changes using the Acquire Module, as opposed to doing it once the image has been brought into Photoshop, is that you can take full advantage of the Photo CD image's original Photo YCC color data, which contains the full range of color and brightness information present in the image. Conversely, certain operations, such as sharpening and color-balance adjustments, can be carried out with greater precision using Photoshop's built-in controls (which are described in detail in Chapter 7).

The Acquire Module's Metric listing includes 21 color-mode options for opening a Photo CD image: RGB, Photo YCC, Grayscale, nine Gamma and White Point options, as well as nine Monitor Setup options. These options modify image information as it's converted from Photo YCC to RGB, affecting the tonality in ways that might provide better results when the file is output to paper or film. One way in which Gamma/White Point information is used to affect tonality is by adjusting the color balance in degrees Kelvin (K°) for measuring the color temperature of light. For example, you can transform a scene in which the skin tones reflect the orange cast of incandescent lighting into one in which the skin tones are pleasingly neutral by raising the White Point setting to a higher Kelvin temperature. Similarly, you can selectively adjust image densities so that skin tones have a more even gradation and better base density by adjusting the Gamma setting to a higher or lower level.

To familiarize yourself with these options and their effects, you might want to output a series of tests showing each of the different Gamma and White Point options, as well as all nine Monitor setups. Doing so will give you a better indication of how to adjust your images at the acquire stage.

83

KODAK CMS PHOTO CD PLUG-IN

The CMS Photo CD plug-in preserves most of the Photo CD image's original color data, which is due primarily to its sophisticated color transformation functions.

To open a file, choose Open or Open As from Photoshop's File menu and select an image to open. All Photo CD files will be listed. When you access a file, the CMS plug-in's dialog box asks you to specify a resolution, as well as an image orientation—either Portrait (vertical) or Landscape (horizontal)—which is the CMS plug-in's only image-editing capability.

The advantage of using the CMS Photo CD plug-in is that it allows you to determine (through the Image Info menu in its dialog box) what film-type parameters and film terms (scanner settings) were used when the image was originally scanned to Photo CD. This information is in turn used to choose a proper Source Option, which affects the way in which the Photo YCC color data are converted into other color modes. This selectivity greatly enhances the amount of color information that is preserved (particularly in the highlight regions of the photo) in the conversion from Photo YCC and is vital for critical applications, such as color separation and high-quality offset printing. Extensive ReadMe data, found in the CMS plug-in folder, will help demystify your options and explain what is meant by specific film types and film terms (also see Chapter 3 for more information on scanning options).

Further fine-tuning of the Photo CD image is achieved by using the CMS plug-in's Destination menu, which lets you specify whether you wish to open the image in RGB or Lab mode, Photoshop's unique version of Photo YCC, designed for Postscript Level II. The Destination option allows you to carefully tailor the image's color data by means of custom color-transformation files, or "transforms," to the specific output device you will be using. Additional transforms, which are necessary for translating Photo YCC directly into CMYK for four color separations and imagesetting, are available by contacting KCMS, a division of Kodak in Billerica, Massachusetts at 1-800-752-6567.

The Kodak CMS Photo CD plug-in for Adobe Photoshop is sophisticated acquisition software that preserves the greatest amount of luma and chroma information of the Photo YCC format. Shown here is a custom transform available for the CMS plug-in that optimizes the color data of the Photo CD image by matching the image's profile to the exact parameters of the intended output device. Such transforms allow the conversion of Photo YCC data directly to CMYK for color separation and imagesetting.

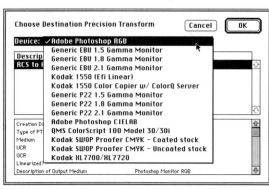

SIDEBAR
A PRACTICAL GUIDE TO RESOLUTIONS

When we talk about Photo CD image pac components, what we're really discussing is a Photo CD image's resolution—the amount of information the image contains. An image that contains a great amount of information (relative to its size) has a high resolution, while an image that contains the minimum amount of information (relative to its size) is low resolution.

When resolution is discussed, it is expressed in terms of dots, pixels, lines, and even elements per inch. For example, a scanner might have a resolution of 1200 dpi (dots per inch), while a digital image in an image-editing application can be given a resolution of 300 ppi (pixels per inch), and a commonly used halftone screen has a resolution of 133 lpi (lines per inch). A computer monitor has a resolution of 72 ppi. This is an important resolution to remember!

Unlike a conventionally scanned image, which consists of a single file with a given resolution, such as 300 dpi, a Photo CD image consists of five (or six) files, representing five (or six) different resolutions. Each resolution is expressed by a specific pixel-by-line image area (see chart below), indicating the maximum usable image size—and here's the trick—at 72 ppi (the standard screen resolution of most computer monitors).

Many of the Photo CD acquisition products available bring the image into the computer environment at 72 ppi, which is ideal for monitor display—but not necessarily the resolution you would choose for high-resolution output. If you're going to be using a Photo CD image for anything other than monitor display, you're going to have to adjust its 72 ppi resolution to suit the higher resolution demands of reproduction, which usually range around 266–300 ppi. To increase the 72 ppi Photo CD image to 300 ppi, for example, simply reduce the dimension of the image. One way to do this is to adjust the image size parameters in Photoshop using the Image Size command (with File Size set to Constrain). This will simultaneously reduce the overall dimensions of the image while maintaining the same amount of information contained in the original image pac file.

When the dimensions of an image are reduced, the pixels making up the image correspondingly become smaller, thus resulting in a higher quality, higher resolution image, in which the total number of pixels remains the same but the number of pixels *per inch* has increased. Think of the resizing process as being like washing a large, loosely woven wool sweater in hot water and then putting it through the dryer. What began as large and

Resolution-to-Size Comparison of Photo CD Image Pac*

Image Pac	Pixels x Lines	Dimensions (in.) at 72 ppi	Dimensions (in.) at 300 ppi	File Size (RGB)
Base/16	192 x 128	2.67 x 1.78	0.64 x 0.43	70 K
Base/4	384 x 256	5.33 x 3.56	1.28 x 0.85	280 K
Base	768 x 512	10.67 x 7.11	2.56 x 1.71	1.12 MB
4XBase	1536 x 1024	21.33 x 14.22	5.12 x 3.41	4.5 MB
16XBase	3072 x 2048	42.66 x 28.44	10.24 x 6.82	18 MB
64XBase**	6144 x 4096	85.33 x 56.89	20.48 x 13.64	72 MB

* Applies to 35mm aspect ratio of 1:1.5. ** Available only on Pro Photo CDs.

Depending on your acquisition software, Photo CD images will enter an image-program at either 72 dpi or 300 dpi. Regardless of which image pac file is being accessed, you can see here that there is a significant difference between the three versions. The Base/16 image on the left is shown at its full size (hence, the 1:1 in parentheses) and is actually less then an inch wide. The Base image had to be reduced four times (1:4) to equal the display size of the Base/16 version, and is actually a little over an inch and a half wide. The 16XBase image required a 16X reduction and is actually about six and a half inches wide. The image pac resolution is also reflected in the file size, shown in the bottom left of each window.

To fully appreciate the practical differences between the files contained in the image pac, magnify a relatively small element and see how much image detail is actually visible. Here, the sun was selected to illustrate this point. In the Base/16 version, the sun was enlarged to Photoshop's maximum 16X magnification and still it remains small and virtually abstract. The sun in the Base version was also enlarged 16X, and, while large in the

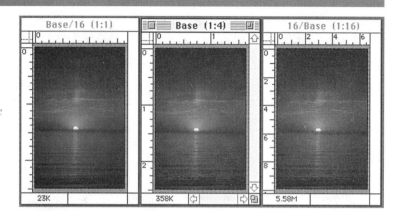

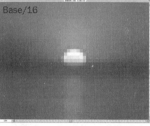

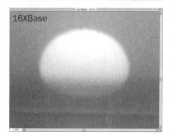

image frame, much of the fine detail is absent and the curve of the sun is distinctly jagged. To fill the frame with the sun in the 16XBase version, the

image required a mere 4X enlargement. Note the lack of "staircasing" present, lending itself to fine-detail work. A 16X enlargement of this

version filled the entire frame with the white of the sun.
(The original image is included here for the sake of reference.)

airy is now very small and so tightly woven that light can no longer pass through it. The sweater has no more wool fibers than it did before, but the fibers have shrunk and in so doing have made the sweater more "densely packed."

Now bearing in mind that Photo CD's image pac components are described in terms of area, which image pac component do you choose, based on your needs? Use the chart on page 85, which defines image pac resolution in terms of area at 72 ppi (low resolution) and 300 ppi (high resolution). Simply determine the final size requirements of the image, whether you need high- or low-resolution output, and choose the corresponding image pac. When images are destined for the printed page, line-screen frequency becomes a factor, and you must choose resolution based on a slightly different set of standards. See Chapter 10 for an in-depth discussion of line screens and resolution.

OTHER PLUG-INS

Besides the plug-ins we've mentioned, Storm Technology has licensed the core code for the Acquire Module from Kodak, which shows up on the market as the SuperMac Accelerated Acquire Module and runs on that company's ThunderStorm accelerator products, as well as on other similar accelerator products from DayStar and Radius, to name a couple.

The Accelerated Acquire Module has essentially the same features as the Kodak Photo CD Acquire Module for Photoshop. However, it actually passes the decompression tasks to the digital-signal processors on the ThunderStorm boards, making the process of opening a Photo CD image dazzlingly fast—about three times the speed of the normal methods.

Human Software, of Saratoga, California, produces a Photo CD plug-in called CD-Q, which adds CMYK-open functions to Photoshop. CD-Q's features include sophisticated color-modification capabilities, unsharp masking, and curve control over the image.

Accessing Photo CD Images in Page Layout Programs

Both QuarkXPress and Aldus PageMaker allow you to import Photo CD images and place them directly into a page-layout application. In PageMaker, this is done with the Place command; Photo CD files appear as a list of readable files that can be imported. However, there is no indication of the file type. In Quark-XPress, importing is achieved with the Get Picture command, which brings up a dialog box featuring a picture preview, under which both the file type and size are displayed along with the

Both Aldus PageMaker (top) and QuarkXPress (bottom) allow the importing of Photo CD images directly into existing page layouts. With PageMaker, acquiring Photo CD images is done using the Place command; in Quark, the Get Picture command is used. Quark's dialog box features a handy image preview, the size and type of the selected file, as well as the color-profile information.

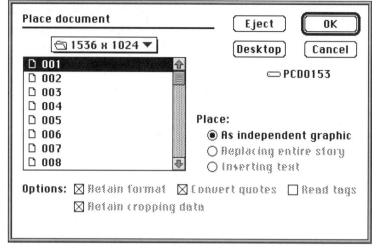

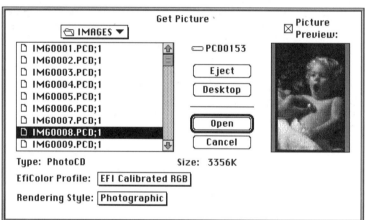

88

color-profile settings. If you will be working with Photo CD images in desktop publishing a great deal, consult Chapter 10 for greater detail on accessing images for popular page layout programs.

7

Editing Photo CD Images

Photo CD delivers an inexpensively obtained digital image library into your own personal desktop environment, where you can make your photo fantasies into a reality. What's more, thanks to Photo CD's image pac of resolutions, you can work with low-resolution versions of your images as "rough drafts," then access the higher-resolution files for the final version.

In this chapter we use Adobe Photoshop (the application of choice among Macintosh users as well as many PC/Windows users) as a guide for navigating through the intricate and exciting realm of image editing and photo manipulation. Although PhotoStyler, also popular among PC/Windows users, shares many similarities with Photoshop, it has enough differences to warrant a discussion of PhotoStyler later on in this chapter.

System Requirements for Image Editing

Image-editing applications are large, sophisticated programs that place huge demands on your computer system. The more power your system has, the more power the application will have for performing complex, otherwise time-consuming operations on high-resolution image files. Here are some basic requirements:

- **The CPU.** The computer's central processing unit (CPU) is the microprocessor chip that processes all the basic operations and calculations your computer performs. It also establishes the clock speed, or rate at which information is processed. Suffice it to say, the more powerful the processing chip, the more powerful your computer will be.

- **Accelerator cards.** One of the tasks that considerably slows down all image-editing programs is redrawing an image every time you make an adjustment to it. As a result, various manufacturers produce accelerator cards specifically designed to speed up the redraw functions in these programs.

- **RAM.** Computers come with RAM installed, but the standard low-end configuration rarely has enough working memory to work efficiently with image-enhancement programs. More RAM can be added to your computer by purchasing the appropriate SIMMs (Single, In-line Memory Modules). To run today's image-editing programs efficiently, you'll need at least 8–16 MB of RAM available for running the program, and you can never have too much.

- **Storage**. The hard disk drive built into your computer provides space for storing image files. The folders on your desktop will tell you how many megabytes of storage space you have available at any given time. Because high-resolution images consume large amounts of memory, your storage space will dwindle rapidly; you will therefore want your computer to have as much hard disk space as you can afford.

- **Peripheral drives**. External hard drives and removable magnetic and optical media are tremendously useful both for increasing storage space and for use as a "scratch disk" (see below).

- **Monitor**. You will need a 24-bit video card in order for your monitor to display the millions of colors contained in a photographic image.

Memory Management

When you're working with an image in Photoshop, the application supplies its own *virtual memory*, a system that permits the computer to access storage memory on the hard drive and use it as RAM, thus significantly increasing the amount of usable RAM, up to the amount of space available on your hard drive. (Keep in mind, however, that actual RAM is accessed more rapidly than virtual RAM and thus is more desirable in the long run.)

Most computer operating systems now come with a built-in ability to create virtual memory. However, this system virtual memory can create conflicts with the virtual memory provided by Photoshop. You will therefore want to turn off your computer's virtual memory so that the two do not conflict. You will also be able to access more memory for Photoshop by selecting *primary* and *secondary scratch disks*. These can be auxiliary disks, such as SyQuest or Bernoulli, or an external hard drive.

The best way to keep your images manageable is to remember

Removable storage media, such as SyQuest disks, are a necessity for working with image-editing programs on the desktop. These disks, which hold 44 MB, 88 MB, or more, can be used as "scratch" disks for temporarily placing files to help ease the demand on the CPU's memory, or they can be used for transferring files to service bureaus or clients.

the basic file-size rule of thumb: Your image should not exceed more than one-third the amount of contiguous space your system has available. Here's why: Photoshop is always working with at least three copies of an image—the copy that's being worked on, the copy for the Undo command, and the copy for the Revert and From Saved commands (discussed later in this chapter). This is not to say that you *can't* work on larger-size images, as Photoshop's virtual memory will kick in and allocate additional disk space for the task at hand. However, you run the risk of running out of working space at any time if you attempt too complex an operation.

91

Photoshop Basics: The Selection Process

Before you get entrenched in the many exciting features and functions Photoshop has to offer, you need a good, solid working familiarity with the basics.

The most important basic task to master is the selection process. To perform complicated tasks on specific, isolated areas within an image, you must be able to easily and precisely select the area you wish to affect. For this purpose, Photoshop supplies a well-rounded array of selection tools. For basic, geometric selections, you will most often use the **elliptical** and **rectangular marquee** tools, located on the toolbar. For irregular selections, the **lasso** tool lets you create a freehand selection.

For precise selection, you can use the **pen** tool, located in the

In addition to the many tools discussed in this chapter, the Photoshop toolbar also features basic painting and drawing tools, as well as a text tool for incorporating type into an image. Here the sponge tool, which provides the ability to increase or decrease a color's saturation, has been selected.

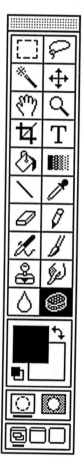

Paths palette, under the Window menu. The pen tool lets you control your selection, point by point. You can then convert the path into a selection, which can then be saved as an *alpha channel* to be used as a *mask* (see below) or saved as a *path* for further editing or for importing into drawing programs, such as Adobe Illustrator.

Another powerful selection tool is the **magic wand,** which lets you select areas of similar tonalities. The tonal sensitivity can be varied from 1 to 255, with 1 being the most restrictive setting, causing the wand to select a single tone of your choosing, and 255 being the most tolerant, selecting a wide range of corresponding tones to the one of your choosing. The Grow and Similar commands in the Selection menu will expand the selection physically or tonally, respectively. Photoshop version 3.0 added the ability to select specific colors, or a range therein, by using the Color Range dialog box under the Select menu.

The rectangular and elliptical tools provide the option of *feathering* the selection, for smooth, gradated vignette effects. Both the lasso and magic wand tools give you the option of making *antialiased* selections, so that the edge of the selection will be smooth and devoid of "jaggies" (the staircase effect). Generally, antialiased selections are preferred for a more natural blending of image elements.

One of Photoshop's niceties is that you can add to or subtract from the original selection, as well as change selection tools, without losing the already selected areas. This versatility is useful in situations where you might want to select a broad, corner-to-corner expanse of sky with the rectangular tool, then *de*-select a mountain range intersecting the sky using the magic wand. Photoshop also gives you the ability to relocate a selection, which is particularly helpful when using the elliptical tool. If your circled selection, for example, does not fall exactly where you need it, you have the ability to move the selection until it is aligned to your liking.

Once you've completed a particularly complex selection (which the mere thought of redoing fills you with a sinking, sickening feeling), it's a good idea to save your selection for future use. There are two ways to do this: (1) save the selection to an alpha channel, or (2) save the selection as a path. When you apply an *alpha channel* to your image, it automatically loads the saved selection. The disadvantages of alpha channels are that they significantly increase file size, and they can be saved only in the TIFF or Photoshop formats. The advantages of using *paths* to save selections are that they can be converted to selections at any time while keeping file size to a minimum; they can be saved in any image format, such as TIFF, EPS, or PICT; and they can be interpreted by a number of other applications.

TIP: *If you are using a version of Photoshop earlier than 3.0, here's a way to simplify the selection process when using the magic wand tool with color images. Observe the image's appearance in its different color channels (an RGB image, for example, contains a red, a green, and a blue channel, in addition to the main RGB channel). If an area you wish to select has a predominance of one color but its tonality closely resembles a neighboring area that you do not wish to select (such as sky and trees, which could be the same tone, despite being different colors), try working in one of the color channels that renders the desired area brighter than the adjacent areas of the image. A single click on the area with the magic wand should select the entire area. When you return to the main channel, you will now have a perfect selection that you can save for later use.*

Another way to select a highly complex area of an image is to select the areas around it, which might prove easier to select than the actual target area, and then choose Inverse from the Select menu. This will swap the selected areas with the unselected area so that you can then make an alpha channel mask for future use.

Making Image Adjustments

Some of the most basic Photoshop functions are similar to techniques used in the darkroom, such as contrast control, color balance, and cropping. Where Photoshop goes the extra mile is in making it as easy to affect an isolated area within an image. In the darkroom, working with localized areas of an image is problematic, requiring time to create cutouts and other such homemade devices. Using Photoshop's extensive selection capabilities, you can quickly and easily alter the appearance of an area without affecting the surrounding areas.

When you bring a Photo CD image into Photoshop, one of the first things you'll probably want to do is verify that the **image density** is to your liking. Obviously, this is a subjective call that

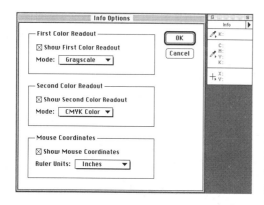

You can access the Info box from the Window menu and configure it according to your needs. This is a very helpful window for determining how the values and colors contained in your image will appear when output.

only you, the photographer/artist, can determine. The best way to determine the density of an image is through the use of the Info box, accessible via the Window menu. It will tell you, in percentages, the density level of the area your cursor is covering. For instance, if your sky is registering a 20 percent density and you want to increase it to a 40 percent density, as if you were intentionally underexposing the image, you would bring up the Brightness/Contrast dialog box under the Image, Adjust menu and lower the brightness until you saw the density change appear both in the image and in the Info box, which will tell you your original density and the new density.

(Note: The Info box is more reliable than your monitor when it comes to conveying realistic color and grayscale data. You may therefore have to take a leap of faith and trust the percentages in the Info Box over how the image actually appears on your screen. It is worth taking the time to have a grayscale strip printed from the medium- to high-end output device you most frequently use for final output, such as a 600 dpi laser printer or Linotronic imagesetter. This way, you'll always have a visual reference point in addition to the Info Box's numerical readouts.)

Just like in the darkroom, you might also want to adjust the image's **contrast,** which can be accomplished via the Brightness/Contrast control. The Levels dialog box (found under the Image, Adjust menu) is a more comprehensive control in that it enables you to make more precise adjustments to both contrast and brightness by affecting shadow, midtone, and highlight areas individually. The Curves control is more sophisticated still, allowing you to adjust contrast and density simultaneously for even greater tonal control. Each of these controls lets you preview your changes before committing to them.

When it comes to **color correction,** Photoshop provides two controls: Color Balance and Hue/Saturation, both located under the Image, Adjust menu. The former lets you control the color balance of an image's or selected area's shadows, midtones, and highlights, while leaving the density, saturation, and brightness unchanged. The latter will let you change the brightness in concert with color alterations. It will even let you go so far as to

You use Photoshop's burning and dodging tools just as a photographer would in the darkroom—and for the same reasons. Here, the original portrait was dodged on the shadow side of the face for a lighter, more evenly lit effect. The second image shows the more dramatic effect achieved by using the burning tool to selectively darken elements and the shadow side of the portrait.

reduce a color image to grayscale in order to colorize it with the hue of your choice.

Of course, if you really want to feel like you're back in the darkroom, you can always resort to your good ol' **burning** and **dodging** tools, located on the toolbar. Just like in the darkroom, however, these tools depend on your ability to wield them. This means choosing the proper size burning or dodging tool for the area you wish to affect, as well as determining how much burning or dodging time the area requires. For more refined adjustments, the sponge tool, accessible through the burn/dodge tool on the toolbar, lets you saturate or desaturate the colors you touch with the tool.

Photoshop gives you many convenient controls over a tool's options. Here, the sponge is the active tool, and the displayed options let you select its opacity, function, and brush size.

CROPPING AND ENLARGING

In the darkroom, enlarging or cropping an image to be printed is a quick, uncomplicated procedure—you merely adjust the height of the enlarger, refocus the enlarging lens, and adjust the position of the easel until the desired magnification, focus, and cropping are achieved. In Photoshop, this process requires a little more thought until you adapt to the procedures. The two ways to change the size or cropping of an image are through the Image, Resize command and with the **cropping** tool. Both let you select the size and resolution parameters for the new image. However, the Image Size control gives you the option of constraining your proportions or file size, so that as one setting changes, the others change proportionately. Furthermore, the Image Size dialog box shows you your original file size as well as the resulting file size, whereas the cropping tool does not display relative changes. Where the Image Size control requires deliberation is taking into account

95

that if the Proportions box is unchecked and a new width or height measurement is entered, the corresponding measurement will not change. Consequently, your resulting image will be stretched or pulled to accommodate the new measurement. The cropping tool will *never* distort your image. (See Chapter 6 for more detailed information on acquiring and resizing Photo CD images.)

TRANSFORMATION EFFECTS

In addition to being able to flip, flop, and rotate a selection, Photoshop provides four ways to alter its physical dimensions: Scale, Skew, Perspective, and Distort, all located under the Image, Effects menu. Each of these commands assigns a "handle" to each of the four corners of the selection marquee. The cursor will automatically become an arrow, enabling you to pull the handles and thus effect the change. If you wait a few seconds before either canceling the operation or okaying it, the image will rebuild itself according to your changes so that you can preview the effect.

RETOUCHING

Photoshop provides some effective ways for removing imperfections or unwanted elements from an image. To eliminate pinholes, for example, you can use the paintbrush tool to "spot" the image, much as you would spot a print or negative. When you select a paintbrush, you can specify the brush shape and size, spacing, fade-out rate, repeat rate, opacity, and mode. Of course, the Dust & Scratches filter, introduced in Photoshop 3.0, has been specifically designed to retouch pinholes and scratches automatically. Through simple adjustments of Radius and Threshold sliders, you will see these blemishes disappear. The Dust & Scratches filter can be found under the Filter, Noise submenu, because it essentially functions as a noise "finder." To emphasize or deemphasize an edge of an image element, you can use the sharpen and blur tools, respectively, just as you would use the paintbrush, with similar options available. The smudge tool can also be used to smooth transitions between or within image areas. Used boldly, the effect can appear very "painterly"; however, it can be used unobtrusively to quickly soften or blend a small imperfection in an image.

If you need to remove unwanted elements, you'll find that the rubber stamp tool permits an exact sampling of an image so that you can "paint" over the distracting element with a nondistracting image area. This is particularly effective, for instance, if you want

The rubber stamp tool is one of Photoshop's most versatile retouching tools. It allows you to "copy" one area of an image and "apply" it to another. Here it was used to remove a dangling wire from the doorscape.

to replace a rock in the foreground with the surrounding dirt from the same area. Used properly, this method makes for seamless cover-ups.

UNDOING AND RESTORING

When you are working in such a complex application as Photoshop, it behooves you to work methodically. Yet on occasion you can find yourself in trouble, finding that you've surpassed the point at which you can "Undo" an unwanted alteration. To cover yourself, it's a good idea to do a number of saves as "Save As." This way, you'll have every stage of your progress saved if you want to return to any given point to proceed from there. There's a big difference between saving as you go and doing a Save As. The former merely updates your document to include all the changes you've made since the last save. A Save As creates a new document with a new name that contains all the new changes while leaving the original document at its previously saved stage.

If you make the mistake of saving instead of using Saving As, there are measures you can take to extricate yourself from these trying circumstances. Here are a few tips that will help you to revert:

- **Revert to Saved**. This global effect returns the image to the last saved state.

- **Magic eraser tool**. You can use this tool to undo only the areas that you "touch" with the tool. The magic eraser's limitations are that its shape, size, and stroke cannot be adjusted and it only produces a hard edge. In Photoshop 3.0, the magic eraser's shape, size, and stroke are adjustable, as is its opacity.

- **Rubber stamp tool**. This tool allows you to restore from a snapshot *or* from the previously saved version—particularly useful if you have not done a Save As. Like the paintbrush, the rubber stamp tool is adjustable.

- **Paste Into command**. You can use this command to paste older versions of the image into the current image document.

97

TIP *(for users of Photoshop 2.5.1 and earlier): To make a number of alterations to a selected image area without having to commit to them, it's helpful to first make the selected area into a floating selection, which is achieved by choosing the Float command from the Select menu. This will create an image overlay identical to the selected area, but it will not replace the underlying pixels until you deselect it. Therefore, if you don't like the alterations you've made, you can simply delete the entire selection and start again.*

Photoshop 3.0 added three new ways of protecting your document: (1) You can duplicate the layer or layers you wish to preserve if anything goes awry; (2) you can duplicate the document using the Duplicate command under the Image menu; this will create an identical copy of the filter that can remain open until you either save or discard it; (3) Save a Copy, under the File menu, will let you save a *closed* copy to a specific destination (such as a folder, the desktop, or a removable disk).

CREATING MASKS

This is one of the many alpha channels saved to create the image on page 107. The more alpha channels a document contains, the more advantageous it is to name them, so that you don't have to rely on your memory, or trial-and-error, every time you want to load a selection.

To work on specific parts of an image without affecting others, you need to be able to create a *mask*. A mask can either block all but the area you wish to affect, or block your affected area so that you can work around it. Once you have saved a selection to an alpha channel (see below), you have created a mask, which can then be loaded into your main channel or loaded into other alpha channels to create sophisticated special effects. You can also save a selection as a Quick Mask, for a one-time use alpha channel mask. Or (with Photoshop 3.0) you can save a selection as a raw layer to affect only that image element (layers are discussed in greater detail later in this chapter).

USING ALPHA CHANNELS

Once you've selected a specific area of an image, such as the sky, and you don't want to have to manually select it every time you wish to manipulate it, the best approach is to save the original sky selection as an *alpha channel*. This creates a new grayscale channel in the image document. When you open your new alpha channel, you will see a white area corresponding to your sky selection and black encompassing the remaining image area. When you return to your main channel, which displays your RGB, CMYK, or grayscale image in its entirety, and you load your new alpha channel into your image, you will notice that the sky has been selected and that everything that appeared black in the alpha channel is now masked. You will therefore be able to manipulate only the sky portion of the image.

> **TIP:** *Because an additional alpha channel increases your document size by approximately 25 percent, it pays to have good alpha channel management skills. In addition to saving alpha channels as paths as a way to keep file size to a minimum, you also have the option of dragging them to a new document, where they can be stored safely intact until you need them. If you are using a version of Photoshop earlier than 3.0, use the Image, Calculate command to select the Duplicate submenu. Choose the channel you want duplicated, then select a new document as the destination. From there, you can delete the channel from the original document and breathe a sigh of relief as you watch your file size decrease.*

By applying a displacement map to your image you can achieve a number of textural effects, such as the jigsaw puzzle pictured here. Using the Distort, Displace command, you can bring in a grayscale pattern that will literally displace the pixels contained in the original image by a specified amount. Additional masks can be used to emphasize the three-dimensional effect. For this image, a ready-made Wow Widget displacement map was used.

Photoshop's Calculate commands, located under the Image menu, were specifically designed to be used with alpha channels to create a whole realm of visual possibilities. Think of the Calculate commands as the ability to interpret specific types of differences between overlapping sheets of film (which, in this case, are alpha channels) and then create a new sheet of film (or alpha channel) representing those differences. Channel operations, often referred to as "chops" (short for CHannel OPerationS), can be most readily used for creating astounding effects with black-and-white, graphic elements. For more practical image-enhancement capabilities, chops can be used to create drop shadows, highlights, and textural effects, also known as *displacements*.

By applying what's known as a "displacement map" to your image, you can create a variety of textural effects, resulting in an image that might look like a jigsaw puzzle, a tapestry, or ice cubes, to name a few. Displacement maps are created from a series of channel operations that produces a final channel that contains a grayscale mask

99

of the texture you wish to apply. When this channel is loaded into the main channel, it *displaces* the image's pixels. How much the original image's pixels are displaced is determined by two factors: the lights and darks of the displacement map's pixels, and the amount of horizontal and vertical scaling you select in the Displace filter's dialog box.

Using Filters

Filters, also known as "plug-ins," perform specific image-altering tasks. Various basic filters are part of the Photoshop package, but a vast array of third-party filters are available as well. Filters are grouped into several different pop-up menu categories found under the Filters menu. As with all of Photoshop's image-adjustment controls, filters can be applied to the entire image or only to selected areas.

TEXTURE FILTERS

Some filters are used for their ability to change the overall "feeling" of an image while leaving its content intact. As you work with these texture-altering filters, it's worth keeping in the back of your mind that the texture need not be applied to all channels. You may find, as you work with color images, that applying the filter to one or two of the channels will be more effective in the long run.

Here are some of the basic filters you'll find in the Photoshop arsenal:

- **Noise**. To make an image appear more grainy or textural, you can apply the Add Noise filter to the desired degree and effect, with the option of Uniform or Gaussian distribution.

- **Blur**. To soften an image, to create a more romantic or ethereal quality, or to simulate selective focus, you have several Blur filters from which to choose. The Blur and Blur More filters soften an image by reducing contrast between adjacent pixels. The Gaussian Blur filter provides the most precise and realistic control. Additionally, there are two special-effects blur filters, Motion and Radial, which can be adjusted and modified for varying effects.

- **Sharpen**. Photoshop provides four sharpening filters. Sharpen

Filters can create some bizarre effects. The filters applied here are (a) Polar, (b) Twirl, (c) Pinch, and (d) Emboss.

(a) (b)

(c) (d)

and Sharpen More increase the overall sharpness of the image by accentuating color differences between differing tonal values. Sharpen Edges and Unsharp Mask work on the edges of an image, increasing contrast between adjacent pixels while leaving areas beyond the edges unchanged. Of these four filters, the Unsharp Mask provides the most realistic effect, because you're controlling the amount, radius, and threshold of the adjacent pixels. Because the Unsharp Mask increases tonal differentiation within the affected areas, it is best applied as a final step in the image-enhancement process, as it would further complicate any selection process using the magic wand tool.

TIP: *As you work with these "texture" filters, you may find that you yield better results by reapplying the filter several times in small increments, as opposed to applying it in one, large increment.*

SPECIAL-EFFECTS FILTERS

Special-effects filters alter the overall appearance of your image rather than subtly enhancing it. Many of these filters have been supplied by Adobe, while others are third-party plug-ins.

Some of the filters that come packaged with Photoshop include Emboss, Wind, Wave, ZigZag, Spherize, Find Edges, Trace Contour, Mosaic, Tiles, Solarize, Pointillize, Pinch, and Extrude. Most of these filters are adjustable and will display a preview of your image in its affected state, so that you don't have to commit to the change until you're satisfied with it.

Third-party filters add even more special-effects possibilities to Photoshop's arsenal. These include Aldus Gallery Effects and Xaos Tools' Paint Alchemy, which produce painting and drawing effects; Andromeda Series I, a set of plug-ins that act much like photographic filters, producing effects such as stars and rainbows; Andromeda Series II, a collection of 3D surface-mapping filters; Wow, a collection of displacement filters; and Kai's Power Tools, from HSC Software.

Kai's Power Tools includes not only a number of stand-alone plug-ins but also some filter-exploring worlds, virtually independent of the application in which they reside. Kai's Gradient Designer, for example, lets you select or create simple-to-complex custom blends that you can save and use again and again. Kai's Texture Explorer functions along the same premise but works with textures instead of gradients. From the textures supplied (of which there are a staggering amount), you can create your own

CASE STUDY

FOCUS ON JEFF BRICE

Seattle-based illustrator Jeff Brice used Photo CD scans as the essential element when he was asked to create a poster for the PBS children's show *Newton's Apple*. Station KTCA in St. Paul, Minnesota wanted Brice to develop something that would be fun as well as represent various aspects of science in the real world. The client also wanted certain aspects of the show stressed in the poster: the apple, the window of the show set, and some opening screens from the show.

Brice used images from the TV show (provided on Photo CDs) as well as images from his own Photo CD library. He imported each of the potential scans to be used into Photoshop using the CMS plug-in in the 16X Base resolution. He then adjusted contrast levels and saved them as Photoshop files.

Here is a step-by-step description of how he created the poster (you can see the full-color poster and the four stages on page C-1 of the color section).

1 The first step was to create a background texture. "This is the canvas for me," says Brice, "and I like to have a field of color and shape to create a basic graphic space to work with." The background was done in Photoshop, using the airbrush and smudge tools. The black gradations were put in using the gradiant tool.

2 All of the images needed to have masks so they would blend together with the background. For Brice this was a somewhat intuitive process, fitting with the vision in his mind of how he wanted the photos to relate to each other. He made a gradation mask for the sky, masked the window so the glass would be transparent, and masked the wall to fade from top to bottom. The images were brought into Specular Collage, where they were put into an image layer list ready for use.

3 The next step was to put the images in place, starting with the larger background images (sky, galaxies, window) and then adding the apple, earths, flamingo, and screen shots. "The logic of placing things is a personal decision," says Brice. "I tried to create an interesting image that moves between flat space and deep space. The screen shots were a good transitional element." Diagrams (created in Free-Hand) were placed last, to provide more graphic shapes and strong colors.

4 Brice input the type in FreeHand, then distorted it using Adobe Dimensions. He added the type last, since it needed to flow around the images in place. He broke the text into four sections and handled each section differently, trying to match relative scale. The wave shape was created in Free-Hand and extruded in Dimensions to map the bottom text to. Once the text had been mapped, it was exported as an Illustrator file and rasterized in Photoshop.

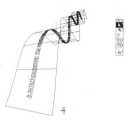

4

2

3

When the collage was complete, it was rendered at 300 dpi. The text was added to the image in Photoshop through an alpha channel. As final Photoshop touches, Brice disorted the flamingo using a wave filter and added ripples to the sky using the ZigZag filter.

"I use Photo CD because it is easy to do and the quality is very good for my purposes," says Brice. "Since my work blends many elements together, the limitations of PCD do not interfere with the overall quality. It is a great alternative to drum scans, which in my case would be very costly as I scan in even more images than the ones I use. It is also an excellent way to create a personal stock library of some of my shots."

Here are some examples of application of Kai's Power Tools plug-ins: (left) Fractal Mandelbrot; (center) Fractal Julia; (right) Find Edges & Invert.

custom variations, via the many controls and options provided. Kai's Fractal Explorer lets you delve into the wild, mysterious world of fractals, which are highly complex, algorithmic painting matrices. These filters can be applied to your image with the same amount of control and flexibility as the other Kai exploration and design tools.

Collaging Images

The digital environment provides a number of ways to combine image elements for seamless results. In the darkroom, such projects invariably require countless hours of masking, pin-registering, and exposure testing to create a result that looks like it was shot in-camera. Between Photo CD and image-manipulation applications, such as Adobe Photoshop and Aldus PhotoStyler, image elements can be blended and merged with precision and ease to achieve virtually any effect you desire.

A collage-specific application, such as Specular Collage, enables you to work with a number of high-resolution image elements relatively quickly and effortlessly as a result of using "proxies," visually accurate stand-ins for the actual high-resolution elements. In combination with Collage's layering and enhancement functions, images can be overlapped and blended much like they would in Photoshop or PhotoStyler.

Photo CD images can also be collaged with illustrations created in Adobe Illustrator or other object-oriented art applications, or with three-dimensional objects created in 3D applications, such as Ray Dream Designer.

When creating collages, you need to keep resolution issues in mind. While you can combine image elements of different resolutions in the same document, you will undoubtedly notice size discrepancies as a result. For example, if you were to paste a 4 x 1½ inch, 300 dpi logo into a 5 x 7 inch, 72 dpi image, the logo would appear enormous relative to the picture, because the logo contains so much more information than the picture. To make the logo accommodate the size of the image, you can (1) resize the logo once it has been brought into the image; (2) reduce the size of the logo prior to pasting it into the image while maintaining a 300 dpi resolution; or (3) reduce the resolution of the logo to 72 dpi while maintaining its original size. (See Chapter 6 for more information on managing image resolutions.)

COMBINING IMAGES IN PHOTOSHOP

Photoshop provides some handy tools and functions for combining and blending image elements on a single canvas.

- **Rubber stamp tool.** This tool can be used effectively for photorealistic painting, selecting an area of the image you wish to clone to another area of the same image or to a new image. You can vary the effects of this tool by choosing among Photoshop's array of brush types (or one of your own custom brushes) for a hard or feathered edge, adjusting the opacity control for an opaque or transparent appearance. This is the ideal tool for blending various image elements.

- **Paste Into/Paste Behind**. These commands can be used to paste another image or image element either into or behind a selected area or areas. Pasting *into* a selection will place the contents of the clipboard directly into the selected area, thus covering the selected portion of the original image. Pasting *behind* a selection will keep the selected area intact while appearing to replace the image behind it with the contents of the clipboard.

  It's important to understand that a pasted image will not replace the original, underlying pixels until it has been deselected. Until then, the pasted portion is actually "floating" above the image plane. Consequently, you can move this floating selection anywhere within the image without creating a blank hole where the selection once was.

- **Clipping paths**. When you want to work with an image element that contains an enclosed area of negative space that you would like to appear transparent when placed atop another image, you must first create a clipping path. This is a function of the Paths palette. You first select the element as you would normally, making sure to exclude the area that you want ren-

SIDEBAR
CREATING A COLLAGE

Preparing the Original

A landscape with distinct image areas (sky, ground, rock) was selected as the basis for the collage. The Photo CD image was then brought into Photoshop at 16XBase in the RGB mode. Each distinct image area was then selected:

- The sky area was selected in the blue channel, using the magic wand tool, and saved as an alpha channel to create a mask.

- The areas of ground were selected with a combination of the magic wand and pen tools, then saved as an alpha channel.

- The rock in the foreground was selected with the pen tool and saved as an alpha channel.

Each alpha channel was then converted into a path. From there, all the paths were loaded into a composite selection, so that the sky, the ground, and the foreground rock were all selected simultaneously. Selection of the remaining rocks in the image was facilitated by selecting Inverse from the Select menu, thus deselecting sky, ground, and foreground rock and selecting everything else. The new selection was then saved as an alpha channel.

Next, the RGB image was converted to grayscale (*a*). Because the sky looked weak, its contrast was increased, via the Levels dialog box, and with guidance from the Info box. The image was then saved in the Photoshop format.

Gathering the Additional Image Elements

The Photo CD image of the water was loaded, just like the original, then cropped to the same size and resolution as the original and converted to grayscale (*b*).

The Photo CD image of the leaves was opened and treated identically to the water image. Next, the water image was made active, selected in its entirety, and copied. The mask of the ground area was then loaded in the original, and Paste Into was selected from the Edit menu. The image of the water now appeared in the ground area.

To position the water within the selected area (*c*), the cursor was placed on top of it and the mouse button held down until the image moved in tandem with the cursor (if you immediately click on the pasted image and try to move it, only the shimmering, "marching ants," indicating the selected area, will move, and you won't see the pasted image until you release the mouse button). Prior to deselecting, the Defringe command was selected for a smooth blend between the water and the abutting elements. At this point, the image was given a new title via Save As.

(a) The original Photo CD image after conversion to grayscale.

(b) The grayscale Photo CD image of the water, cropped to the same size and resolution as the original.

(c) The original image after pasting the water into the ground selection and increasing the contrast of the sky.

106

The image of the leaves was then made active, selected in its entirety, and copied (*d*). The mask of the sky area was loaded in the original, and Paste Into was selected. This made the image of the leaves appear in the sky selection. The leaves were then positioned in the same manner as the water image. To reduce some of the tonal detail in the leaves, the highlight areas were darkened using the Levels controls.

Next, the Composite Controls dialog box was opened, and Multiply was selected from the mode menu, keeping the opacity at 100 percent. This operation made the leaves appear to blend with the sky, while adding a sense of three dimensionality (*e*). Finally, the sky area was defringed, and the image was given yet another title with Save As.

Finishing Touches

To better complement the tonality of the sky, the appropriate alpha channel was reloaded, and the contrast of the water increased, using Levels.

To heighten the contrast between the background rocks, sky, and water, the midtones of the rocks were lightened by 15 percent (according to the Info box), using the Input slider in the Levels dialog box. To subtly enhance the texture of these rocks, the Unsharp Mask was applied in a small increment.

To appreciably enhance the prominence of the foreground rock, the appropriate mask was loaded, and Unsharp Mask was applied at the default setting. The selection was then defringed, and the image was again given a new title under Save As.

Final steps included using the rubber stamp tool to remove tiny imperfections and saving all the alpha channels to a new document using the Image, Calculate, Duplicate command. From here, the alpha channels contained in the original document could be deleted, thus reducing the file size from over 27 MB to under 6 MB. This final stage was saved as a new title in the EPS format, for reproduction (*f*).

107

(*d*) The grayscale Photo CD image of the leaves, cropped to the same size and resolution of the original.

(*e*) This is what a mask looks like when it's visible. Here, the mask is indicating that only the darkened area of the image can be affected.

(*f*) The final image.

dered transparent. You then convert the selection into a path (if it isn't a path already) and convert the path into a clipping path. This operation makes the element into a cutout, in which the "clipped-out" area or areas register as nonexistent. Clipping paths can also be translated by other art and page layout applications, preserving the transparent area so that you can see the elements behind it.

BLENDING IMAGES IN PHOTOSHOP

As you combine elements into a single image using Photoshop's various selection and paste tools, you may want to integrate them using subtle, gradating blends, or hard-edged, distinct boundaries. You may want image elements to fade in and out of other elements or appear translucent against an underlying image. Photoshop makes all of these effects easily attainable.

One of the keys to controlling the blending process is via the Composite Controls dialog box (in the Edit menu), which is only accessible with floating selections. This one control is quite powerful, as it allows you to affect both layers individually or collectively; this includes being able to change overall opacity and to exclude specific tones or colors in one or more of the channels composing the image elements. All modifications can be previewed as you make them and can be reset to the starting point if you go too far.

108

```
╔══════ Composite Controls ══════╗
║                                 ║
║  ┌─ Blend If:  [ Black ⌘1 ▼ ]  ─┐    ┌────────┐
║  │   Floating:    0      255    │    │   OK   │
║  │  ▲─────────────────────△     │    └────────┘
║  │   Underlying:  0      255    │    ┌────────┐
║  │  ▲─────────────────────△     │    │ Cancel │
║  └─────────────────────────┘    └────────┘
║                                 ⊠ Preview
║  Opacity: [100] %   Mode: [ Normal    ▼ ]
╚═════════════════════════════════╝
```

The Composite Controls dialog box features nearly everything you need for precision blending of overlapping image elements. Note the two slider bars, which let you control how specific tones or colors contained in both the floating and underlying images interact.

Once you have a floating selection (which you can make simply by selecting Float from the Select menu) that you want to blend softly with the background, you can choose Feather from the Select menu. This will produce a soft edge around the selection by a specified number of pixels, which will not be apparent until the selection is moved or modified.

Your final step in the blending process is to apply the Defringe command (also located in the Select menu); like Feather, it only works with a floating selection. Defringe is the most effective way to eliminate a hard, distracting edge around a selection and blend it, to a specified degree, with the underlying image. This step will create smooth, realistic transitions between image elements.

For a step-by-step example of how to combine images in Photoshop, see the sidebar on pages 106–107.

USING LAYERS

Photoshop's layers feature (introduced in version 3.0) makes it possible to experiment with an image all you want without actually altering the original. What's more, layers enable you to move, edit, and blend individual picture elements independently without having to load alpha channels or create floating selections.

Layers function much like transparent acetate overlays; where there is pixel data, the "acetate" (or layer) is opaque, and where there is an absence of pixel data, the layer is transparent. Consequently, as layers are "stacked" on top of one another, the transparent areas enable the underlying image elements to remain visible (and you can select which layers you wish to be visible at any time). To prevent "sullying" transparent areas of a layer as you apply various effects, simply check the Preserve Transparency box on the Layers palette bar. This ensures that only the existing pixels will be affected—the transparent areas will be left untouched.

When you open an image, it automatically registers on the Layers palette as the Background layer. This is the base level of the document and is thus the only layer that cannot be made transparent. From there, layers can be added. (Note: A layer cannot be added beneath the background, and there need not be an actual background layer.) Each subsequent layer added to the document is, by default, transparent. There are three ways to place an image onto a layer: (1) by pasting, (2) by dragging a selection from another document into the destination document, or (3) by dragging a layer from the Layers palette of another document into the destination document. When a selection is pasted onto a layer, it automatically registers in the Layers palette as a Floating Selection.

The order in which the layers are stacked in a document can be crucial or irrelevant, depending on your goals. If you intend to do a lot of blending between layers, it's important to remember that a layer can only be blended with the layer beneath it. Layers can easily be reordered within the document with a simple drag-and-drop action within the palette.

With the addition of the Layers palette

Photoshop's Layers palette lets you control, with drag-and-drop ease, how the layers contained in a document are organized and how they interact with each other. Note that the Channels and Paths palettes are combined in this palette, although they can be separated or reordered for your convenience.

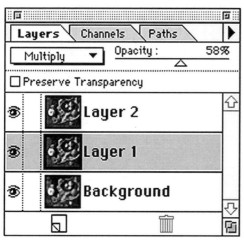

109

in Photoshop 3.0, the Composite Controls are now divided between the Layers palette and the Layer Options menu. On the palette bar itself are the opacity-control slider, as well as a pull-down menu of all the blending modes available, which can be applied to any layer (except the Background) at any time. The slider bars let you control the way in which the two layers interact on a particular layer.

Further control of a layer's appearance—by itself or in relation to another layer—is afforded by the Layer Mask. A layer mask functions like an alpha channel, using black and white pixels either to subtract from, or mask, the pixels on the active layer. When you create a layer mask, it automatically appears in the Channels palette as an alpha channel, which can subsequently be loaded as a selection, should you need it. This temporary alpha channel will remain in the Channels palette until you either apply the mask to the image or discard it. It can be made into a permanent alpha channel simply by duplicating it.

TIP: *Just like alpha channels, layers eat up memory. One way to help keep your file size manageable is to consolidate your layers as you go: Make visible only the layers you have no further intention of affecting, and select Merge Layers from the Layers palette. The selected layers will combine, forming a single layer represented on the Layers palette. The more complex and "layered" your image is, the more you will benefit from merging completed layers as you work.*

When your image is complete, you have several options for saving the final version. If the image is going to be sent out for proofing, in which case the file should be presented in a single layer, you can save a copy of the file with the Flatten Image box checked. This will automatically create a new document in which all the layers have been merged into a single "flat" piece of art. Meanwhile, you still have the original layered file for future use. You can also choose to flatten the image file at any time using the Flatten Image command in the Layers palette. (Note: Layers will automatically flatten upon any color mode change.)

Aldus PhotoStyler

PhotoStyler is every bit as sophisticated and powerful as Adobe Photoshop and, for the most part, the applications operate similarly in terms of its tools, commands, and capabilities. However, there are

110

some significant differences between the programs worth mentioning here.

Many of PhotoStyler's advantages are memory-allocation conveniences that allow you to optimize your system's memory while working in the program. Other PhotoStyler advantages are simply niceties that make the working process go more smoothly.

Some of PhotoStyler's memory-enhancement features include (1) the ability to load only the portions of an image (masks, paths, selections) you want to work on, (2) a memory-usage indicator that helps you keep track of available RAM, (3) the ability to disable the Undo function (which doubles the working file's size) to increase available memory, (4) the ability to dump the Undo buffer to temporarily free up more memory when you don't want to disable the Undo command, and (5) the ability to support up to four hard drives simultaneously for swapping-out virtual memory and to reconfigure the virtual-memory drives without having to quit the application.

Some of PhotoStyler's features that make the image-enhancement and selection processes more convenient include:

- Three previews of the image in each dialog box—one containing the original settings and two test copies that can be individually adjusted.

- A Multi-Transform dialog box that lets you experiment with multiple transformations on low-resolution versions of the image, so that you can then view the cumulative effect and apply all the changes at once.

- A Magnification Loupe that can be moved over part of an image, enlarging, from 1X to 4X, only that portion of the image.

- A more flexible magic wand tool, with adjustable tolerance levels, that can select colors or grayscale values based on one pixel or an average of an area.

- The ability to choose how much information you wish to restore during a Revert to Saved

- The ability to Undo an accidental Save.

PhotoStyler also has some useful features for outputting images, such as the ability to create a Sketch Overlay that acts as a tissue overlay for your artwork, where you can provide printing instructions or other pertinent comments; a Print Preview that

111

displays all the elements that will be printed on the page, including the image itself, printer's crop marks, labels, tiling breaks, and so on; and the ability to "soft proof" an image on screen, so that you can see an accurate representation of what the image will look like on any CMYK-output device supported by Kodak's Precision Color-Management System (CMS).

Output

While it's easy enough to create an image that looks great on screen, making sure that image will look the same when it's output can be an entirely different matter. A little knowledge can go a long way in reducing the amount of time, money, and angst spent in pursuit of a specific outcome.

CALIBRATION AND COLOR MANAGEMENT

When it comes to color management, predictability is the name of the game, and calibration is the secret of success. When all hardware and software components in the imaging chain are aligned, in terms of standardized values and measures, you can consider your system calibrated. It is particularly important that your system be calibrated to the output device that will produce your final-form image. Check with your service bureau regarding equipment specifications and recommendations. For more on calibration and color management, see Chapter 10.

FILE FORMATS

When you save an edited image in Photoshop, whether it is a completed image or one that is still in progress, you will be presented with a list of file-format options. The most important consideration in choosing a file format is how you intend to output your final image. Since you can change the file format at any time, you may decide to use one format in which to save individual changes as you go and then switch to another format in which to save your final image. Here are some of the options Photoshop gives you:

- **PICT.** Smaller than most other formats, PICTs are the only format that most multimedia applications will read. However, while the PICT format will allow you to save alpha channels (as long as JPEG compression is not selected) it will *not* allow you

112

to save your image in the CMYK color mode. Furthermore the PICT format can be highly unreliable if your image contains PostScript text or graphics and you plan to export it to an illustration or page layout application.

- **Photoshop**. This is the ideal format for saving your work as you go. The Photoshop format will produce files that are roughly the same size as PICT files and will allow you to save your alpha channels, which are indispensable for images in progress. Because Photoshop is not exportable to other applications, you should not use this format for your final image.

- **EPS**. Specifically designed as a graphics format, EPS is the format of choice if you plan to bring your image into a page layout or illustration program. It also lets you take advantage of clipping paths for "dropping out" part of an image. With EPS, your image is really saved in two forms—a PostScript file and a bitmapped representation of that file, which can be easily read and displayed by your page layout application. The actual Post-Script file is "device and resolution independent," meaning it will print at whatever resolution the printer happens to be. The EPS format will not save alpha channels; however, once your image is finished, this should not be a problem.

- **TIFF**. Designed primarily as a format for scanning images, TIFF is also a highly useful format for layout or illustration applications. Although the PostScript language of the EPS files is generally preferred for high-end printing, TIFF images are high-resolution, bitmapped images that will also produce excellent results. Two key advantages to using TIFF over EPS are its ability to save alpha channels and its incorporation of LZW compression—a "nonlossy" means of compression (which suffers no information loss upon restoration) that can significantly reduce your file size for storage.

- **JPEG**. A "lossy" compression scheme (meaning it actually throws away data to save space), JPEG (also accessible through the PICT format's save options) gives you compression options ranging from fair to excellent. The JPEG format should be avoided if you plan to go to any output device other than a video or computer monitor. In addition to the TIFF-LZW and JPEG compression formats, there are various third-party compres-

113

sion applications that can save you considerable disk space and are considered nonlossy. These include DiskDoubler (Symantec), Now Compress (Now Software), and Stuffit (Aladdin Systems).

- **Photo YCC.** Your final image can be written back to Photo CD's Photo YCC format at any time simply by bringing the file to a Photo CD service bureau, which will rebuild the image's Photo YCC data, build a new image pac, and write the new file to a Portfolio CD, which will support most of the other formats mentioned above. Check with your service bureau for specific recommendations and how to supply the files.

Once you have edited your Photo CD images and stored them in the desired format, you can use them for a wide variety of applications, from print to multimedia. We'll be looking at a number of these uses in the rest of this book.

8

Image Management

If you store your digital images on Photo CDs or other electronic media, you will eventually find that you need a means of keeping track of your ever-increasing number of images. Image-management applications are sophisticated database programs that allow you to pinpoint the location of specific images. Most of these applications locate and retrieve not only Photo CD images but images saved in other conventional formats (PICT, TIFF, EPS, DCS, JPEG, and so on), as well. Such programs allow you to scan the image library using keywords—one-word descriptors—or combinations of keywords to call up custom selections of images.

A good image-management application is essential to anyone who wants electronic access to a large number of images. Those who already make extensive use of professional photography—art directors in advertising agencies or in-house art departments, graphic designers, textbook publishers, greeting card and calendar publishers, and so on—are a ready-made market for image-management software.

Up to now, these professionals have tended to farm out their picture research to stock photography houses or independent researchers, partly because they didn't have the image libraries in-house and partly because they couldn't devote the time to the labor-intensive practice of having to search it for particular images. Photo CD can bring the image library in-house. And using a good image-management program can automate picture research so that the creative individuals or teams can have more direct involvement in the process. By bringing image libraries in-house and offering fast, economical access to large volumes of still photography, Photo CD also opens new possibilities to desktop publishers and other producers of low-cost, low-distribution projects who, up to now, have been unable to afford most professional image resources.

Photo CD and Image Management

Photo CD was a revolutionary development in computerized image management and distribution. By pushing the limits of existing thinking on how CD imaging could be used, its standards defined how image-management applications would proceed in the immediate future.

The multisession feature in Photo CD (the ability to add more images at any time until the disc is full) greatly expanded the usefulness of CD technology. Picture researchers could now combine images from various sources on a single customized, special-subject or special-project disc—thus reducing their need to remember which images were to be found in which catalogs. But this development required them to coordinate a single image-management system for their images from various sources, so that they could use a consistent search-and-retrieval procedure.

Kodak's solution to this image-management problem is to support the creation of CD catalogs, which consist of multimedia files on a CD along with software and indexes to provide dynamic search and retrieval capability for the end-user. Kodak is developing its Browser Photo CD Catalog software for this purpose.

Kodak Browser is a companion to Kodak's Shoebox Photo CD Image Manager software. It is intended for use with Photo CD Portfolio discs when the publishers want to provide indexed-search access to their images. It can also be used with other multimedia CD-ROM discs. Kodak Browser allows the end-user to search through the content files, using keywords and indexes created in advance by the publisher.

The type of CD catalog that you will be able to have written by a service provider will contain Kodak's own Browser software. Having the software encoded on the disc itself eliminates the need for separate image-management software to conduct picture research on the disc. You can also have a service bureau put images on a Portfolio disc (up to 700 Base-only versions), along with Browser software.

Photo CD Catalog is an obvious tool for stock photo agencies (libraries of copyrighted images available for professional use) because it puts in digital format what previously required thick paper catalogs. The Catalog disc provides thumbnails adequate for previewing thousands of images and Base/4 versions suitable for using as position prints (FPOs) in page layouts. Chapter 9 provides detailed coverage on how stock agencies are using Catalog discs and other PCD media for delivery of photographs.

Kodak has also expanded Photo CD's potential beyond the

116

PCD FORMAT 3
PHOTO CD PORTFOLIO II FOR CATALOGING

Image source: Photo CD or other digital image files

Playback: Photo CD players, CD-I player, 3DO player, Photo CD–compatible CD-ROM with Photo CD acquisition software

Authoring system: Kodak Build-It authoring software.

Storage capacity: About 4,400 low-resolution images

Optional features: Audio; programmed access (branching menus); text and graphics

Description: Using the Photo CD Portfolio II disc for cataloging provides a way to circulate large numbers of images in a compact, economical form.

Portfolio II discs are created at a Kodak Build-It Workstation using special software to assemble the photos from Photo CD Master discs, Pro Photo CD Master discs, Print Photo CD discs, and other digital files. The plan is for Kodak Browser software to accompany each Portfolio II disc, allowing the user to manage the thousands of images than can be stored.

Stock photo agencies, libraries, museums, and mail-order houses are among the main users of the cataloging aspects of Portfolio II discs. They can store and organize large numbers of images for a wide variety of purposes. Stock photo houses, for example, can supply catalogs on Portfolio II discs to clients, who can browse through images on their computer or TV (with appropriate Photo CD playing equipment), then order originals in either traditional or digital form.

117

individual disc by offering the Kodak Professional Photo CD Image Library, a system designed to store up to 100 Photo CDs (or other CDs, including CD-ROM, CD-I, and Kodak Writable CD discs) in a "jukebox" to provide on-site or on-line access to 10,000 or more full-resolution images. Once an image is selected from the system, it can be exported at any of its image pac resolutions to another application or output to various peripherals such as printers or film recorders.

Right now most organizations and individuals who need to manage large numbers of images do not have the ability to produce catalogs and do not need an elaborate hardware setup. They

Kodak's Photo CD "juke-box" holds up to 100 CDs that can be accessed by a computer. It is one component of Kodak's Professional Image Library 30, which also includes juke-box manager software (which can actually keep track of information regarding up to 2400 discs) and Kodak Shoebox information-management software. The system is available for both Macintosh and Windows.

tem. In the remainder of this chapter we look at what an image-management system consists of, what applications are currently available, and how such a system is used.

Image-Management Approaches

There are a number of image-management applications to choose from out there in the digital marketplace. How do you decide which one is best for you? Any good image-management application should include the following elements:

- Handy mechanisms for searching image databases, locating needed files, copying them to where you need them, and then finding them again when you need them for another application.

- Methods for you to preview and edit selections of images before manipulating or exporting them to page layout, multimedia, or art programs.

- The ability to display an abbreviated version of the image that doesn't require retrieval of the entire image file

- The ability to accommodate other types of files—sound, text, and/or video—in addition to images

No currently available image-management software can give you all the features that make for perfect image management. Some programs are advertised as capable of managing tens of thousands of images from multiple sources, yet slow down un-

118

acceptably when only a few thousand images are put into the system. Some corporate- or library-level programs can manage hundreds of thousands of images but lack many useful features of smaller-scope programs and also lack modules that work well with Photo CD.

Given that the perfect software application is still a few years away, here are some factors that you should take into consideration when selecting from existing image-management applications:

- How much memory and RAM does a given application require? Will you be dedicating a hard drive to image management?

- What is the maximum number of images you expect to incorporate in your system?

- What is the maximum number of keywords and other data fields you expect to use in your image-management system? (Many early software developers underestimated their clients' needs in this area.)

- How fast will you need the screen display to be? (Remember, no operation can proceed faster than its slowest step.)

- Will you be pressing your own Photo CD discs? If so, does your image-management system accommodate authoring software?

- Will you need to encrypt high-resolution files?

- Do you intend to network your system so that several members of a creative team can have access to the same digital files from different computer workstations? If so, are the image-management system's security features adequate to prevent team members from accidentally altering each others' work?

- Will you be transmitting or receiving images over a modem?

- Is the given system compatible with your computer platform, CD-ROM drives, scanners, printers, and any other hardware or software with which it must interface? Can it handle the kinds of files that you work with most often?

A final factor is how well an application works with what you intend to include on your discs. The more platforms and formats with which it is compatible, the less storage space for images. On Catalog discs, where only lower-resolution images are used, few users will mind if their disc only contains 2,000 images instead of 5,000. But on high-resolution compact discs—those that will be

119

used to print high-quality artwork larger than 8 x 11, for example—the difference in image capacity will be noticeable.

Now that we have described some of the basic features of image-management applications, let's see what's currently available.

Best-Known Image-Management Systems

Most image-management products are specifically geared toward working with Photo CD images and discs and include PCD among their compatible formats. But otherwise they may take entirely different approaches to problem solving for the image user. Here are a number of popular existing image-management systems and how they approach the organization of digital images.

KODAK SHOEBOX

Shoebox is the search-and-retrieval software that Kodak developed for working with Photo CD. It is available for both Macintosh and Windows. Its name suggests the common practice of keeping old family photos in a shoebox—how do you find the ones you want, when you want them?

Shoebox offers a virtually unlimited keywording capacity. Since Photo CD was originally conceived as a consumer product, the developers assumed that everyone's keywords (labels they assign

Shoebox allows you to assign your own keywords to images.

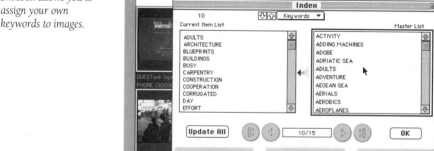

Shoebox also allows you to define your own data fields.

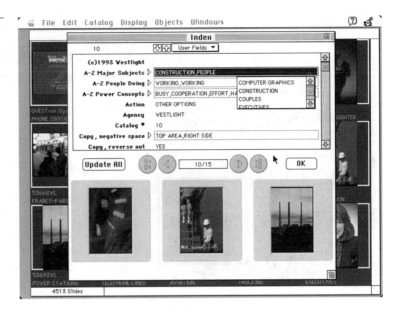

to images) would be different: "Roger's wedding," "Janet's graduation," "Mom and Dad's anniversary."

This is a departure from one preoccupation of image management, which is to get as much consistency as possible among the keywords. After all, when you ask for "horses," you want to get *all* the horses; you don't want to miss the ones for which someone used the keyword "horseback riding." But the departure has considerable potential benefit in image management for industries with specialized needs. Few image users, for example, would need separate keywords for each botanical species of flower, but a horticultural magazine might. With Shoebox, whatever keywords you want to use to search for pictures, you can add them to the list, as long as you stay under 33 characters per keyword.

The flexibility to customize the search-and-retrieval system with Shoebox goes well beyond keywords alone. The software also offers the option of customizing your own data fields, separate of keywords. And here is where the possibilities really expand. If, for example, you will want to review only horizontal or only vertical images for certain projects, you can set up "orientation" as a data field. Or perhaps you will sometimes need images of people in certain demographic groups. In that case you might set up "age," "ethnicity," or "clothing style" as a data field. Shoebox allows users to define up to 100 different customized data fields without overtaxing the system. Once you begin analyzing the possibilities among user-defined data fields, searching by keywords alone may seem primitive.

In addition to searching through images on an existing Photo CD Catalog disc, Shoebox also allows you to create customized catalogs—designed around individual projects, around individual team members' favorite photo sources, or what have you. With this possibility, you can retrieve digitized images from various sources—several discs, on-line services, and so on—and copy them to a file on the computer's hard drive or other storage medium.

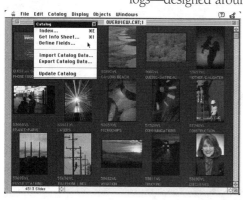

Shoebox allows you to create customized catalogs.

This approach gives you several advantages. First, you can consolidate in one catalog the images you would like to consider seriously. Second, with your customized catalog on the hard drive, you have the option of opening more than one catalog at a time. This feature can be particularly helpful if you tend to work on several projects at once.

The built-in flexibility of creating customized catalogs was intended to allow team members to share their catalogs (by putting them on CD-ROM discs) without having to set up a computer network. Networking is not one of the Shoebox options.

Shoebox was developed with the graphics formats EPS, PICT, TIFF, and of course Photo CD. Although it accommodates the audio format AIFF and the QuickTime video format, it was not intended to accommodate a wide range of multimedia files; management of still photography remains its main focus.

Unlike some other programs on the market, Shoebox is intended for image management only and thus does not provide image manipulation or project/client management features. Shoebox (and Browser) do include the most basic editing features of zooming and cropping, but for more complicated editing and layout work, you'll need to export PCD images to an application such as Photoshop.

Like many image-management applications, Shoebox has many operations that work by "drag and drop." To use this procedure for moving or resizing an image, you bring the cursor to whatever you want to move around on the screen, then click the mouse and hold it down to carry out your operation.

If you spend hours at a time in front of your computer screen, you'll appreciate the many options for controlling on-screen dis-

122

play. You can modify the size of the thumbnails, and you can change the background color and text color at will.

FETCH AND IMAGE BROWSER

In the Photo CD image-management arena, the other two major applications are Fetch and Kudo Image Browser. In this section, in order to avoid repetition, we will emphasize how these systems differ from Shoebox.

Developed by Multi-Ad Services and currently owned by Aldus, Fetch has as close ties with the computer world as Shoebox has with the photographic world. Both applications are excellent, but the differences in their corporate backing are reflected in their designs.

Fetch is currently limited in that it works only with Macintosh-compatible computer systems, but a Windows version is expected soon. However, it interfaces with a wider range of file formats than does Shoebox. For graphics, it is compatible with 8BPS, 8BIM, PICT, RIFF, TIFF, PICT and PCD; GIF and JPEG; and the full gamut of EPS files, including Freehand, PageMaker, Persuasion, Illustrator, Macpaint, and Multi-Ad Creator files. Compatible video formats are MooV (QuickTime) and PICS. Audio formats are AIFF and SND. For text, it interfaces with Text Preview. Fetch also features Image Integrator, MacEasy Open, and Quark Xtensions.

123

With Fetch, you enter your search parameters (such as "people and beaches and ocean") on the Search screen.

Fetch has good keywording and captioning features, but unlike Shoebox, they are not oriented around highly customizable, user-defined data fields. Fetch does include over a dozen preprogrammed data fields, in addition to keywords, and the data fields are extremely well thought out according to how image users are likely to define their searches. You can also add two user-defined data fields, should you wish.

Fetch also offers the option of putting the image-management software on a network, where members of a creative team can have access to the same files. It uses a password-based security system to help prevent team members from altering each other's work. It also has the option of setting up the network so that some team members can review all the files but can't change anything.

Kudo Image Browser, an application that creates thumbnail catalogs of image and movie clips, is both Macintosh and Windows compatible. Like Fetch, Image Browser supports a wide range of formats, though not always the same ones that Fetch supports. For Image Browser, compatible file formats in addition to Photo CD are 8BPS, 8BIM, RIFF, TIFF, and PICT; GIF and JPEG; BMP; PCX; and a range of EPS files. Compatible animation/video formats are PICS and QuickTime. Compatible audio formats are AIFF, SoundEdit, SND, and SFIL. Image Browser also features Quark Document and Template for text, and the Macintosh version has AppleScript support.

With Kudo Image Browser, you enter search parameters on the Find Screen.

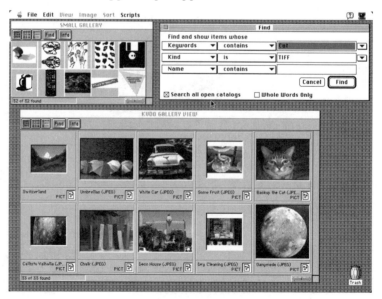

Searches can be made on ten data fields, in addition to keywords, although none of them can be customized. Image Browser can be networked as a viewing system, with the useful feature that only one person on a network can alter the files. This could be a real asset to creative teams in which there are more decision makers than designers.

Image Browser is set up to work with on-line digital transmission services and can access files both on and off line.

Other Image-Management Applications

A number of other image-management applications are available for working with Photo CD files. We focus on some of the better-known ones here, but keep in mind that this listing is not exhaustive.

IMAGEAXS

ImageAXS, from Digital Collections, Inc., is a cross-platform (Macintosh and Windows) image-management application with a unique interface that is designed to enhance the quality of the images within the database. Images are organized into collections, from which projects can be created, each containing diverse file formats and creator applications. Macintosh-supported file formats include PICT, TIFF, EPS, JPEG, RJPG, QuickTime, and Photoshop. Windows files include BMP, TIF, TGA, PCX, GIF, EPS, JPG, WMF, JIF, AVI, and WAV. PCD is supported on both platforms.

All windows in ImageAXS can be arranged to fit the way you work. In the list view (right), it can be configured to display and print the information you need.

Files, folders, or entire volumes can be cataloged with a simple drag and drop. Seven user-configurable data fields are available, along with a long text field that can contain up to 25 pages of text.

125

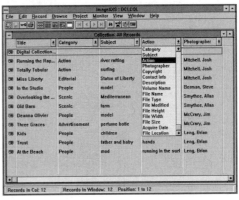

In addition, "smart" keywords allow simplified and automated data entry, and batch operations can be used to attach and detach keywords to a selection of images. Complex searches can be built using any combination of keywords, data fields, description, or file information. Images and data can be viewed in any of five ways, and views are configurable for a customized display.

ImageAXS's cross-platform design allows collections to be shared between Macintosh and Windows users without incurring data incompatibility. Its automatic tiling of up to four images on-screen and a built-in slideshow feature make this a good choice for mixed environments. It also interfaces with Nikon's line of scanners.

CUMULUS

Cumulus, by Canto Software, Inc., is designed for networking and on-line use. The basic software package accommodates up to five users; an auxiliary package adds five more computer workstations at which users can view but not alter the work in progress. Cumulus comes in two versions: PowerPro and PowerLite (both for the Mac). PowerLite is the single user version.

The system was designed to manage both images and multimedia and to facilitate client relations and record-keeping on projects. Artwork can be transmitted to clients over a modem. The software can create a record of a user's past activities, so that you can keep track of the various stages of a project and how you got to

Cumulus PowerPro is a high-end product that boosts powerful networking features and impressive speed in finding and retrieving images and other documents.

126

where you are now. Though it is not part of the basic software package, a transaction protocol can be added to track which images have been used by which clients.

Cumulus comes with a dozen preprogrammed data fields in addition to keywords and offers the option of customizing three more data fields. It also offers the benefit of having keywords arranged hierarchically, so that users can choose how specific they wish to be in their searches. Here's an example of how it works:

Hierarchical arrangement:	*Nonhierarchical arrangement:*
Trees	Oak Trees
Aspens	Oregon
Oaks	Palm Trees
Palms	Parks
Coconut	Spruce Trees
Date	Teak
Spruce	Toys
Teak	Trees

Cumulus also offers the option of searching and retrieving images based on their similarity to another selected image. Here the search criterion is defined overwhelmingly by graphics, rather than by words. This can be a tremendous benefit for projects in which the transitioning or mood-setting characteristics of an image matter more than the subject itself.

The graphic formats compatible with Cumulus are EPSF, Free-Hand, IsoDraw, JPEG, JFIF, PageMaker, Photo CD, Photoshop, PICT, RIFF, Quark XPress, Scitex CT, and TIFF. Compatible video formats are QuickTime, PICS, and Persuasion. For audio, Cumulus is compatible with AIFF. To add other formats you can buy a developer kit for writing your own file type filters. Cumulus's files can be accessed with Quark XPress, Photoshop, PageMaker, FrameMaker, IsoDraw, RagTime, or the manufacturer's own art program, Cirrus.

COMPASSPOINT

CompassPoint, by Northpoint Software, was designed by a professional photographer and is a Macintosh-only system for cataloging both digital and film-based images. Supported file formats include TIFF, PICT, PCS, and EPS formats, and JPEG compressed files through QuickTime. Searches are accomplished via keyword, and up to 12 thumbnails are viewable on screen at a time.

THUMBS UP

Thumbs Up, by Graphic Detail, is a relational image-management system originally developed for university use; it is designed with speed of display in mind. The Macintosh-only application supports the standard Macintosh file formats, including PCD. Searching can be done using keywords and Boolean logic.

IMAGEPALS2

ImagePals2 for Windows, by U-Lead Systems, was designed to meet the needs of individual graphic artists, desktop publishers, and designers. It is intended to be used as both an image-management application and as a basic art program. In practical terms, this means that the graphic artists doesn't need to export images from the program in order to edit or manipulate them.

Image-Pals2 can organize files from any registered Windows application. For nonimage files, it uses icons in place of thumbnails. The program can convert between a wide range of media files. Supported file formats include BMP, DXF, EPS, PCX, GIF, JPEG, Targa, TIFF, and PCD. The program also supports AVI and WAV (sound) files.

In the area of search and retrieval, the software allows you to create complex sets of queries and then save them for future use. If you need to make numerous similar searches, this feature can be a tremendous time saver—you don't need to create a written record of every successful search parameter or reinvent the wheel with every search.

ImagePals 2 is designed as much for multimedia as for image management and thus accommodates numerous video and sound files. With built-in soundtrack controls and transitional effects between images, it can be used as-is for building sophisticated multimedia shows.

The art side of the program provides a complete set of tools to capture, manage, edit, and convert files from different media, plus special-effects filters for manipulating layouts. The program can import files directly from scanners, digital cameras, video-frame grabbers, or Photo CD discs. It allows you to preview an effect before applying it to an image, thereby increasing the opportunity to experiment without being stuck with overambitious mistakes. It can clone images within or between documents and drag and drop thumbnails to outside publishing, presentation, or multimedia applications.

GRAPHICS TOOLS

Graphics Tools, by Delta Point Software, in a Windows-only application that also includes full image-editing, file conversion, and processing capabilities and allows cataloging of a range of graphics and image files formats, including PCD. Special effects, color control, and full TWAIN compatibility for easy scanning interface are features of the application.

MEDIAORGANIZER AND MPCORGANIZER

MediaOrganizer and MpcOrganizer, by Lenel Systems, Inc. are a Windows-based industrial-strength application and a consumer-oriented application, respectively. Both allow drag and drop image, sound, animation, and video file management, searching for files with keywords, and previewing media. Like CompassPoint, both applications allow for cataloging nondigital objects. Media Organizer supports video and audio hardware, including the Sony 8mm VISCA devices and the Sony and Pioneer videodisc players, and the Truevision Bravado and New Media Graphics Super Video Windows capture boards.

VIDEOBASE

Videobase, by Videomail, is a Windows database with the ability to capture, store, and display media files. Although it lacks OLE support, the user can import BMP, WAV, AVI, and JPEG compressed files. It also interfaces with sound boards, laserdisc players, VCRs, video cameras, video capture boards, and scanners with a separate video capture board.

LEADVIEW

Leadview, by LEAD Technologies, is another Windows-only application. In designing it, LEAD Technologies aimed at a combined market: graphic arts users new to digital technology (and therefore needing simple, easy-to-learn operations with the familiar Windows screen features) and experienced users who had outgrown programs with fewer art features.

LEAD has developed its own image compression format, LEAD CMP, pushing further the limits of lossless compression. In practical terms, this means faster speed of operations. Leadview can accept images in color, halftone or grayscale from scanners with OLE 2.0, DDE, or TWAIN standards.

The software includes a paint program and a broad range of

129

drawing and editing tools, for those who would like to manipulate and enhance their artwork in the image-management program itself rather than exporting it to an editing or art application. Leadview also includes a number of standard transitional effects for building slide shows. A screen grab can send images directly to a slide show, a printer, a disc, or a clipboard. But the focus of the software is graphic arts, not multimedia.

MEDIA CATALOGER

Media Cataloger, by Interactive Media, Inc. is a Macintosh-only application designed to track files with keywords and display them as thumbnails. It employs the Claris XTND translator and supports all compatible file formats, including PICT, TIFF, EPS, and MacPaint. It also supports QuickTime and SND files.

Organizing Images

Up to now, we have covered image management as if it were something that software manufacturers organize for you. In this section, we will address it as something you can do for yourself, by customizing both keywording and user-defined fields.

Once you have images in digital format, organizing them and then being able to retrieve them easily depends on having an internally consistent and broadly used search language. To demonstrate why, let's begin with the most elementary method of searching for images, keywording.

KEYWORDING

Virtually all management systems offer the option of searching on keywords. Type in the keyword "teenagers" and the system will retrieve all images containing the keyword "teenagers"; type the keywords "teenagers" and "beach," and the system will retrieve all images on file of teenagers at the beach.

A search language, like a language between peoples, must be inclusive enough to take in all anticipated communication between the user and the computer's search-and-retrieval system. Whatever rules you develop for the search language, they must be applied to each and every image you have digitized. If you are inconsistent, the process will quickly become arbitrary.

Keywording images is a very repetitive process, but yielding to the temptation to take shortcuts may have undesirable conse-

SIDEBAR

SOME TIPS ON CHOOSING KEYWORDS

Like any other form of communication, keywords work only if they are consistently applied. It is necessary to check and recheck keywording methods by observing their effects on many people. Dictionary definitions don't always apply in an environment that is directed not at the masses but a specific industry, where everyday words are sometimes more restricted in their meanings.

Plural versus Singular. At some point you will have to decide whether all common nouns should be singular, plural, or both. This may seem trivial, but your decision will affect hundreds and possibly thousands of words, so users need to know where you stand. Unless all nouns are handled in the same way, users will never know which form to try first.

Whichever you decide, you probably will need the help of thesaurus or spell-checking software (see below) to ensure consistency. This is especially true if you plan to include both singulars and plurals.

Using a Thesaurus to Add Words. Some words naturally go together: all birds are animals, many mountain shots contain snow, and so on. There are so many examples of such associations that the use of thesaurus software can significantly reduce data entry time. A thesaurus program can automatically generate keywords without your having to think of them.

Several thesaurus programs on the market are specifically written to aid in image keywording, but they are expensive. Absolutely essential to such a program is the ability to customize it to match your individual situation. There is no way a generic thesaurus can address all your personal needs right out of the box, without adjustment.

Each user's goals are different. There will be entire categories of words that you do not need

at all, and other categories that you will want to break down further than someone else would. There will be times when you want the program to add a particular word in all cases and other times when you will want to make exceptions.

Although one normally thinks of a thesaurus as supplying only synonyms, for the most part you are concerned with words that are associated in other ways, such as the group to which something belongs, or a concept that describes an object. You can carry this as far as you want, to include associations that would not exist at all for other users.

Consider a keyword that has several meanings, such as "stars." This could mean celestial bodies, pointed figures, or movie actors. Suppose that when you use the word "star," you mean it in the first sense 80 percent of the time and in the second sense the rest of the time. A generic thesaurus, even if it recognized all the various definitions of "stars," would have no way of knowing which definitions you use, and how often. A customized program could produce two separate lists of optional words for each of your two uses, ignoring all other definitions. It is unlikely that a generic product could adequately deal with concepts. A customized program can suggest "vast" as a probable concept for "stars" and "patriotism" as a less probable concept.

A thesaurus can be of tremendous help in entering locations. For example, it should never be necessary for you to enter continents, because the thesaurus can be made to enter them automatically based on the country. (This won't work with Russia and Turkey, the only countries that lie on two continents, but with these you can use the city to determine the continent. In the case of the U.S., you have to use the state to determine the continent because of the lone exception, Hawaii.)

131

A complete thesaurus can do a lot with a single entry; for example, simply by entering "Grand Canyon," you can automatically get "Arizona," "locations," "National Parks," "North America," "parks," "Southwest," and "United States." A customized program can even recommend concepts based on the location, such as "romance" for the Eiffel Tower.

Using a Spell Checker. The same factors that make a generic thesaurus ineffective are also applicable to spell checkers. In fact, you will find that most of the corrections you want to make to words do not involve spelling at all, but style. You may want a device that changes singulars to plurals, changes adjectives to nouns, or allows the use of shorthand terms for quicker data entry. These all fall under the same operating principle as a spell checker, but no generic spell checker would do them. A generic product would have no reason to treat a singular noun as a misspelling.

Together, a customized spell checker and thesaurus can be used to impose editorial decisions as a defense against data entry that does not follow the agreed-upon style. And because you created them, you have the freedom to change them.

Suppose, for example, you always want to include both "medicine" and "medical" as keywords. This is handled by putting both terms in the thesaurus. Whichever spelling you enter, the thesaurus will automatically put in the other as well. But what if, after entering hundreds of images this way, you change your mind and decide you want only "medicine"? You can then delete these words from the thesaurus and put them in the spell checker instead, telling it to "correct" the unwanted spelling wherever it appears.

quences. For example, you might think that because you have given the keyword "trees" to several dozen forest shots, you have a good representative selection and can stop using that keyword. But what if a situation arises where you specifically don't want to see trees? The Query Link function of Kodak Browser includes a "But not" search option, and the Windows version has a "Does not equal" option, enabling the user to omit images with a given keyword. When you search on "people but not trees," for example, you will still get hundreds of shots that have trees in them if you have not been meticulous and consistent in your keywording.

USER-DEFINED FIELDS

Not all your image searches will be strictly keyword based. If you were seeking images for packaging, for example, or for an advertising background, the color scheme or the mood-setting qualities might matter more than the subject itself. Or you may want to find images for which type will fit in a certain area. So it's definitely an advantage to be able to add other, user-defined fields for search and retrieval, ones that cover the kind of information you would commonly include in picture requests.

In setting up user-defined fields, you need to give a great deal of thought to your long-term uses of the search language. After all, if you entered 5,000 digital scans in your image library and then decided that you needed a new user-defined field, you would have to go back and enter new data on those 5,000 images.

If you are a graphic arts professional setting up a digital database of your own, you might include fields such as:

• Your **client** for whom the image was licensed.

• The **product** with which the image was associated.

• The **media** in which the image was published.

• The **branch office** through which the project was coordinated.

You might also include such photographic elements as lighting angle, color scheme, negative space, and reverse-out capability.

The point is to examine the ways in which you would normally ask for photographs and to start from there. At the outset, you should set no limitations on the number of variables. Write down all that comes to mind, being as specific as you need to be. Once you have begun your data entry, it will be easier to consolidate small categories than to split up large ones.

SEARCH AND RETRIEVAL WITH KODAK BROWSER

Flexibility can be a boon in structuring your own keywords and data fields, but the search and retrieval process itself should not be so free-form. Remember, when a computer is conducting a search, it is reading binary code, not English. It doesn't know that "teen-agers" are the same as "teens" or even that "jewelry-making" and "jewelry making" are the same. So rather than having you type in keywords and data fields that might be one keystroke off from what you entered yesterday, it is helpful to work from a list of the choices you or the manufacturer have already defined.

Let's look at the computer screen as it will appear using Kodak's Browser software. When you begin a search, a list of the data fields will appear on the left side of the screen. You scroll through the list and select a data field on which you want to search. You can search on many data fields at once, but for this example, let's begin with "keywords."

At the bottom of the screen, as soon as "keywords" has been selected, there appear the words, "Keywords equals . . ." (When you first begin searching for images, the query link will default to "equals." Other possible query links are "does not equal," "contains," "does not contain," "begins with," and "ends with.") At the same time, a list of the keywords that are already in memory appears on the right side of the screen. Again, you scroll through the list and make a selection—let's say "executives." The words at the bottom now say "keyword equals executives." If you want to narrow the selection further, you now hit "add another query."

With Kodak's Browser, you begin by entering a keyword, such as "Keyword equals beaches."

If you add another query, there will appear at the bottom of the screen, below "keyword equals executives," the words "and keyword equals…"—and those words will remain there unless you scroll through the list of data fields and select another one on which you want to search.

Suppose your layout is for a magazine cover and you can only use verticals. For the second query, you might select "and orientation equals vertical." As soon as you've selected "orientation" as your data field, the list of keywords on the right side of the screen will be replaced by a list of choices for orientation. A third query might give you "and gender equals both." You can add as many queries as you want.

You can narrow your search with various query links. To get an empty beach, you add "but not keyword equals people."

In setting up the queries, there is another set of choices that we haven't covered yet. On the computer screen is a list with three possibilities: "and," "or," and "but not." These are the query links. Here is how they work:

You are creating a layout in which you need endearing photos of common household pets. Your first query is "keyword equals dogs." If your second query is "and keyword equals cats," you will retrieve only the images in which both dogs and cats appear together. If you also want to see photos of dogs and cats separately, you would change from "and" to "or." Thus the two queries would read, "keyword equals dogs" followed by "or keyword equals cats."

The option "but not" offers equally important possibilities. For pristine, empty beaches, try "keyword equals beaches," followed by "but not keyword equals people."

134

There will always be times when you have called up a selection of images and then decided you want to narrow it further—or broaden it if you decide you have narrowed it too far. Kodak Browser offers you several search options: "Search entire catalog," which will have the computer start over and search the entire catalog; "Search displayed list," which will have the computer search only those images that were called up in the previous selection; or "Add to displayed list," which will allow you to add more images without losing your initial selection.

Suppose, for example, you had used three different queries in your search but had been afraid to add a fourth for fear the selection would be too narrow. The search turned up so many images that you decided you could throw in that fourth query. You would add the fourth query and hit "Search displayed list."

In addition to the search menu, the display menu offers convenient options for picture research. For a multi-image project, no one search would call up each and every subject you wished to cover, yet you would want the images to coordinate well together. In this case you would carry out a number of searches and mark those images you wanted to consider further. When you were finished, you would use the "Display marked" option to get a thumbnail display of all the images you were considering for your final work. As you eliminated photos, you would simply unmark them and later redo the "Display marked" option.

Now let's suppose you have already selected an image and want to export it to a graphics program for layout and manipulation. You must first copy the image from the disc to the hard drive, where it will be accessible when the graphics program is open. Clicking twice on the image will not only select the image but indicate that you want to load it at the higher Base/4 resolution (the resolution normally used for comprehensive layouts). You then use Browser's "Save object as" dialog box to tell the computer your desired file format and where to put the image on your hard drive.

COORDINATING AN IMAGE-MANAGEMENT TEAM

If you will be the only person using your image database, it won't matter if anyone else understands your system. But if you are part of a team, you will have to have ways of arriving at agreements so the system works to everyone's benefit. Here are some pointers:

1. Get more than one point of view. Brainstorming with other

135

For many stock photography agencies, the next step in marketing their services is to circulate Photo CD catalog discs among the regular users of stock photography. After all, glossy paper catalogs of their best images have, up to now, been the agencies' most effective marketing vehicle. And the industries that use stock photog-

raphy are rapidly turning to digital technology. A number of Photo CD Catalog discs have already been released by American and international stock agencies.

One recently released Photo CD Catalog is called Questock, issued by the Los Angeles–based stock photography agency Westlight. Questock is both the name of the disc and of the search language that Westlight developed. Unlike some agencies, Westlight saw Questock not merely as a catalog of photographs but as a

new kind of tool that would have to integrate with other new electronic tools. Thus, the Questock search language was developed not only to locate images on the Westlight disc but also to locate them on any customized catalog that graphics professionals might create for their own use.

How does a graphics professional look for photographs? The keyword list includes subjects, activities, concepts, locations—virtually any idea that might come to mind as one tries to define his or her needs. Questock's other data fields—arranged as yes/no or multiple-choice options—help narrow the selection, while at the same time prompting the user to include all the parameters he or she will need to use. Does the artistic style matter? If not, skip that data field; if so, select the style you need. What about dominant color? Or mood? Do you need negative space, a place in the image where you can drop in type or a product and have it stand out well? If so, where in the image? Is this for a magazine cover? Does the image have to read easily small? For some uses, there's no point in selecting a photograph if you can't tell what it is without blowing it up! For photographs of people, should they be posed or candid? Do demographics matter, and does style of dress matter? For scenics, does the season matter, or the weather conditions? Does the horizon line have

people may bring out important ideas and perceptions you never considered before.

2. Define terms exactly and make sure everyone agrees to the definition. There can be no room for interpretation. Set the rules and stick to them. With more abstract words, it may not be possible to agree in advance but only after some experimentation. Realize that a certain amount of trial and error is normal and be prepared to deal with it, but always with the goal of arriving at a clear understanding.

IMAGE	COMPONENT	DOMINANT COLORS		ENVIRONMENT	HORIZON LINE	LIGHTING ANGLE	LIGHTING LOOK	POINT OF VIEW
A-Z MAJOR SUBJECTS	DOZENS OF CHOICES	RED	BROWN	INDOOR	TOP	FRONTLIT	DAY	HIGH
A-Z PEOPLE DOING	DOZENS OF CHOICES	YELLOW	GRAY		MIDDLE	BACKLIT	NIGHT	LEVEL
POWER CONCEPTS	HUNDREDS OF CHOICES	BLUE	WHITE	OUTDOOR	BOTTOM	TOPLIT	SUNRISE/SUNSET	LOW
			BLACK			SIDELIT		
KEYWORDS	THOUSANDS OF CHOICES	ORANGE	MAGENTA		ANGLE TILT	FLAT	TWILIGHT	AERIAL
		GREEN	MULTI COLORED	OTHER OPTIONS		SUBJECT IS SOURCE	INTERIOR	
		VIOLET	NEUTRAL		OTHER OPTIONS	OTHER OPTIONS	OTHER OPTIONS	CLOSE-UP DETAIL
LOCATION	REGION	CITY		STATE OR PROVINCE		COUNTRY		CONTINENT
STYLE	ABSTRACT	COMPOSITE	CONTEMPORARY	EYESTOPPER	GALLERY	GRAPHIC	PROGRESSIVE	STILL LIFE
SETTING	SCENICS	SEASON	WEATHER		FORMAL	BABIES	BOTH	NONE
					CASUAL	CHILDREN		ONE
DATABASE OF THOUSANDS OF IMAGES	ALL NATURE	WINTER	SUNNY	HAZY/FOG	SEMI-FORMAL	TEENS	FEMALE ONLY	TWO
		SPRING		STORMY	UNIFORM			
	NATURE W/ MANMADE	SUMMER	CLEAR	RAIN	BUSINESS	ADULTS		GROUP
		FALL					MALE ONLY	
	ALL MANMADE	OTHER	OVERCAST	SNOW	COSTUME	SENIORS		CROWD
PEOPLE	POSED OR CANDID	MODELS OR REAL			CLOTHING	AGE	GENDER	NUMBER
SOUND VALUE	SILENT	QUIET			LOUD		VERY LOUD	
READ EASILY SMALL	TOP AREA	BOTTOM AREA		MIDDLE AREA	LEFT AREA	RIGHT AREA		ALL AREAS
COPY	NEGATIVE SPACE	REVERSE OUT CAPABLE		VERTICAL				
				HORIZONTAL				
ACTION	NONE	BLUR ACTION	STOP ACTION	VERTICAL & CROPS				
				HORIZONTAL & CROPS				
MOOD	BRIGHT & FRIENDLY	DARK & SOMBER	NEUTRAL	ALL CROPS				
LAYOUT	BACKGROUND	COVER	TEXTURE	ORIENTATION				

TABLE FOR CONVERTING IDEAS TO IMAGES

After organizing images according to all possible options, each situation's unique requirements can be met by mixing and cross-referencing search paths. The process is designed to be an adventure in creative stimulation and idea prompting. The Questock system is available on an interactive compact disk. The Questock search system is based on years of research into graphic problems and creative visual solutions.

800 • 622 • 2028

©1994 Westlight

just as the cymbals crash in the background music? If so, do you need only images which support a loud sound value?

Some new converts to digital imaging have been bewildered that Westlight included as many search parameters as they did. The data fields, they felt, went well beyond what would be needed to manage the 5,000 or fewer low-resolution images that would fit on a Photo CD Catalog disc. But Questock was developed not around the needs of the disc itself but around the needs of the art directors and graphic designers who would use the language. The Questock disc gives the purchaser the option of importing its search language and using it for all his or her in-house image management, without additional licensing costs. The language may also be licensed for bundling with other catalog discs or image-management software that will be distributed commercially.

137

to coordinate with that of other images which have already been selected? Do you need a background to combine with a subject for which the lighting angle is obvious? If so, with what lighting angle do you need to coordinate? Will the photograph appear in a multimedia sequence

3. Don't make snap judgments. If you come across a new situation the group didn't foresee, stop what you're doing and call a conference. Discuss it openly and make sure everyone contributes to the discussion. Don't go any further until everyone agrees to the new policy.

4. Appoint specialists. Have each participant be in charge of a specific group of search fields. The person in charge will have the responsibility of enforcing the previously agreed-upon standards. When disagreements arise, this person will remind others of their commitment.

5. Build in quality control at several points. There are always going to be little mistakes—typos, judgment errors, and so on—so create a system to find and correct them before you're done.

6. Draw the line somewhere. No search language is ever going to be perfect, especially if some of the categories are very subjective. Fine-tuning is a neverending process. At some point you just have to say, "This is good enough," and move on.

9

Photo Delivery and Photo CD

Thousands—possibly millions—of photographs change hands daily in the United States. At any given moment during the business day, designers and editors at newspapers, magazines, book publishers, ad agencies, corporations, and multimedia production houses are busy looking for and choosing photos for immediate and future use. Although a number of these photos are shot on assignment by staffers or freelancers, many more are existing shots purchased or licensed from individual photographers or from stock photo agencies.

Although Photo CD technology has not yet taken the field of stock photography by storm, several photographers and agencies at the vanguard have begun to use Photo CD discs both as a way to organize and catalog their images and to make them available to clients. Some agencies are using Photo CD discs as a way for clients to preview and choose from low-resolution images; others are actually providing the complete image pacs. In addition, "clip photos" are being delivered in Photo CD format. And perhaps one of the most exciting developments in this area is the fledgling on-line photo delivery industry, which brings hundreds of thousands of images to the potential user's desktop for preview and selection.

In this chapter we see how individual photographers can use Photo CD discs as a delivery medium, how stock photo agencies are incorporating PCD technology in their methods of operation, and how the new on-line services are delivering PCD images via the digital highway.

Photo CD Delivery by Photographers

When photographers solicit new business, they often have to carry around bulky portfolios of their past work to show what they can do. With Photo CD Master or Portfolio discs, they can carry hundreds to thousands of images on a single disc. In addition, the images on a CD can be displayed much more entertainingly, since the photographer can use Kodak's Portfolio authoring system to add music and special effects to support the transition between pictures.

Shifting the photographer's portfolio to a more easily carried and entertaining medium can change the whole atmosphere of the portfolio review, in a way that benefits photographer and prospective client alike. Up to now, commercial color photographers have worked overwhelmingly in transparency format. When a photographer has presented his or her work to a prospective client, the company's art directors, account executives, photo buyers, and other decision makers have had to crowd around a small light table to see the images as best they could. In showing a portfolio on Photo CD, the photographer can invite decision makers to sit comfortably before a large-screen television and review the work in large format. He or she can make a better impression on more decision makers at once, and the increased comfort of the situation may make them more favorably disposed toward the work. And a PCD portfolio offers the photographer an opportunity to show off other multimedia skills he or she might have.

For many photographers, Photo CD may also be a good medium for the final product delivered to clients. For instance, photographers can create Photo CD "photo albums" for sale to clients. The major milestones of life—graduations, weddings, christenings, bar mitzvahs, and so on—already provide a substantial part of consumer photographers' business; imagine that increased business if photographers could also sell dynamic multimedia shows of those events on Photo CD!

Virginia Beach–based photographer Chris Crumley has found numerous uses for Photo CD. The underwater photographer shoots images all over the world. He selects the top images to be written to Photo CD discs, then uses Shoebox on the Macintosh for cataloging and organizing them. Crumley has produced four-color brochures and other promotional materials containing the PCD images, and his agency, EarthWater, has supplied some 5,000 PCD images to go on-line with Kodak Picture Exchange.

Corporate clients, rather than having a few photographs taken for brochures, might have their full product lines shot and written to Photo CD. These images could then be used for a multitude of purposes, from print to simple presentations to multimedia productions.

Then there is the advantage of being able to deliver digital files to art directors and designers on Photo CD Master or Pro discs. The more that art directors and designers can do with photographs, the better they look in the eyes of their employers and their clients. Images delivered in high-resolution digital format invite graphics professionals to manipulate them at will, without incurring too much expense. Once art directors and designers have become adept at working with digital files, they may not want to accept transparencies or prints anymore. They can already get as high quality prepress work from high-resolution digital files as they can from transparencies. Ultimately, the advantages of Photo CD far outweigh both photographers' and clients' reluctance to change media.

Disc Delivery of Stock Photography and Clip Photos

A stock photography agency maintains a library of photographs that can be licensed for professional use. An agency may have a generalized file of commonly sought subjects, or it may specialize—regional scenics, sports, celebrities, news, and historical subjects are common specialties. Images may be straightforward representations of particular subjects, or they may be unexpected expressions of special concepts—a businessman climbing a ladder, for example, or a child stepping through a doorway into an endless field of stars. Except for some early historical material, the photographers themselves usually earn a percentage of the licensing fees that stock agencies charge their clients to publish the images.

Stock photography agencies are just beginning to explore the variety of uses of Photo CD media in their business. A stock agency can significantly reduce its labor costs if its clients are able to select images from Photo CD Portfolio II discs (described in Chapter 8) and then receive high-resolution files on Photo CD Master or Pro discs. With Photo CD, the cost per megabyte of storage space is very low, and the costs of writing images onto a new disc are far lower than the costs involved in traditional research and delivery methods.

Some clients may select a photograph in transparency format but ask to have it digitized. The image can be written to a Photo CD

Master or Pro disc in less than a minute. Although the cost for an agency to have its own PIW is many times that for regular desktop scanners, those scanning in volume may find that the upfront expense is worth it. Currently only one stock agency, Westlight, has a Pro Photo Imaging Workstation in-house.

Among stock agencies, Photo CD is in the early stages as a medium for both image management and image delivery, primarily because of the newness of the medium but also because many stock photographers still have ingrained suspicions of how digital imaging will affect their livelihood. With the new tools at their disposal, many clients can draw images from several sources, create their own collections of images on their hard drives, and then copy the images onto compact discs for future use. This possibility makes many stock agencies and photographers nervous, especially if they have supplied the clients with high-resolution reproduction-quality digital files. An age-old problem for stock agencies is clients making copies of images and then forgetting where the originals came from and assuming that they own the copyright.

Nevertheless, many stock agencies are jumping on the Photo CD bandwagon. As of late 1994, three major stock agencies (Image Bank, a subsidiary of Eastman Kodak; ProFiles West; and Westlight) and six clip photo distributors (Corel Corporation, Digital Stock, CMCD, DiAMAR, Pacific Publishing, and Digital Zone) had released catalogs of images on Photo CD. Four other stock agencies (Allstock, FPG, Stock Market, and Tony Stone Worldwide) produce CD-ROM catalogs on a comparable digital imaging disc developed by 3M, and two agencies (Comstock and the newly formed Digital Stock Connection) have developed their own digital imaging disc systems. These systems are all flexible enough that discs can be general catalogs of available images or can be specialized to specific markets or types of requests.

CLIP PHOTOS

Clip photo discs contain images that can be used freely by the purchaser without additional payment. The subject matter of clip photo discs varies, but the subjects tend to be frequently published, inexpensive to shoot, and unlikely to be litigious. Nature and travel are popular subjects; celebrities and professional sports are generally too risky, while peoples of the Yucatan, for example, would be too specialized. Also likely subjects are public domain images, such

SIDEBAR

STOCK PHOTOGRAPHY AND MULTIMEDIA

Except for one factor, stock photography agencies are extremely well positioned to meet the needs of the newly expanded multimedia industry. The one problem is pricing.

Interactive CD-ROM publishers use a large number of images for each of their projects. If they followed traditional pricing standards for licensing images—standards that were established around projects that use far fewer images—the cost of their products would be prohibitive for the consumer market. At the same time, stock photography agencies are extremely skilled-labor intensive. They can ill afford to drop their prices significantly unless they can substantially reduce their labor costs. And photographers depend on their commissions from licensing fees to finance future stock shooting. If good photographers are not paid adequately for their work, the sources of professional quality images will dry up.

If pricing images for electronic media is the problem, Photo CD Portfolio II discs may well be the answer. If electronic publishers can be persuaded to do their own picture research on Photo CD discs and to select a substantial number of their images from a single catalog, then stock photography agencies may be able to reduce their labor costs, and both photographers and agencies might let volume sales offset a reduction in price per image.

In practical terms, this means that stock photography agencies and multimedia producers can, indeed, meet each others' needs, as long as they are conscious of both the benefits and limitations they offer each other.

143

as NASA space photos. It can be a hassle for individuals to go through the red tape to obtain professional-quality versions of such images from the federal government, but they are easily obtainable from stock houses that have already gone through the hassles.

Corel Corporation offers two major clip art products: Corel Gallery, a disc with over 10,000 color and black-and-white images for only $59, and Corel Professional Photo CD, a set of Master discs each containing about 100 copyright-free photos for $24.95 per disc. (Note: All prices quoted are subject to change.)

3G Graphics offers its Art à la Carte discs at $49.95 for over 150 images per disc. Art Films Inc. puts an average of 35 high-resolution images on each of its Art Files Clip Art Library discs and charges $9.95 per disc.

CMCD's Visual Symbols Library consists of seven collections of Photo CD images, including three discs of everyday objects plus single discs of "Just Tools," "Just Hands," "Just Documents," and "Metaphorically Speaking" (containing visual puns). The royalty-free photos were selected by award-winning designer Clement Mok. The list price on these discs is $129 each.

FOCUS ON DIGITAL STOCK

Digital Stock, in Solana Beach, California, publishes royalty-free stock photographic image discs using Kodak's Photo CD technology. Its comprehensive image library is organized into easily accessible categories, such as Animals, Transportation, and Landscapes. Each Digital Stock disc is a Photo CD Master disc containing 100 images from a selection of America's premier photographers. A catalog disc is also available containing thumbnail previews of the more than 2,000 images available in the library. The ability to browse the images by keyword with the software included on the disc (Fetch) represents a distinct advantage over the old way of choosing a photo by paging through the thousands of images contained in stock photo books.

Principal Charles Smith is responsible for acquiring new images, conceptualizing the categories of work, and overseeing the production of the discs. As a well-recognized professional photographer himself, Smith brings a unique sensibility to Digital Stock: "With over 20 years in the business of making photographs, I know how important the quality of the images is to the photographer, and how hard it is to translate that quality to the printed page, so we are always asking imaging professionals about

how they work, what they need, and why they need it. For example, we know that most stock photographs are being used for some kind of output, so we collaborated with Kodak on a special Kodak Color Management System (KCMS) Transform that converts Digital Stock's images into RGB for monitor display or into CMYK for printing. That way, the user sees perfect color reproduction and shadow detail from start to finish."

The concept for a Digital Stock Photo CD can come from a request from the market or may arise from a particular or obvious theme, such as flowers. It can even emerge from a capricious thought or comment, such as "The 100 Best Photographs of Killer Whales." Depending on the theme, it can take from three to six months from conception to completion of a disc.

According to Smith, the key to any Digital Stock CD's development is the availability of suitable content and the ability to access it. First a photographer must be identified, contacted, and possibly educated to the Photo CD stock concept. Some photographers are resistant to the thought of publishing their photographs on Photo CD at all. "The most common myth they've expressed is that the integrity of the images can't be preserved, or that only drum scanners produce high quality," Smith says. Photographers also fear loss of control of their images, seeing the virtually unlimited availability on the disc as a license to steal.

Smith acknowledges that it is of the utmost importance to provide high-quality images. That means finding a service bureau that meets the highest quality standards for processing Photo CD scans and writing them to disc. Digital Stock tested five service bureaus before they found one that performed to their exacting standards.

In answer to photographers' concerns about possible "theft" of their images, Smith notes that because the images are royalty-free, clients purchase the right to use the images in whatever way they want, including electronically combining and manipulating them and using them multiple times. Digital Stock therefore works to negotiate a fair royalty with photographers at the outset to ensure their continued participation. Smith points out that the competition for image use means that only 1 in 20,000 images will ever be licenced by the traditional stock agency, so that the increased exposure for the photographer's work outweighs the disadvantages.

Digital Stock has been so convincing with this argument that a number of noted photographers have signed on to provide images for specialty discs. These photographers include Robert Yin, a master of underwater photography; Joshua Ets-Hokin, a noted food photographer; and Mike Sedam, whose human interest

photographs have appeared in such publications as *National Geographic* and *Newsweek*.

Smith believes that products such as his company's will change the business of stock photography by providing new quality, economy, and availability to more and more publishers, ad agencies, corporations, multimedia developers, and other major users of photographic images. And Photo CD technology is playing a key part in that quality, economy, and availability.

145

DiAMAR Portfolios each contain 54 royalty-free images (in both PCD and CMYK TIFF formats) from award-winning professional photographers. Six discs are currently available: Backgrounds & Textures, Cities & Castles, Flowers, Landscapes & Scenery, Nature & Animals, and People & Lifestyles. The suggested retail price for each disc is $79.95.

Pacific Publishing's Blue Ribbon Photography Series offers royalty-free Photo CD images from such well-known photographers as Barbara Sansome and Lee Hinton. The discs retail at $49.95.

Digital Zone's Digital Sampler series also emphasizes specific photographers. Its series includes discs devoted to internationally acclaimed travel photographers Kevin Morris and Cliff Hollenbeck. These discs, with 50 images each, are rather steeply priced at $599.

Digital Stock delivers not only standard stock subjects on Photo CD but also specialized topics by well-known photographers. This agency is profiled in the above case study.

LICENSING FEES

Like books and audio materials, a digital image is considered *intellectual property*—that is, material that can be copyrighted by the author (in this case, the photographer) and subject to payment of a licensing fee for its use. Permission to use a digital image and the negotiation of fees is generally handled directly by the photographer or with the photographer's agent, most often the stock photography agency. Although many Photo CD discs contain digital images that are distributed royalty-free (the licensing fee has already been paid by the publisher of the disc), some do not. In some cases, a Photo CD disc may be distributed for its promotional value, accompanied by a grant of license to use the images it contains free of charge in specific media, such as newsletters or magazines, but prohibiting use in other media, such as corporate reports or television.

An important concern with each Photo CD disc in your library is to check the licensing information on the disc to see what you've actually bought—and to keep that information intact whenever you copy an image to your hard drive or import it to another image-management or multimedia program.

When using images obtained from such outside sources, be sure to ask these questions:

- What permission for use is included in the purchase price of a particular Photo CD disc? If the disc was distributed as part of a promotion, what publishing restrictions are included with it? Does the permission cover the uses you want to make of the images?

- If images must be licensed directly, did the publisher include sufficient information to contact the photographer, agent, or agency?

Never forget the principle of "caveat emptor." Photo CD technology is a new field; many people may try to jump into the business without knowing what they are doing. Some of them may be appallingly ignorant of intellectual property law. Consider the existing reputation of the publisher of any Photo CD disc. These practices could save you major headaches!

On-Line Delivery

The 90s have seen the introduction of a new method of providing images for professional use: digital transmission services that allow

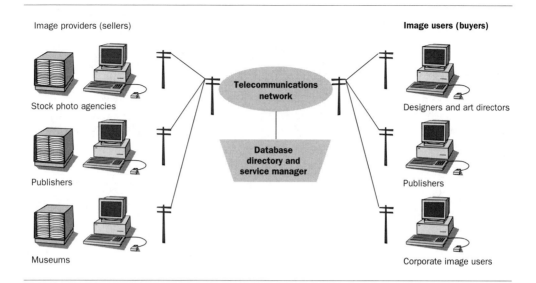

Image providers (sellers)

Image users (buyers)

Stock photo agencies

Publishers

Museums

Telecommunications network

Database directory and service manager

Designers and art directors

Publishers

Corporate image users

Kodak Picture Exchange is a global imaging service that links image providers with image users. Agencies whose images are already available include Archive Photos, Light Sources, Photobank Inc., Ewing Galloway, FPG International, Hulton Deutsch Picture Library, The Image Works, International Stock, Profiles West, Ro-Ma Stock, The Stock Shop, and Tom Stack and Associates.

on-line searching, browsing, and retrieval of print-quality image files. Like stock photography agencies, these on-line libraries offer copyrighted images available for licensing. But these images can be delivered directly to clients' workstations via modems. Kodak Picture Exchange (KPX) and Picture Network International (PNI) are currently on line and other such services can be expected soon. In this section, we will cover some of the features of and some of the challenges faced by these digital transmission services.

HOW DIGITAL TRANSMISSION SERVICES WORK

To acquire images from a digital transmission service, you, the subscriber, must have a desktop computer equipped with a modem and the transmission service's software. You contact the service by modem and, using keywords and other data fields, describe the pictures you need. Depending on the service, a list of images that match the search criteria or small representations of the images (thumbnails) are displayed. Larger representations (position prints, or FPOs) can also be downloaded for easier off-line editorial selection.

Once you've chosen the image you wish to use, the procedure varies according to the service. With KPX, you contact the stock photo agency that represents the image to order the high-quality transparency and to negotiate a licensing fee. Most reputable stock photo agencies can send transparencies, prints, or negatives within hours by express delivery; a few can deliver Photo CD discs con-

147

taining high-resolution versions equally fast. Or you can have KPX download the high-resolution file to you via modem and alert the stock agency that you will need to license the image. PNI, on the other hand, offers the user an on-line ordering form that includes such questions as the number of uses of the image, the type of media in which it will be used, and whether the use will be domestic or international. The licensing fee for the specific use is then calculated and displayed for the client's approval.

DRAWBACKS TO ON-LINE DELIVERY

Photo delivery on-line does have its drawbacks. Anyone who has ever gotten an illegible fax transmission knows how on-line noise—from whatever source—can corrupt files that go over the telephone lines. Another obstacle in the utilization of picture networks is the time it takes to transmit images. If the selection by keyword comes up with 100 images and transmission from provider to user takes three seconds per image, you'll spend five minutes in front of the computer just to get a look at thumbnails. For higher resolution, downloading the images will take even longer—fifteen minutes to several hours currently, depending upon the speed of your modem and the complexity of the image file.

Costs can also be daunting. All services currently on line carry per minute or per hour access fees for the user, and some also require annual membership or subscription fees. Image providers can be charged an annual per image storage fee plus a referral fee for each picture request the service forwards from a prospective client. So image providers may not be motivated to put anything on line that would not move quickly and in volume.

SELECTING A DIGITAL TRANSMISSION SERVICE

In selecting the best transmission services for your needs, it is important to consider how each service had dealt with potential problems that could hamper the efforts of their subscribers. Quality control and control of the photo files are potential problem areas.

- **Quality control.** Unless transmissions services oversee scanning quality, some digital scans will be adequate for prepress use, and others won't be—and when graphics professionals are on line, they won't be able to tell easily which is which. They also won't be able to tell which photographers use adequate model releases, which images are backed up with adequate

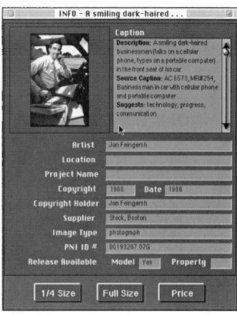

(left) PIN's Image Browser window displays the images you've selected in thumbnail size. You can now retrieve them in either quarter-page or full-page size or else open an Info window for an image after selecting it. (right) The Info window displays a selected image with its detailed caption and reference information. You can retrieve the image at this point and also initiate the pricing sequence.

duplicates, which stock agencies keep reasonable hours and have reliable service, and so on. So the question is, does a digital transmission service enforce consistent standards among its suppliers?

- **Who controls the files?** Does the transmission service allow each supplier to decide which images to place on line, and how to cross-reference them, while no one oversees the balance of the entire file? Does the transmission service edit all keywording or allow each supplier to make its own keywording decisions? If the picture exchange does not maintain tight controls over the organization of files, it will mean additional labor costs for those seeking images.

NEW OPPORTUNITIES

Because of the limitations in the speed and quality of image transmission over existing telephone lines, digital transmission services are currently used primarily for reviewing and editing available photographs from many suppliers. But as existing telephone lines and switching equipment are replaced by fiber optic cable, these services will be used extensively to transmit high-resolution digital images to clients' modems. Established digital transmission

149

services are preparing for the day when they can provide this service to a broad market, and they expect Photo CD to be the most cost-effective and time-effective medium for storing their high-resolution image libraries.

On-line delivery and Photo CD Portfolio II have the potential to be used together for greater efficiency in picture research. Here's how a combined effort might work: A subscriber has the Portfolio catalog of a favorite stock agency, which is also a contributing member of KPX. The subscriber pops the agency's catalog in a CD-ROM drive for a quick and cost-free review of the images. A little experimentation will reveal which combinations of keywords and other data fields will produce the best selection. Then if the subscriber is still not satisfied with what's available on the disc or wants to see what else is available, he or she can use a menu option that will automatically call KPX. Since the subscriber will have already worked out the search parameters with the disc, on-line search time will be minimized.

As the systems for digital transmission become streamlined, some types of photographs may actually become easier to get. News and documentary photography, for example, are particularly well suited to the new on-line services, because of the fast delivery available. An electronic picture exchange can have news images on-line the same day they are submitted.

Good-quality clip photos may also become more widely disseminated via digital transmission services. Universities and other institutions may even provide images for free, a development of potential benefit to both the on-line service and the subscribers. However, this possibility raises questions about who will absorb the cost of putting the images on line, whether the images will be interesting enough to be usable, whether model releases have been obtained, and whether any other intellectual property rights are being violated.

Looking to the Future

On both the consumer and the commercial level, many potential buyers of photography may be a bit leery at first of receiving images on Photo CD discs or from files archived on Photo CD media. After all, they cannot hold CDs up to the light and see instantly what they have. They have to invest in previously unnecessary electronic equipment to use the medium. Business has gone along just fine up to now without Photo CD technology.

Many professional photographers express reluctance to use Photo CD as a medium of delivering their images to clients. If a client doesn't have a CD-ROM drive that can display the images, what happens to the client presentation? Few photographers can afford to buy their own Photo Imaging Workstations, making them dependent on service bureaus to create their Photo CD discs. Few currently have the skills in other media to create professional-quality multimedia consumer products. And again, business has gone along just fine up to now without the medium.

But think of how fast the public shifted from vinyl records to CDs for musical entertainment!

In the future there will be many sources of electronic imaging, but Photo CD will remain the most basic and most efficient medium for storing and delivering digitized photography. A few clients, both consumer and commercial, will invest only in Photo CD players, and for them Photo CD will be the only medium they have to read digital imagery. But most clients will upgrade their computer technology in general. Most will likely install CD-ROM drives in computers with modems, so that they can have information transmitted to them over telephone lines. This is, after all, what the much-vaunted information superhighway is all about.

151

Part III

PRINT MEDIA APPLICATIONS OF PHOTO CD

10

Desktop Publishing with Photo CD

Desktop publishers, whether of magazines, books, catalogs, brochures, or other printed matter, are finding that Photo CD technology is allowing them to use color images in a variety of ways that they simply couldn't afford before. The ease, speed, and low cost of having color slides and negatives scanned to Photo CD has been a boon for magazines from low print-run local monthlies to high print-run, high-profile national weeklies.

Here are just a few examples of how desktop publishers are incorporating Photo CD technology into their production process:

- Cole & Weber, a Seattle ad agency, produced the program for the Northwest Addy Awards, which needed to depict 186 entries, by having all the entries shot to 35mm transparency film, scanned to Photo CD discs, converted to black and white in Photoshop, and imported into QuarkXPress for the page layout. The whole production was completed in five days.

- The Taunton Press, publishers of *Fine Gardening, Fine Homebuilding,* and *Fine Cooking,* among other consumer magazines, have their assignment photographers shoot pictures with Photo CD in mind. The photos are all shot on color negative film, written to Photo CD discs, and imported into QuarkXPress for page makeup.

- A real estate rental outfit in Florida publishes a regular color newsprint booklet of available properties. All property shots are now written to Photo CD and stored in a database. As properties become available, the digital images are easily inserted into the listing page layouts. The publishers have cut their costs considerably by using Photo CD scans rather than traditional scans.

- All the product shots in a recent catalog for No Fear Sports Gear are Photo CD scans. Since switching to Photo CD, No Fear is able to include many more photos in the catalog and to produce

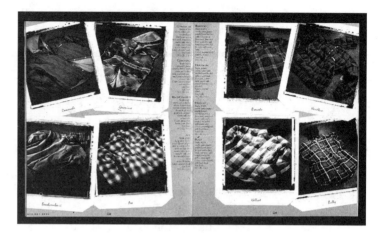

All product shots in a recent No Fear Sports Gear catalog were Photo CD scans. Designer Brent Stickels brought the PCD images into Photoshop, where he color-corrected them using a set of curves he had developed. He then applied Unsharp Mask at about 75 percent to compensate for the general softness the images had acquired in the scanning process.

it more quickly. Photo CD technology also allowed the catalog to expand 40 percent in size while still costing the same to produce.

- Book publishers are also taking advantage of the quality and cost effectiveness of Photo CD scans. Noted photographer Rick Smolan used Photo CD scans for his highly acclaimed book *From Alice to Ocean* and for his newest book, *Passage to Vietnam.* His incorporation of Photo CD in this project is described in detail in the case study on page 174.

Our descriptions of publishers and designers at the vanguard of Photo CD applications in desktop production could go on for pages, but you get the idea: *everyone* is coming up with ways to apply Photo CD technology to his or her particular needs. In this chapter we cover the nuts and bolts of what's involved in working with Photo CD in desktop publishing. In Chapter 11 we get into the more complex area of Photo CD's role in high-end prepress.

To fully exploit Photo CD technology's potential for desktop publishing, it pays to have an understanding of the procedures and processes involved in this medium, which begins with an electronic file and ends with a printed page. This journey from electronic image to printed page involves an incredibly diverse range of control factors designed to preserve the original integrity of the image, from the pixel data of the Photo CD image to the four-color printing plates that define the image in print.

Making Photo CD images part of a printed publication is essentially a five-stage process:

1. Acquiring the image from the Photo CD disc

2. Adjusting the image's color balance or altering it in other ways for optimum workability in the computer environment

3. Customizing the image's characteristics for the specific output device you will be using

4. Incorporating the image into an electronic page layout application

5. Outputting the electronic layout to a short-run color printer and eventually as four-color separations (film) from which printing plates can be made

The most formidable obstacle in converting Photo CD images into color separations is the myriad ways in which color information can be misinterpreted among the many devices an image will encounter from input to output. While attaining a perfect level of consistency throughout all these devices is virtually impossible, there are ways of overcoming the obstacles to make your results predictable. Through a system of color management, you can obtain the highest quality reproduction of your Photo CD images.

Overview of Color Management

Because your goal as a desktop publisher is to obtain the highest-quality color reproduction, you need a good color management system to predictably control color throughout the input-to-output process. In a color management system, each input, display, or output device is characterized in terms of its color *gamut,* or the range of colors it can reproduce. Through a set of tables of color data for these devices, the system "knows" what kinds of color characteristics to expect from each device and can translate between them. It can analyze the color data gathered by a Photo CD scanner, for instance, predict how a particular imagesetter (high-end printer) will output that data, and figure out how to accurately preview the image on screen.

Where Photo CD is concerned, the term *color management* has become synonymous with Kodak's Color Management System, also known as KCMS, which is used in a number of Photo CD–related desktop publishing products. KCMS supplies a set of precision transforms (PTs) capable of providing a means of precise color data translation between the various devices in your desktop color system.

To describe specific devices, KCMS uses numerous **precision device color profiles (DCPs)**. These are description files used to characterize input sources and output destinations and are available from KCMS for a wide range of printing and proofing devices. Furthermore, makers of Photo CD acquisition products understand that the fewer color mode changes an image undergoes, the less image and color data will be lost—not to mention that each time an image is converted to a new color mode it must be color corrected to match the original. Therefore, many of the high-end acquisition products described here convert a Photo CD image from Photo YCC to CMYK (the format needed for four-color separations) directly and are capable of customizing the data to specific output devices for the highest quality color match of the original.

We should note here that Photo CD images require their own unique form of color management. If the Photo YCC information is not customized to the destination color space as it is acquired, much of the original image data will be lost, either getting compressed in the transition or "averaged to white," a phenomenon known as highlight *clipping*. Because the perceived quality of a printed image depends, to a great degree, on the delicacy and detail of its highlight areas, clipping is disastrous to Photo CD images intended to be color separated and subsequently printed. KCMS products, as well as a host of independent software products, perform a customized acquisition of the Photo CD image such that its individual characteristics, as well as those of the various devices it interacts with, are defined and used as a means of translating the Photo YCC data into a form usable in the computer environment.

THE SCANNING STAGE

You can optimize your images for desktop publishing by taking a few precautions at the Photo CD scanning stage.

First, be sure to take your slides or negatives to a service bureau that will *clean* the images before scanning them. Dust can be a major problem with Photo CD scans, and if the images are not thoroughly cleaned, pinholes and specks will need to be removed later, on your time and at your expense.

Second, it helps to use a service provider that knows you and the type of work you do, as well as the destination of the scans—magazine, book, newsletter, or whatever. Some service bureaus do prescans, so that the operator can correct for color and density differences between the scan and the original slide. And whereas most consumer Photo CD scans are done with the scene balance algorithm (SBA) turned on, a professionally done Photo CD scan will involve turning that feature off, so that the operator sees what the photographer intended to capture on film and can manually color correct the image. As we saw in Chapter 5, such professional service usually costs more than the average Photo CD scan, but it is money well spent for higher-quality, individualized scans.

MONITOR CALIBRATION

Simply put, if your monitor is not calibrated to reflect true color values, it doesn't matter how extensively you color correct a PCD image, either in the acquisition stage or later in Photoshop—you will not get in print what you see on the screen. For this reason, a variety of high-end monitor-to-output calibration systems are available, such as Daystar's ColorMatch system and Radius's Precision-Color system, and many of the acquisition plug-ins and applications described in this chapter feature monitor calibration and characterization as part of the color management system the applications provide.

159

If you lack the means or the inclination to invest in an elaborate calibration system, here's a simple, low-cost alternative:

The Radius PrecisionColor Calibrator is a device that attaches to a color monitor and evaluates and then corrects variations in color that occur over time. Calibrating your monitor is an essential part of an overall color management system.

1. Have a MatchPrint made from an image you have on your hard drive—the image should be in its final CMYK form, and it should be output from a device you intend to use frequently.

2. Compare the MatchPrint to the on-screen image and use the Gamma control panel (included with Adobe Photoshop) to adjust the color balance of your monitor until the on-screen image matches the proof.

3. Save your new Gamma settings (if the Gamma control switch is ever turned off, you will need to reload your settings). For each device used to output your images, you can create a new Gamma file, which can be loaded on an as-needed basis.

Image Acquisition

A number of the acquisition products discussed in Chapter 6 use KCMS technology to avoid unnecessary and unwanted image data loss while maintaining as much of the original Photo YCC information as possible. KCMS software is available in upgrade kits for a variety of existing Photo CD acquisition products and is included free with certain image-editing software, such as Aldus PhotoStyler, Migrografix Picture Publisher, and Adobe Photoshop (in the form of the Kodak CMS plug-in for opening Photo CD images).

STAND-ALONE SOFTWARE

Turn to the color section for a comparative view of the various methods of acquiring Photo CD images.

If you have **Access Plus** software, you can make the transition from Photo YCC to CMYK without missing a beat, simply by obtaining the Kodak Precision CMYK Starter Pack, which provides a Kodak Precision Color Processor for making the conversion. The pack also includes a number of DCPs (device color profiles) for proofing on U.S., Japanese, and European devices. When used with the latest version of Access Plus, 2.0, you can also take advantage of a selection of look-up tables (LUTs), which will adjust an image's color balance to match a particular monitor's display attributes. This upgrade package is currently the only way to access Kodak's Precision CMS conversion in Windows, besides Aldus PhotoStyler 2.0.

On a more sophisticated level, **Purup's PhotoImpress** automatically and directly converts the Photo CD image's Photo YCC data to CMYK and provides both a complete color management system and a closed-loop calibration system from input to output. All image

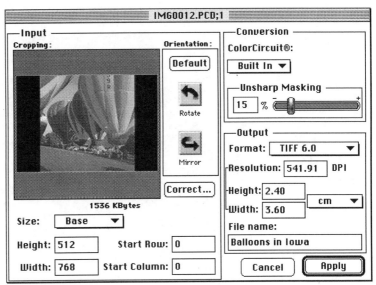

Each image opened by PhotoImpress software can have custom settings, including resolution, rotation, unsharp masking, and color corrections. Purup's software also allows resolution modification on-the-fly, a feature unique to this product.

editing and data conversions, which include unsharp masking, input and output options (such as resolution and data formatting), and color corrections, are done in PhotoImpress's oversize Correct Image window, which features before-and-after image previews so you can monitor the effect without having to commit to it. What's more, PhotoImpress also provides a densitometer function, scanner and printer calibrations, interfaces with spectrophotometers (for measuring printer response), gamut mapping (between scanner and printer gamuts), and a number of options for generating the black color separation. You can also create custom color transformations by combining scanner and printer profiles.

Another product that lets you acquire Photo CD images directly in the CMYK format for color separation is Human Software's **Color Extreme**, a full-featured image-manipulation application that, among other things, lets you crop, resize, mirror, apply unsharp masking, adjust black generation, and change output formats and other parameters before acquiring the image. You can also record and script different color correction curves (custom set-ups) for each image, as well as adjust the Input Options, such as the Scene Settings used by the PIW scanner operator. Color Extreme also includes a monitor/output calibration system and an oversize preview window in which to view image-editing effects.

One of the newer products on the market is Apple **PhotoFlash**, which is designed specifically for acquiring images and placing them directly into page layout documents. A Browser feature al-

161

PhotoFlash offers a variety of options for image editing during the acquisition process.

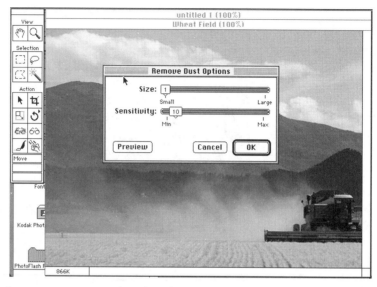

PhotoStep calculates and constructs custom look-up tables for the Kodak Photo CD Acquire Module. You enter the metric used to open the test file, the values measured for black and white, and then click on "Calc" to create a custom look-up table, which is used the second time to open the image from the Photo CD disc. The image appears dramatically different in the second pass (see the color section, page C3).

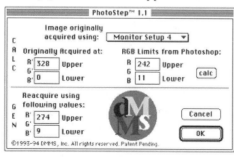

lows you to view thumbnail versions of Photo CD images (or images saved in other formats, including PICT, TIFF, EPS, DECS, JPEG, etc.) and sort them by date or name. The browser also allows you to link directly to other applications, so you merely have to drag and drop images into existing layouts.

Among PhotoFlash's more interesting features are its automated enhancement options: not only the usual crop, rotate, sharpen, blur, resize, zoom, and brightness/contrast correction but also DeDust and DeScratch tools that automatically remove pinholes and scratches from your images.

Because the program supports AppleScript, PhotoFlash lets you use scripting and recording capabilities to automate repetitive tasks and streamline workflow. With a single click of the mouse button, you can take advantage of a feature called the Automatic Folder, which will automatically perform assigned operations to an image dropped into it. It also acknowledges Photoshop plug-ins, so Kodak's Photo CD Acquire module and CD-Q will also work inside Photoflash.

To preserve the uniqueness of a Photo CD image, **DMMS PhotoStep** (which requires the use of the Kodak Photo CD Acquire Module 2.2) builds individual look-up tables that customize the path by which the Photo YCC information is translated to the desktop color space. The advantage of custom LUTs is that you can apply a specific table to a series of Photo CD images, providing they have all been scanned in the same session. It also gives you the ability to work with problematic images that require more correction than normal.

PLUG-INS

For sophisticated color transformation functions, the **Kodak CMS Photo CD plug-in** features the Kodak Precision Color Management System. The main advantage of this plug-in is that it allows you to define Source information (such as scanner settings, film type, etc.) and Destination options (including destination mode and output device) independently, enabling you to create your own device-specific precision transforms through which the Photo YCC image data are processed. The Kodak Precision Starter Pack, a software enhancement for Adobe Photoshop (a Starter Pack for the Windows-based Migrografix Picture Publisher is also available), provides six RGB profiles, all with different appearance characteristics, and a number of DCPs that allow you to convert Photo YCC directly to CMYK for four-color separations. Once you select a Destination option, the image will automatically be opened in CMYK.

Although earlier versions of the **Kodak Photo CD Acquire Module** (1.0 and 2.0) exhibited severe highlight clipping, the Acquire Module 2.2 takes full advantage of the extended range of the Photo YCC data when the appropriate mapping, density, and color changes are applied at the Photo CD acquisition stage. This module also provides 21 display options (look-up tables) for opening

163

The CMS window is the control that appears when you choose to open a Photo CD image in Photoshop. It features controls for resolution as well as both source and destination profiles. Several profiles are provided with the basic product; additional profiles can be purchased, including the CMYK options used for this illustration.

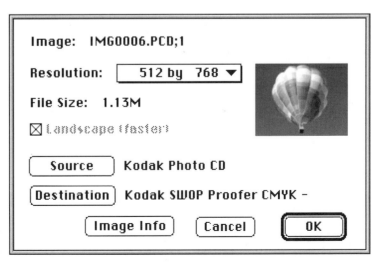

The Edit Window of the Acquire Module allows cropping, resolution selection, control over color and brightness, sharpening, and selection of the many metrics that affect the way a Photo CD image is imported. This plug-in results in RGB images only, which must be converted into CMYK in another process.

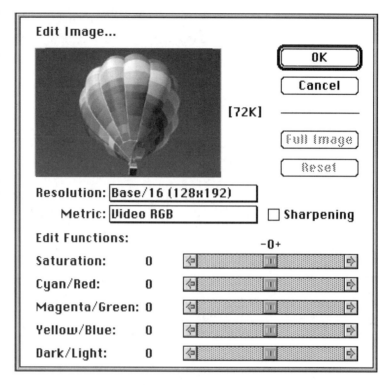

a Photo CD image and converting it to RGB. By using the Gamma and White Point settings, and by accessing the nine Monitor setups, you can customize the appearance of the image as it is converted from Photo YCC to RGB.

Human Software's **CD-Q Plug-in,** for Adobe Photoshop, also features sophisticated CMYK color modification capabilities, as well as unsharp masking, black-level adjustment, white and black point setting, cropping, rotating, resolution (image and output) and dot-shape adjustments. It, too, lets you open Photo CD images in CMYK.

DEVICE COLOR PROFILES (DCPS)

The KCMS group offers a wide range of precision DCPs written for specific output devices that will greatly enhance the final color quality of the color-separated Photo CD image. KCMS Product kits include:

• The Professional Proofing Pack—provides optional DCPs for generating CMYK separations from specific proofing devices, such as Agfa Proof, 3M MatchPrint II, Japanese Standard (DIC

164

Human Software's CD-Q plug-in allows users to open any Photo CD image at any resolution, including Pro Photo CD resolution, in either RGB or CMYK in one pass. It has controls for unsharp masking, will convert to GCR (gray-component replacement) simultaneously, and has very sophisticated controls for adjusting the color of the image on import (see the color section, page C3).

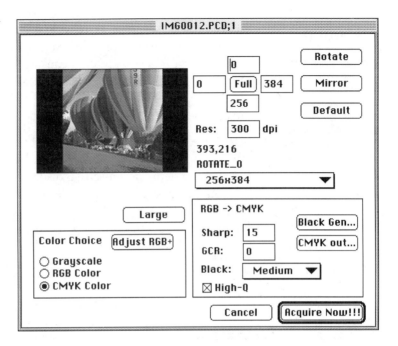

165

Press), Du Pont Cromalin, Fuji Color-Art, Enco PressMatch, Kodak (Approval, Contract, and Signature), European Match-Print, and European Cromalin. You can also choose from 15 undercolor removal (UCR) and gray-component replacement (GCR) combinations to optimize color for final separations.

- The CMYK Pro-Pack—designed to color manage U.S. generic CMYK proofing systems; also offers a selection of six GCR and UCR settings.

- Individual Scanner and Printer DCPs—provides scanner DCPs for various models of HP, PixelCraft ProImage, Howtek, Kodak, Microtek, and Nikon scanners, plus printer DCPs for various models of Apple, CalComp, Canon, Fargo, HP, Kodak, QMS, SuperMac, and Tektronix printers. Additional device profiles are available for LVT Digital Film Recorders and NEC Multi-Sync monitors. Most of these products are available for both Mac and Windows.

- Precision Input Color Characterization (PICC)—a custom-profile tool that utilizes the KCMS to achieve high-quality color matching from the original photograph (negative or slide) to the acquired image by allowing you to build custom precision

Photoshop's Open command uses the CMS plug-in to access the Photo CD image. Accessory packs can be purchased from Kodak's CMS Division that expand the range of options available in the Open window, including a variety of CMYK formats as shown in this screen capture. The selection shown is for Kodak Contract CMYK, a photomechanical proofing process.

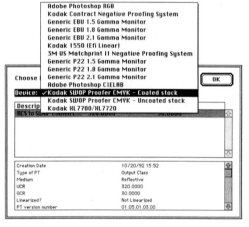

transforms for scanners or individual Photo CDs. Once you've created a custom PT for your scanner or a Photo CD disc, it stays in your system, and you can use it for all images input from that scanner or disc, thus dramatically reducing the amount of time spent color editing images to make them more closely match the original.

• DayStar ColorMatch—a system that builds on the capabilities provided by the Kodak CMS plug-in by adding a color management system for on-screen display of Photo CD images. DayStar is designed to provide WYSIWYG color between monitor and printer. Included in the ColorMatch package is a monitor calibration set-up, a set of Kodak Precision DCPs, and a ColorMatch Quark extension for accessing Precision CMS from within QuarkXPress 3.2 or later.

• KEPS PCS100 Kit—an upgrade kit for separators who use Adobe Photoshop. It uses KCMS to provide a color reference for viewing and editing color, with on-screen, interactive, output simulation, and monitor-to-proof results—all done using Photoshop (2.0.1 or later). And because the kit contains KEPS color calibration and color management technology, you can accurately acquire, retouch, export, and separate continuous-tone color images, all with the flexibility of working in Photoshop's CMYK mode. The kit will operate with any Macintosh II-family, Quadra, or PowerMac computer.

Image Editing at the Acquisition Stage

Generally speaking, the more image editing you can do before the Photo CD image is acquired, the less work you will need to do later. Also, the more you can do to tailor the Photo CD image to the various environments it will inhabit, the better the result will be. Depending on the features of your acquisition software, here are some things you will want to do to the image at the acquisition stage.

- Image orientation. You will want to take this opportunity to rotate the image to proper orientation.

- Cropping. If you loosely frame the image as it will appear on the printed page, you can also reduce the file size of the image as it is acquired.

- Color cast correction. Often images on a Photo CD disc, or those written to a disc during a single session, will have a color cast that can be easily corrected at this stage.

- Color match. If your software has look-up tables, as with the Photo CD Acquire Module 2.2, use them to color match the screen image to the original image. If you are working with a monitor calibrated to output, you will drastically reduce the amount of color correction needed in Photoshop by acquiring an image that closely matches the original.

- Color mode. Set the color mode (i.e., RGB or CMYK). Note: Many people like to work in Photoshop in RGB, preferring the smaller file size and ease of operation. However, if the image's final destination is CMYK, you will have to repeat at least some of the adjustments done in RGB in the CMYK mode in order to fine-tune the color for separation.

167

- Input profile. If your acquisition software uses custom transformations that define input sources, such as the KCMS Photo CD

The CD-Q plug-in for Photoshop affords the user powerful controls over the color of the resulting image. Each color can be magnified with the curves shown (either singly or in combination) or automatic adjustments can be made. The lower windows allow before and after views of the image so you can make on-screen decisions about the color corrections being made.

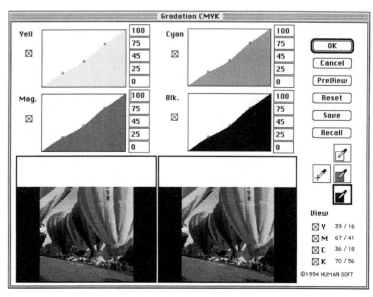

SIDEBAR

WORKING WITH RESOLUTION AND LINE SCREENS

To decide which image pac resolution to use when going to print from a Photo CD image, you should first determine the final output size and the line screen that will be used to reproduce the image. The generally accepted rule of thumb is this: The best quality (i.e., high-resolution) output is achieved when you have a 2:1 ratio of pixels to line screen (ppi:lpi). For example, with a 150-line (lpi) screen, your image should have a resolution of 300 pixels per inch. (Acceptable results can be obtained with a lower ratio. You should test various ratios for yourself. It is possible to obtain excellent images with much less resolution—going as low as a ratio of 1.25:1—if you use one or two passes of Unsharp Mask in Photoshop.)

Because Photo CD's image pac components are described in terms of *area* (i.e., the resolution of a 16XBase image is 2048 x 3072 pixels), which image pac version do you choose, based on required output size and line-screen criteria? Here's a simple formula: Multiply each dimension of the final image by twice the halftone screen to obtain the maximum resolution required, in pixels, for a high-quality output.

Example: To reproduce a Photo CD image at 4 x 5 inches with a 150 lpi screen, you would multiply 4 x 150 x 2, to equal 1200 pixels; then you would multiply 5 x 150 x 2, to equal 1500 pixels. From the accompanying chart, you can see that the resulting measurements place the desired image pac version somewhere between 4XBase and 16XBase. The 4XBase component falls just short of the 2:1 ratio, whereas the 16XBase component has more image information than needed. This being the case, you could easily select either version, with a slight increase in the dimensions of the 4XBase version, or a significant decrease in the dimensions of the 16XBase version.

Maximum Output Size per Halftone Screen

Resolution	Lines x Pixels	175 lpi	150 lpi	133 lpi
Base/16	128 x 192	N/A	N/A	N/A
Base/4	256 x 384	0.8 x 1.1 in	1 x 1.5 in.	1.3 x 1.9 in.
Base	512 x 768	1.5 x 2.2 in.	1.7 x 2.5 in.	2.5 x 3.8 in.
4XBase	1024 x 1536	3 x 4.5 in.	3.5 x 5 in.	5 x 7.5 in.
16XBase	2048 x 3072	6 x 9 in.	7 x 10 in.	10 x 15 in.
64XBase	4096 x 6144	12 x 18 in.	14 x 20 in.	20 x 30 in.

Plug-in or Kodak's Precision Input Color Characterization software, this is the time to establish these parameters.

- Resolution. Determine and select the image pac resolution you wish to acquire, based on the anticipated size of the final, separated image. If you have an option for output resolution in your acquisition software, set it now. Output resolution should be 1.5 to 2 times the line-screen frequency used to reproduce the image (see sidebar).

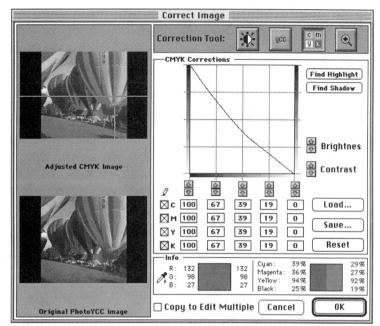

Purup's PhotoImpress allows a tremendous degree of control over the color of each image opened by the program. As with CD-Q, there are before and after images and controls for each color, including automatic controls for maximizing the quality of the image. All of the color editing settings can be saved for application to a variety of images. The on-screen densitometer also reveals before-and-after values for the pixels under the eyedropper.

- Brightness and saturation. Perform major image adjustments for brightness and saturation. Note: Because more control is afforded in Photoshop, you should delay any fine adjustments until after the image is acquired.

- Unsharp masking. Since Photo CD scans are not sharpened as part of the process, whereas drum scans are, some image sharpening is usually required. Sharpening should be done as either a first or last step in the image-editing process, because it produces artifacts that may be emphasized by other image manipulations. Depending on output requirements, a good rule of thumb is to sharpen once at the acquisition stage, and then again, if required, when you are finished fine-tuning the image in Photoshop.

Image Adjustments in Photoshop

Once a Photo CD image has been acquired in Photoshop, it can be brought to an even higher level of "print readiness." Although varying output requirements necessitate different procedures, the following are general guidelines for achieving optimum results.

SIZING THE IMAGE

Depending on how large the image is going to appear in print, now is the time to make sure the image is sized accordingly, so that it neither requires too much reduction (making for unnecessarily large files and slow processing times) or too much enlargement (resulting in lower-quality reproduction).

COLOR CORRECTION

There are several ways to use Photoshop's color correction tools to affect an image's color balance without sacrificing image data in the process. Both Photoshop's Info and Levels boxes should be used often to determine true image values and color densities as you make adjustments to an image's color balance.

Newcomers to color correction will undoubtedly appreciate the **Variations** dialog box (Under Image, Adjust, Variations), which provides multiple previews and lets you compare the modified image with the original. Variations also lets you preview multiple corrections at the same time. It allows you to adjust highlights, midtones, and shadows independently with a fine-to-coarse control; avoid using the Lighter and Darker controls, as these are global commands that delete image information from one end of the scale or the other. Worth noting is the Show Clipping box. When activated, this function indicates where color data will be clipped as a result of a particular adjustment.

The **Hue/Saturation** control is an effective means of controlling the appearance of individual colors contained in the image while leaving other colors unaffected. For example, by clicking on the Magenta button, you can now control the lightness, color value, and saturation of *only* the magenta hues contained in the image. This control is therefore ideal for removing, subduing, or altering unwanted colors without globally affecting the others.

Other than for neutralizing highlights and other small, isolated corrections, we don't recommend using Photoshop's **Color Balance** control, for the simple reason that to use it effectively, you need to be able to determine—yourself—exactly where in the image the shadows end and midtones begin, and where the midtones end and highlights begin. What's more, there is no black-point control whatsoever, as there is in the Levels and Curves controls, for example.

Speaking of **Levels** and **Curves**, you will probably want to do the majority of your color corrections using one or both of these controls. Why? Because they afford the ability to affect an image's midtones without altering either the highlights or the shadows. Levels tends to be more user-friendly than Curves, simply because it displays a histogram that enables you to see how the colors are distributed throughout the image and where image data may have been "clipped" as a result of an adjustment. Both the Curves and the Levels controls allow you to affect either a single color component or all simultaneously, and both permit the saving and subsequent loading of custom settings. Where the Curves control is more comprehensive is that it enables contrast and density to be adjusted in tandem (whereas these are two separate controls in the Levels box), by your adjusting the shape of the image's characteristic curve.

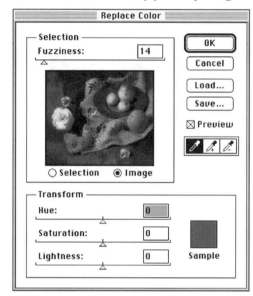

Photoshop's Replace Color command lets you adjust the hue, saturation, and lightness value of a specific color without altering any other color.

The **Replace Color** command lets you create a mask based on specific colors and then adjust the hue, saturation, and lightness values to correct the color. With this control you can adjust a specific color without altering any other color.

The **Selective Color** command lets you modify colors by changing the amount of "ink" used to make a specific color. This control can be used in conjunction with printer proofs, to add or subtract color in each of the four separations.

The **CMYK Preview** will allow you to see what the image will look like after it has been converted from RGB to CMYK without actually converting it. By creating a new window, you have the ability to work on an RGB image while previewing the CMYK output without actually having made the conversion.

If you need to verify whether the colors in your document will reproduce (based on the selected output device, paper stock, and printing inks established in Photoshop's Preferences), check Gamut Warning in the Mode menu. Any color outside the printing gamut will appear highlighted in the color or tone of your choosing.

FILE FORMATS

There are several viable file formats in which you can save your Photoshop images for page layout and eventual color separation. The traditional choices are EPS and TIFF. With EPS you also get a low-resolution version of the image, capable of serving as an FPO (for position only) in a page layout application. Another option is DCS (desktop color separation), which can be accessed by saving the image as an EPS with the Desktop Color Separation option selected. This will produce a master low-resolution file of the image and four high-resolution separation files, one each for cyan, magenta, yellow, and black. When you import the DCS file into QuarkXPress, for example, the low-res master file is accessed. When the document is sent to an output device, the high-resolution versions of the image will automatically be accessed as needed. DCS and EPS files separate identically, although an EPS image is much larger in use. DCS lets you work on a relatively small master file, while the huge CMYK files are not being accessed. The latest version of DCS (2.0) allows you to add spot colors as separate files. Note: Before saving your images in specific formats, be sure you have checked with your printer and separator as to their file-format preferences.

Another format that is very useful (yet seldom used) is the Scitex CT format in Photoshop. This format records CMYK data in the same manner as the other formats, is accessible to QuarkXPress and PageMaker, and is a single file, compact and convenient to output on PostScript imagesetters.

Bringing Images into a Page Layout

It is important to realize that your objective—from scanning to final reproduction—is to preserve and display as much of the original image data as possible. For this reason, you will not want to import Photo CD images into a page layout application directly from a Photo CD.

If you have already converted your images to CMYK—which depends, to a large degree, on how you acquired the images (i.e., as CMYK or RGB) and on how you like to work on them in Photoshop—you are now ready to import pictures into your page layout program. Although Aldus PageMaker and QuarkXPress are similar in the ways in which they import and display photos, we will primarily address Quark, currently the market leader, and include some additional comments about PageMaker at the end of this section. We will also assume that the images have been preseparated in Photoshop and saved as DCS files. Although you can postseparate the images, allowing Quark to convert them in separation, the files have to be translated from RGB to CMYK each time you print. This is done either with the EfiColor XTension (located in your Quark XTension folder, with the EfiColor Processor and database in your system folder) or with Aldus PrePrint or Kodak Prophecy. Since the translation process is rather time consuming, many people prefer to preseparate in Photoshop, having to make the conversion only once.

How an image appears in QuarkXPress is very much affected by its file format and the way in which it is brought into the application. For example, an EPS imported into QuarkXPress is ragged and thus difficult to evaluate (the reason being that Quark is accessing a low-resolution, 72 dpi preview of the actual image). A TIFF, on the other hand, is truer to the actual image than its EPS counterpart but is rather finicky (especially if it is repositioned within its picture box or rotated at an angle) and subject to producing strange anomalies that appear on screen and sometimes even show up when printed from consumer-level laser printers.

Publish and Subscribe functions (System 7.0 and later for Mac) add a whole new level of quality to the appearance of images on screen in Quark, facilitating more precise layout control, such as framing and text wraps, as well as the finest possible low-resolution output.

EfiColor, now bundled with QuarkXPress versions 3.2 and later, is a powerful color management system designed to provide color consistency from monitor to proofing device to the final output device, given the specific characteristics of each. The result is that what you see on screen and in your color proofs will bear a happy resemblance to your final output. Like KCMS, EfiColor employs device profiles to characterize screen and output devices. EfiColor, however, will not affect or influence EPS files. Where EfiColor might also prove worthwhile is in its ability to convert RGB files to CMYK *within* QuarkXPress—which means you don't have to use Photoshop or another high-end image-editing application to perform this operation prior to importing the image into Quark documents. But be warned: this may produce unpredictable and potentially undesirable surprises.

Bringing images into Aldus PageMaker documents is similar, but not identical to, the methods required by QuarkXPress. While you can import EPS and TIFFs the way you would in Quark, DCS files and subscriber editions will appear as a gray box with appropriate tags. What's more, PageMaker cannot separate RGB TIFFs as will the Quark/EfiColor combination. PageMaker is, however, able to separate CMYK EPS, DCS, and TIFF files.

FOCUS ON PASSAGE TO VIETNAM

Rick Smolan, the photographer best known for his **A Day in the Life of . . .** series of coffeetable books, has become a Photo CD convert. He first used Photo CD technology for his "interactive coffeetable book" *From Alice to Ocean*, which consisted of a four-color book accompanied by two discs: a Photo CD Portfolio disc and a CD-ROM disc. Smolan's images of Robyn Davidson's 1700-mile journey across the Aus-

© 1994, Catherine Karnow, Passage to Vietnam

Phuong Anh Nguyen escaped to California with her family when she was 13 years old. After graduating from San Jose State College, she returned to her native Vietnam in 1990 as part of a medical relief group. She now lives in Ho Chi Minh City, where she designs bars and restaurants.

tralian outback were scanned to Photo CD for use in the book and on both discs.

Smolan's latest project, *Passage to Vietnam*, again makes use of Photo CD technology for both publishing and multimedia. *Passage to Vietnam* features photos taken by 70 photographers who were allowed unlimited access to the country for seven days in March 1994. The more than 200 images in the book where culled from approximately 200,000 that were taken during that week. Tom Walker, the New York-based art director who worked with Smolan on his previous projects, decided which of the images to consider for the book.

"I chose five or six hundred from the thousands, sent them off to be scanned onto Photo CD discs, then put the slides away and didn't worry about them," says Walker. "I don't have to worry about the original slides, I don't lose track of the images I scanned, and I can retrieve them easily." He uses Kodak Shoebox to organize the images.

Production of the Vietnam book was done at Smolan's own publishing company, Against All Odds Productions, in conjunction with Charles

Short-Run Desktop Color

The advent and development of desktop publishing has been accompanied by technological advancements for printing color pages. Instead of using printing plates on a press to put ink on paper, new methods produce color pages in other ways, opening up the possibilities for color print projects that require relatively few copies and have budgets that wouldn't otherwise allow for color. In addition, short-run color printers can be used early in the development of a project to produce *design comps* that look very much like the printed page.

Short-run color printers are typically low-resolution devices putting 200 to 600 dots per inch on the page, compared to

© 1994, Harry Gruyaert, Passage to Vietnam

In the book's cover photo, a woman throws her whole body weight behind the oars of her boat as she rushes to beat nightfall on the Mekong Delta.

Melcher's Melcher Media. The chosen Photo CD images were brought into Photoshop, where they were cropped and the color and contrast were enhanced. They were then imported into PageMaker on a Macintosh. The final pages

were output to a Majestic color printer to produce "advance copies" of the book to show to stores months before its actual publication date. While orders from bookstores were processed, the electronic files were sent to Hong Kong for color separation and printing.

Smolan says about Photo CD technology in general that "it's still hard to believe how many uses we find for the same scans—that something that cost a dollar or two saves us a fortune in time and money for subsequent scanning."

The scans of the photos for *From Alice to Ocean,* for example, have been used not only for the book and the two discs but for making prints for an exhibit at the International Center for Photography in New York City. The scans for the Vietnam project have been used for color comps, publicity materials, and an interactive CD-ROM disc as well as the book. The disc, which is sold separately as well as being bundled with the book, interweaves video, still images, and narration to involve viewers in an interactive visit to today's Vietnam. The viewer joins photographers on their assignments, shares their experiences, and learns about their photographic techniques.

175

medium-resolution devices that print 1000 to 1600 dpi and high-resolution imagesetters that produce 2000 to 3600 dpi for traditional printing processes. Some color printers are priced low enough for many design studios or publishers to include them in their desktop publishing setup. Others are usually available at photocopying or imagesetting service bureaus.

COLOR PRINTERS

The three main types of short-run color printers you are likely to encounter are color thermal transfer printers, dye sublimation printers, and color copiers. **Thermal transfer printers** use thermally sensitive color sheeting. The printer *rasterizes* a digital im-

The Kodak XLS 8600 PS printer is a thermal transfer printer that outputs photographic quility prints and transparencies from virtually all presentation and image-editing software.

age from a graphics or page layout file—that is, it turns the image file's instructions into a dot pattern specific for that printer. To print each of the four process colors (cyan, magenta, yellow, and black), the dot pattern for the color is applied to the page by heat and pressure from the pins in a printhead that fuses dots of color to the page. As the color sheet moves past the printhead, each pin in the printhead is either heated (to put a dot on the page) or not heated (to leave the dot space blank). The page makes four passes through the printer, with one color applied on each pass, resulting in a four-color print. A full range of colors is produced when the tiny dots of the process colors, all the same size, are mixed on the page in "dithered" patterns.

Dye sublimation printers also use heat to apply color to the page. In this case, although the printer produces a relatively low number of dots per inch, the color print looks like the continuous tone of a photograph. That's because the pins in the printhead can be heated to many different temperatures. The degree of heat applied to the pin determines how much of the dye or ink from a color transfer ribbon is applied to the dot. By controlling the amount of dye released, dye sublimation printers can mix colors without "dithering" to produce a continuous-tone image.

Because thermal transfer and dye sublimation prints cost more per copy than pages produced on color photocopiers, one way to print short-run color is to produce an "original" with a thermal transfer or dye sublimation printer and then use a color copier to

The Kodak Color Edge copier can produce images directly from disk at 300 dpi.

reproduce it in quantity. Color copiers can work by thermal transfer, photographic, or xerographic processes. The xerographic process uses a laser to set up a dot pattern on a printing drum, with toner bound or repelled according to the charge at each dot location. Heat is then used to fuse the toner to the paper.

As desktop color has developed into a major force in publishing and printing, color copiers have been adapted to receive the information for printing from a digital file. For example, the Kodak ColorEdge copier can accept graphics files stored on disk. Another interesting development is printers that combine technologies. The Seiko Professional Color Point 2 PSF, for example, is a 300 dpi printer that allows users to switch between dye sublimation and thermal transfer printing simply by changing an interior cartridge and the paper type. The less-expensive thermal prints can be used for proofing, then the more expensive dye sublimation version can be printed for the final copies.

177

LOW-RESOLUTION PROOFING

Using low-resolution, FPO images in your page layouts gives you the option of outputting the files onto short-run color printers for proofing purposes. If high-res files were used, the total size of the page layout files—and the images they would be accessing— would be so large that they would be impossible to output on

The Seiko Professional ColorPoint 2 PSF Model 14 is the first Adobe PostScript Level 2 color printer to offer multiple printing technologies— thermal transfer and dye sublimation—in one printer.

conventional printers, which often have a meager memory buffer. Low-res proofing also provides an inexpensive means by which a client can approve a basic design and evaluate your efforts.

> **TIP:** *Instead of substituting your high-res images for low-res, FPO counterparts capable of being spooled and printed by commercial printers, select Low Resolution from the Output pop-up menu in Quark's Print dialog box. You can select this option regardless of whether your images have been saved as EPS or TIFF files. Now, rather than the printer accessing the high-res image file, only the picture-preview file will be accessed, permitting the entire page to be printed easily, more quickly, and without incident. Of course, files saved as DCS automatically provide a low-res FPO in the layout.*

Color Separation on the Desktop

The most commonly used method for producing printed pages from desktop publishing systems is to produce digitally separated film from which printing plates are made. Because the imagesetting equipment that makes these separations is complex and relatively expensive, film is often produced by service bureaus specially equipped to accept desktop color files and deliver separated film.

Once you've completed the layout for an ad, brochure, poster, or publication, proofed it at low resolution, and corrected any problems, it is time to send the digital pages to the service bureau for film output. Here is where coordination with your color house and printer will save you time and money, since you can make a lot of the final preparation changes yourself.

Through discussions with the printer, you will have arrived at decisions as to paper stock—weight, coating, surface texture—and printing ink. Each of these decisions is based on cost, the printer's equipment, and the desired appearance of the final product. Furthermore, each of these decisions involves a different set of options in regard to the images. The ways in which certain inks combine with certain papers produces one set of variables, as do the characteristics of the press itself. Using Photoshop's Separation Preferences, you can input the data the printer gives you. Under Printer's Ink Setup, you'll find options for the all-important dot-gain percentage (how much darker the piece will look once on press), gray-balance coordinates (affected by the actual color of the ink and the paper), and various ink/separation options. In Separation Setup, you will find GCR (gray component replacement) and UCR (undercolor removal) options, black ink limits (in percentages), total ink limit, and black-generation settings. You will also have the option of creating a custom Separation Table, or using a combination of default and custom settings.

Color Separation Software

A variety of software packages are available to help you prepare your digital page layout files for color separation and subsequent printing on an imagesetter.

SPECTREPRINT PRO

SpectrePrint Pro (version 4.0), from Prepress Technologies, can open a Photo CD using any acquire module that works with Photoshop. It performs an automatic "enter-white" and an automatic "enter black" and can subsequently make a color separation correctly for any specific printing condition. Because CMYK is different for every use, SpectrePrint allows the user to fine-tune color separations to the intended output device whether it is a dye sublimation printer or a printing press.

This approach to color separation makes the results from QuarkXPress documents more consistent and the color more reliable. Using current techniques, QuarkXPress documents are separated inconsistently, with compensation being applied for continuous-tone and illustrations being separated verbatim without compensation. The SpectreSeps technique treats all components of the document consistently.

SpectrePrint Pro also offers batch processing capabilities, making light work of multiple image separations and improving productivity.

SPECTRESEPS QX

SpectreSeps QX (version 2.0) is an XTension to QuarkXPress that lets you separate directly from the QuarkXPress application. It controls UCR (undercolor removal), dot gain, and gray balance within color separation controls. All artwork, including continuous-tone images and synthetic art (screen tints, EPS graphics, etc.) is filtered through the SpectreSeps separation process, making the color separation of the entire document consistent and of equal quality.

SPECTRECAL

Another product from Prepress Technologies is SpectreCal, a calibration product/service that allows you to precisely calibrate a scanner, computer, and output device to deliver the best possible color separations.

SpectreCal includes an IT8 transparency or reflective original for testing the scanner. After you scan this target, you send the resulting file to Prepress Technologies, where they create a corrective curve using an X-Rite colorimeter. This transfer file is returned to you for adding to your SpectreSeps or SpectrePrint software.

COLOR ACCESS

Pixel Craft, a division of Xerox Corp., produces Color Access, another powerful color separation program. With control over the most subtle nuance in color and contamination, Color Access is considered by many to be the most effective color separation program on the market. It provides control over dot gains, press and paper combinations, and ink contamination.

Originally billed as a color retouching program, Color Access has focused more recently on color separation, leaving retouching and creative image manipulation to the other popular products on the market.

PHOTONE PREPRESS

Photone Prepress and Photone Lite are color separation programs that bring professional-level color separation to the Macintosh. Photone products include a comprehensive approach to color separation, with applications and documents for color calibration of imagesetters and printing presses and paper/ink combinations.

Photone's on-screen manual explains the process of calibration and preparation in fine detail, with discussions of each topic in concise terms, and describes the technique for making the best color separations from digital files.

180

Photone Prepress is a color separation package that gives perhaps more control over the separation of images than any competitive product. Based on high-end scanner controls, the Photone control windows allow you to create and balance such components of the separation process as ink calibration, halftone screens and angles, and dot gain.

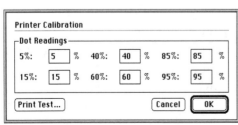

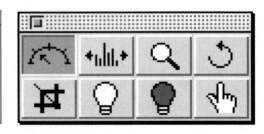

THE KOLORIST

FSI Software from Columbia, Georgia, has produced The Kolorist for Macintosh and Windows. Kolorist bills itself as the only 100-percent mathematical solution to color separation, and those who use the product are impressed with the accuracy of the work it produces. It sports many of the controls found on conventional drum scanners, such as contamination control, undercolor removal, gray-component replacement, and dot gain compensation.

Besides short-run color prints and proofing and output through an imagesetting service bureau, desktop color files can be output on "high-end" color systems. Desktop computer-based systems can be linked to more expensive proprietary systems, such as those of Scitex and Linotype Hell. How Photo CD fits into this high-end printing approach is addressed in the next chapter.

11

Photo CD and High-End Prepress

Although it is beyond the scope of this book to go into detail about color printing processes and all the ins and outs of preparing electronic files for high-end color printing, we do want to introduce you to two Photo CD products that are having a significant impact in the prepress marketplace: Pro Photo CD and Photo CD Portfolio II.

Pro Photo CD in Printing and Publishing

As soon as the photographic and imaging communities were aware of the existence of Photo CD, they asked for more—more resolution and more film sizes supported. The Pro Photo CD system was developed to fill the void created by Master Photo CD scanners being able to scan only 35mm film.

Pro Photo CD uses a larger-format scanner called the Photo CD Scanner 4045, with image scanning capacity of films up to 4 x 5 inches. The 4045 also has a trilinear CCD array with twice the density of sensors of the 35mm version (4096 sensors, or 4K along the short dimension of the film). This gives the Pro Photo CD an imaging capacity of up to 72 MB when scanning a 35mm negative or transparency in RGB format. Different film sizes yield different net file sizes, but all images are stored in 3:2 ratio (4096 x 6144 pixels) size. Where 35mm yields a full-frame image, other formats—4 x 5, 6 x 6, 6 x 9—are "padded" with black nonimage pixels from the end of the film frame to the full proportion of the Photo CD image space.

Using films with image proportions other than 3:2 requires cropping, and a proportionately smaller file size will result. Opening Pro Photo CD images in CMYK format with software that supports such transfers results in a larger file—96 MB for films that match the 3:2 proportions of the file format.

Pro format discs have a proportionately smaller capacity than their 35mm Master counterparts. Where the Master disc can accommodate about 100 images, the Pro Photo CD disc can accommodate approximately 25 images.

ACCESSING PRO IMAGES

Because file sizes are larger than for the Photo CD Master image pacs, the time it takes to access a Pro image is similarly longer, with access times on the more powerful Macintosh and Windows machines of 9 minutes or more. The 16XBase image pac is accessed to read these files, and an additional file called an image pac extension (IPE) is added to complete the 64 MB restoration of the original image.

The IPE files are stored in a separate directory on the Pro Photo CD disc, making them accessible only when the file is opened from an actual Pro Photo CD disc. Transferring these images to a hard disc won't work, because the file structure is incorrect for Photo CD access software to recognize the location of the IPE.

Some Photo CD access software (both plug-in and stand-alone) cannot access the 64XBase image because the authors of these products did not include the code necessary for such access. As PCD-capable products mature, access to the Pro files will be included in all software. The Kodak CMS Photo CD Plug-in that shipped with Photoshop 2.5.1 and later could not access Pro images. The new version, 2.1, not only accesses Pro level discs but also runs more quickly and efficiently than its predecessor.

The Photo CD Acquire Module for Photoshop has been able to read Pro images on Macintosh since 1993, and on Windows since mid-1994. All versions after 2.0.1 have Pro support built-in.

Purup PhotoImpress 1.1 and the PowerMac 2.0 both read Pro Photo CD discs, as does Human Software's CD-Q 1.18 and later. Human Software's Color Extreme accepts Pro Photo CD discs, as does Corel's Photo CD Workshop.

Apple Computer's System-level Slide Show Viewer and Quick-Time Extension did not support 64XBase files as of late 1994. If you insert a Pro Photo CD into a Macintosh computer, the Finder creates folders of PICT images in the five basic resolutions only—the Pro level IPE file is ignored.

FILE SIZE

Pro Photo CD images open in RGB at 72 MB (if the proportion of the film is 3:2). Many computers have difficulty managing files of this size. Even *opening* a 72 MB file is a challenge for entry-level computers. While it is possible to lower the resolution after opening the image in Photoshop, getting to that point can be difficult on computers with marginal RAM and hard disk space.

A fast processor, at least 20 MB of RAM, and a multisession CD-ROM are minimum requirements for opening a Pro Photo CD file.

Using a sampling ratio of 2:1, a Master Photo CD file can be reproduced as large as 6.82 x 10.24 inches in size. The Pro image is four times as large (64XBase) and will result in a reproduction capacity of 13.65 x 20.48 inches at that same 2:1 pixel-to-halftone-dot ratio.

But, sampling an image at 2:1 is a very conservative thing to do. Many tests have shown that this ratio of sampling for most printing projects is excessive. By sampling at lower ratios, it is possible to increase the size of reproduction to a huge degree. For example, if a sample rate of 1.5:1 pixels to halftone dots is accepted, the image size increases to 13.65 x 9.1 inches. And, sampling at 1.25:1 (the lowest sampling factor we recommend) yields an acceptable image at 150 halftone dots per inch of 16.34 x 10.89 inches—easily full-bleed for a letter-size page. Pro images are twice that large at 32.68 x 21.78 inches. Sizable!

Pro Photo CD scans are useful not only for scanning larger-format negatives and transparencies but for providing the kinds of high-resolution image files that many publishers of four-color books, magazines, calendars, posters, and other works want and need—and at a much lower cost than traditional drum scans.

Photo CD and Electronic Prepress Systems

For years the prepress industry has fought with nonstandard "standards," those methods by which files can be transferred from one high-end prepress system to another. Most of these "standard" file formats have not worked, and those that have worked at all, have not worked well, because of variants of the standard adopted by individual manufacturers.

The traditional method for image file storage has been nine-track magnetic tape. These half-inch tapes typically hold one image and its associated files and represent an investment of about $25. But storage and retrieval problems abound with these tapes, as magnetic tapes suffer from long-term image loss due to print-through, a problem caused by magnetized layers of tape passing their magnetic patterns to adjacent tape layers in the roll.

Photo CD discs, on the other hand, offer a 100-year shelf-life and unalterable data. At a cost of about $20 each, Kodak's Portfolio II discs represent an improvement in storage security, speed of image access, and the solution to the interplatform file protocol problems that have beset the prepress industry for decades.

Kodak has effectively added a standard for CMYK files written to the disc, in addition to the normal selection of files found on Photo CD Master discs made directly from film.

Kodak has enlisted the four major prepress manufacturers—Linotype-Hell, Du Pont Crosfield, Scitex, and Dainippon Screen—to agree not only to support Photo CD in its standard ramifications but to support a new four-color standard that all are able to read and write.

Portfolio II has the potential to hold a CMYK image as well as the standard image pac that is written to all Master Photo CD discs. This same Portfolio II disc can also be played in a television player.

The basic hardware for writing a Portfolio II disc for prepress.

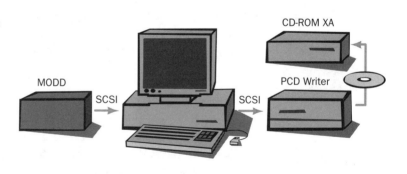

PCD FORMAT 4
PHOTO CD PRTFOLIO II FOR PREPRESS

Image source: Negatives, transparencies, photographic prints, printed pages, electronic files

Playback: Print Photo CD–compatible CD-ROM drive

Authoring system: Photo CD authoring workstations connected to high-end scanning systems of Du Pont–Crosfield, Dainippon Screen, Linotype Hell, or Scitex

Storage capacity: Up to 100 images, depending on resolution and on size of CMYK files

Optional features: Can store Photo CD and Pro Photo CD files, CMYK files, and text, graphics, page layout, and data files

Description: Portfolio II incorporates features developed specifically to meet color prepress needs. It provides scans that have been color corrected, retouched, and color separated, ready to be published.

The standard format for CMYK files has been agreed to by the four main manufacturers of color electronic prepress systems (CEPS): Du Pont–Crosfield, Dainippon Screen, Linotype Hell, and Scitex. To produce the discs, a Kodak Portfolio Photo CD workstation is connected to one of these standard high-end scanning systems.

In addition to providing print-ready images, Portfolio II can act as a "job jacket" that accumulates not only Photo CD files but the kinds of CMYK files familiar to the desktop publishing environment. Prepress operators can use Portfolio II discs to store images from Photo CD and Pro Photo Master discs that have been retouched and prepared for printing; to store scanned input from all four manufacturers' prepress systems; and to accommodate graphics, text, and other page elements. This capability thus allows prepress houses to store all job-related files together in a convenient, inexpensive, and durable form.

BREAKING THE REFLECTIVE AND LARGE ORIGINAL BARRIER

Systems for producing Portfolio II discs are sold as an add-on component of prepress systems manufactured by Linotype-Hell, Du Pont Crosfield, Scitex, and Dainippon Screen. Kodak's KEPS products will also support the creation of Portfolio II discs.

Systems from the major prepress suppliers are typically connected to conventional drum scanners. Portfolio II has the ability to accept a document that has been scanned from any original that the drum scanner can accommodate. On a Crosfield 646 drum scanner, for example, the original can be as large as 24 x 28 inches, either transparent or reflective.

Retouched images, those already run through the CEPS (color electronic prepress system), can also be written to the Photo CD disc—a first among source images that can be written to the Photo CD series. In fact, the Portfolio II system cannot be connected to a stand-alone scanner, so images must first be scanned and stored on a CEPS computer system before being passed to the Kodak-built Photo CD mastering platform.

The first of the four major prepress companies to release a Portfolio II authoring system is Screen (USA), a subsidiary of Dainippon Screen. Screen's Print Photo CD Input & Authoring

Screen is the first of the four prepress manufacturers to release Photo CD Portfolio II authoring system. Images from drum scanners and from other sources (including such proprietary sources as TaigaSPACE) are written to the CD disc at a PIW. The images can be accessed and manipulated on a desktop system; they are then rewritten to the disc or directly output to the prepress system.

188

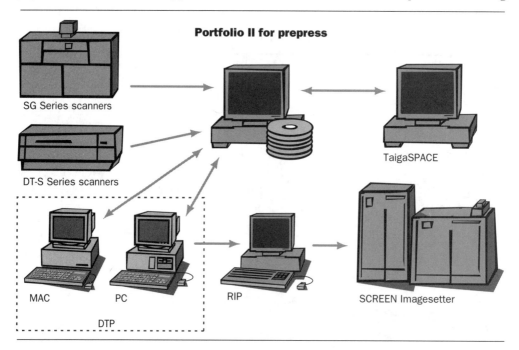

Portfolio II for prepress

SG Series scanners

DT-S Series scanners

TaigaSPACE

MAC   PC   RIP   SCREEN Imagesetter

DTP

System, termed PrintCD Master, can accommodate a wide range of image information input from scanners and digital cameras. It also accepts information from proprietary CEPS formats, including Screen's OMEGA and TaigaSPACE formats. Screen's PrintCD Master runs on the standard Sun SPARCstation (UNIX) platform and authors CDs via a Kodak PCD Writer.

HIGH END TALKS TO HIGH END

Kodak's Portfolio II offers a solution to the dilemma of interplatform file exchange with a standardized file protocol that can be read and written by all the participating manufacturers as well as by desktop computer systems. The four-color standard, called TIFF/IT P1, is legible to virtually all computer systems that can manage prepress graphics. Scitex, Du Pont, Linotype-Hell, and Dainippon Screen have all agreed to work closely with Kodak to implement that standard so that cross-platform compatibility becomes practice rather than a promise.

When a prepress firm scans an original and passes it to a desktop production person on a Portfolio II disc, that person has access not only to the original file stored in CMYK format but also to the Photo CD image pac containing the basic five resolutions of the same image for position—or for reproduction.

If the production designer wants to use the Photo CD images from the image pac to build a color document, the files are easily accessible and work in the same way that Photo CD images work from other source discs. The largest file available now from the Portfolio disc is 16XBase, but that yields a big enough file for most graphic arts applications.

The desktop designer also has the option with page layout software or photo manipulation software to open the CMYK image at its full resolution. This poses a potentially daunting problem for some desktop computer systems. If the full-size file in CMYK is 200, 300, or 400 MB, the desktop computer must be able to accommodate this size of file.

Managing such large files in most desktop applications is potentially difficult and often inappropriate. More appropriate, perhaps, is the acceptance of the Photo CD image pac with its 18 MB image as a reproduction image on the desktop system.

This is not to say that the full-resolution files cannot be used by desktop systems. Adobe Photoshop running on a properly outfitted computer (adequate RAM, hard disk, fast processor and dis-

189

CASE STUDY

FOCUS ON APPLIED GRAPHICS TECHNOLOGIES

Applied Graphics Technologies (AGT), a leading provider of prepress and printing services, immediately recognized the value of Photo CD in its industry and adopted it as an alternate source of scans suitable for many prepress applications. But AGT also recognized one latent potential of Photo CD: as *the* barrier-breaking technology that could solve problems unique to the high-volume imaging requirements of many publishers, especially of weekly magazines.

In 1994 key members of Kodak's original Photo CD team formed AGT's Digital Imaging Systems Division (DISD) to push Photo CD technology in these new directions. Within a few months, DISD unveiled its premier product, the Digital Link Gateway System, a complete solution for rapid image capture, editing, management, and archiving. Although designed primarily for use by news publications, the system has a variety of secondary applications that may have an even greater impact on how digital images can be used.

The Gateway System is an integrated set of Windows NT-based software that runs on standard PC-based hardware. The system integrates components of the Kodak PCD system to capture more than 250 color images an hour—but with a twist. Instead of writing Photo CD image pacs directly to discs, the Gateway System stores them on a server hard disk for on-line editing. The system also groups related images into jobs and appends annotations to each image during capture—critical advantages for subsequent editing and archiving.

After images are captured, they are immediately available for editing at networked workstations. In fact, in less than 10 seconds an image can move from film to full-color display on any or all workstations in a network. AGT's Photo Editor software provides complete tools for viewing, sorting, annotating, and adjusting images (and will soon support images from other scanners and wire services). Editors can attach production notes, crop the image, set the output

size, and delete unwanted images. When images are ready to go, they can be converted to TIFF and transferred for further production and use in page layout or new media applications at any workstation on the network—PC or Macintosh.

After editing and annotation, images can be archived from the server to writable CD media using a Kodak or other writer. The Gateway System can be integrated with database software and supports multidisc changers to provide a complete archiving and retrieval system.

By integrating Photo CD's high-speed, high-quality scanning technology, the Gateway System offers one of the few viable solutions for demanding commercial imaging use—as Gateway customers such as *The New York Daily News, U.S. News & World Report,* and *Newsweek* have discovered. But the system also has wider applications, including distributed image capture and remote photo editing. For example, a photojournalist on assignment in California might take late-breaking news film to a Gateway-equipped lab, where the images can be digitized and then edited remotely by a photo editor on the East Coast. After editing, selected photos can be archived to disc and shipped—or, better yet, transmitted electronically to the publisher.

AGT is also using the system to provide affordable digital archiving services. Because the Gateway System scans very rapidly and automates much of the annotation process, it can meet the needs of vast libraries, even those containing millions of images. As part of its archiving strategy, AGT can cost-effectively recapture—on 35mm film—originals in a variety of formats (various film sizes, reflective art, even glass plates) for subsequent high-speed capture on the Gateway System. In a related application, the Gateway System is being used in a new all-digital stock agency, MP©A In View, a subsidiary of the American Society of Media Photographers, both to create the photo archive and to fulfill customer requests by producing custom Photo CDs on demand.

190

play card) or KPT's Live Picture can both handle multi-hundred megabyte files without serious difficulty. In fact, Live Picture with its FITS technology is better suited to handle such large files than many prepress systems are.

FILE SERVERS AND PRINT PHOTO CD

Though not available at present, print servers such as Color Central from Adobe, Helios, and Archetype will likely be able to use the Photo CD image from a Portfolio II disc in RGB format (perhaps at 4XBase resolution) to build the page, then substitute the CMYK TIFF IT-8 file at the time of output to the imagesetter. Making Photo CD Portfolio assume the role of OPI (open prepress interface) is a logical move on the part of high-productivity print server systems.

Using the Portfolio images as FPO (for position only) images is more likely than the same scenario with standard Photo CD images because the image can be scanned and retouched on a CEPS system before being written to the disc, making the image on the Portfolio disc a more reliable image than one scanned directly from film, with its potential for dust and image flaws that need to be retouched.

Combine this better quality feature with the ability to download a full-resolution post-CEPS image in CMYK format while using a space-efficient Photo CD image in RGB format for position, and you have a very workable and professional system for color reproduction.

191

Part IV

CREATING PRESENTATIONS WITH PHOTO CD

12

Photo CD and Desktop Presentations

You've probably seen hundreds of presentations in your lifetime and maybe even given a few. Simply defined, a *presentation* is a slide show. It might be as elementary as showing a few dozen slides on a portable screen with a standard carousel projector, or as sophisticated as using multiple projectors, controlled by a computer, for elaborate programs that include music, narrative, and visual effects.

Presentations are pervasive in the business world. Corporate accounting departments use presentations to show cost/benefit analyses in visual formats. Marketing departments use simple presentations for informal meetings and more complex marketing and sales presentations for trade shows. In the educational sphere, instructors find that slide shows enhance classroom lectures and aid in the learning process. Similarly, scientists use presentations to demonstrate new ideas to colleagues; ophthalmologists use slide shows to advise patients on forthcoming cataract surgery; urban planners find that slides aid in discussions between various groups involved in both the political and design processes; lawyers use slides to present evidence in court. Even the family photo album can be shown to friends and relatives as a slide show.

Slide-show presentations are more or less static when compared to the user participation characteristic of most multimedia programs. When a slide show is presented, the audience can only view what is shown; they have no other options. Productions that *do* allow for audience interaction and that incorporate video and animation as well as sound and graphics are usually classified as *multimedia*, a topic we cover in Chapters 14 and 15. Here we will concentrate on the less complicated types of presentations that you can develop incorporating Photo CD images.

Whatever your purpose in developing a presentation, you will find Photo CD useful as a source of images, as an authoring tool, or as an output medium.

Linear Presentations on Photo CD Master Discs

If your goal is to show fewer than 100 images in linear order without sound, you can put your presentation on a Photo CD Master disc. Choose the 35mm images you want in the show (whether negatives or slides), indicate the order in which you want them to appear, then take them to a service bureau to have them converted to Photo CD. You can then simply play the disc as is, or you can "edit" your show by using the remote control on a Photo CD player to crop or enlarge photos, change the order, and so on (see Chapter 6). Keep in mind, however, that to play back your "programmed" show on a TV set, you will need to use the same Photo CD player on which it was programmed.

Presentation Software

If your slide show is to consist of more than just photos, incorporating text and graphics, for example, you'll want to create it with a presentation software package. Such packages now come equipped with a wide range of capabilities, including visual effects, sound, and the ability to import photographic and illustration files and even video.

With so much complexity added to presentation software, you may think that it has also become more difficult for the average person to use. Not so. As computer presentation applications have become more powerful, they have also been made easier for users to work with.

Software packages provide you with predesigned background templates if you do not have the time or the ability to design your own. In addition, most applications include a clip art library, some graphics tools, and built-in color palettes guaranteed not to embarrass the black-thumb visual presenter. Templates for printing audience handouts and speaker notes are generally included as well. In addition, a variety of designs for charts, graphs, and tables are part of most popular software packages. With this level of help, all you have to do is insert the content in the spaces provided.

BASIC FEATURES

The basic features of any presentation package include templates, transition effects, builds, clip art, and chart-making tools.

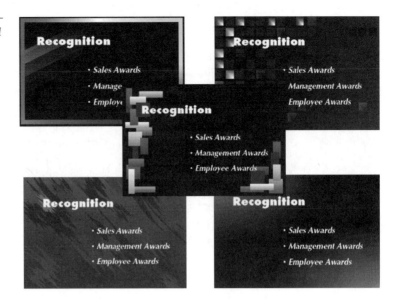

Various color scheme and design templates are included as part of presentation packages.

- **Templates.** Presentation packages provide a variety of templates based on preset typography and color palettes. Each template includes a background design and placeholders for up to five or six levels of text. Each text level has a preformatted typeface and size assigned to it. Type colors are chosen to be easily read. Bullets can be applied to highlight important text items.

- **Transition effects.** A *transition* is a visual effect that softens the abrupt change that occurs when you switch directly from one slide to another. The most commonly used transition is the *dissolve,* based on the movie technique of fading out from one scene while overlapping it with the gradual appearance of another. Available transition effects range from simple dissolves to wipes, zooms, page turns, and splits. A *wipe* is an effect in which a slide appears gradually onto a blank screen from a preselected direction, as if you were *wiping* it on. If you select a vertical wipe from bottom to top, it will look as if you are pulling up a window shade. *Iris* transitions come in two styles, in and out. When an "iris in" transition is applied, the scene gradually disappears into a circle in the center of the screen. "Iris out" has the opposite effect.

- **Builds.** With a *build,* the individual bulleted text items on a slide are moved in one at a time, building up to the completed text. Builds can be combined with other slide transitions, such

197

that each time a new text item swings on to the screen, a dissolve or other effect can be applied.

TIP: *Builds and transitions add interest and movement to a slide presentation. However, it is easy to create appalling effects if you apply them thoughtlessly. Try to keep the direction path the same throughout a build, and use the same transition effect throughout a slide sequence. Change the visual transition when a new major topic appears.*

- **Clip art.** Most presentation software includes a clip art library; their usefulness varies from application to application. You can augment these images by importing art from commercial clip art libraries, photos from Photo CDs, and images created in sophisticated graphics applications. Most packages will allow you to import QuickTime movies, although these need to be constructed in another software environment. You will need to check your software for the specific import formats it allows.

- **Chart-making tools.** The variety of supplied chart types depends on the package you use. Again, if you prefer to use a separate program for constructing charts, they can usually be imported to your slide show.

LEADING PACKAGES

The leading presentation authoring packages are Persuasion, PowerPoint, Astound, and Create-It.

Aldus Persuasion is perhaps the most popular presentation software, especially for Macintosh users. Persuasion has a filter that allows you to access Photo CD images directly from within the application. However, if you want to crop or otherwise manipulate the image, you will have to so with other software, such as Photoshop. Other features include a hefty set of slide templates, a variety of color palettes, an extensive clip art library, graphics, color blends, and OLE (object linking and embedding) for working with Cricket Graph and Microsoft Word while you are in Persuasion.

Microsoft PowerPoint features a color palette married to the template of your choice. Individual colors in a palette can be changed or an entirely new palette selected.

Microsoft PowerPoint has its own library of ready-made slide design templates that can speed the job of producing a presentation.

198

PowerPoint contains a large clip art library with segments including business, school, nature, men, and women. It also includes a filter for importing Photo CD files. Most of the items on a PowerPoint slide, including the clip art library, are object-based, allowing you to scale them. You can also group and ungroup them and change their color. Backgrounds and certain objects can be filled with graduated color tints. The graphics tools include a cropping function. Like Persuasion, PowerPoint has OLE available for working with Graph and Word while you are in PowerPoint.

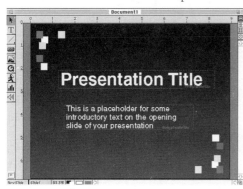

Astound is another popular presentation application.

The Macintosh version of PowerPoint (3.0) lacks some of the features in the Windows version (4.0), but an upgrade is in the works.

Astound is a presentation program that includes most of the basic features described above. Its unique addition consists of some sophisticated animation techniques and interactivity usually associated with multimedia applications. A packet of simple animations, called Actors, is included. Astound also contains a graphics library that provides animations as well as still images. New objects can be added to the library. Astound is no Macromedia Director (see Chapter 14), and it lacks some of the more powerful features found in Persuasion and PowerPoint (such as a built-in color palette), but it serves as a useful introduction to multimedia that newcomers will find easier to use than Director.

If you have a Macintosh computer, you can also create presentations using Kodak's **Create-It** software. This authoring program has many powerful features for working with photographic images, and your slide show can be output to regular slides or to a Photo CD Portfolio disc. Chapter 13 provides detailed information on Create-It and Portfolio.

Other well-known presentation packages include Macromedia's Action!, Corel Presents, Harvard Graphics, and Tempra Show. (For more information on these software programs, see Appendix IV.)

199

Planning Your Presentation

Before you start making slides, you'll need to develop the content for your show. What is the purpose of your presentation? Do you want to sell an idea or a product? Get a budget approved? Train

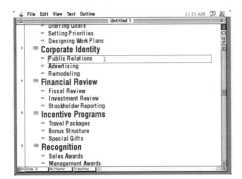

The outline view in Aldus Persuasion allows word processor–style editing of slide text.

The slide sorter view allows rearrangement and sequence editing of a presentation.

employees to deal with customer problems? Do you want to concentrate on photographic images with a minimum of text, or will text slides be an important consideration? Will the presentation be directed to a small group or to a crowd in a large hall? Make your slide show relevant and to the point, based on its purpose and intended audience.

Most presentation packages come with a ready-to-use outliner for keying in text, slide by slide. Text can include the slide title, main items, and secondary items. It can also include a short paragraph describing the illustration you want to insert. (The description can be removed once the image is in place.) At this point you shouldn't be concerned about getting your slides prettied up and in perfect order. The aim is to get what is in your mind into the software!

As you develop the text, indicate where you would like to see a photograph, illustration, or graph. You can edit and rearrange the slide sequence with a mouse drag as needed while you compose the text outline for your presentation. Items within a slide can be shifted around as well.

When you are satisfied with the basic text, it's time to go on to the visuals. If you prefer, you can develop content in the slide view as well as the outliner. You can continue to make changes in text and slide sequence at any time during the authoring process, either in outline or in slide view.

TIPS: *Robert D. Hall, a senior consultant at Decision Solutions, a part of AT&T Global Information Solutions, makes the following suggestions for authoring presentation content:*

• *Limit the number of items on each slide—communicate one idea at a time.*

• *For each major topic, plan a slide that lists the topic title with its major components. These can be listed as bulleted items.*

• *List no more than three or four items to a slide. If you find that the slide runs over that limit, add a new topic slide.*

- *Include relevant graphics wherever possible. If your slide contains a graphic image, confine the text to a title and a brief description.*

- *Save your work frequently, and proof it for accuracy.*

PLANNING THE DESIGN

Although the most popular applications offer many templates to choose from, you will still have to make some design choices. Before selecting a template, consider your audience, the content of your slide show, and what you hope to accomplish with the presentation.

Dave Perrell, of Hearn/Perrell Art Associates, is a graphic designer who constructs presentations for various audiences and purposes. For a client that delivers technical seminars at major corporations, Perrell produces slides that are clean and corporate looking, with no superfluous graphic distractions. For presentations shown at trade shows. however, he designs slides that are glitzy and full of motion, as suits the trade show environment and audience.

If you are designing your own templates, limit the number of typefaces you plan to use. If you are going to be projecting the presentation in a large room, make sure the type is large enough to read in the back of the room.

Once you have chosen a template or created a basic background and type design for your presentation, you will need to plan the appearance of photographs, illustrations, and charts.

Photographs are used in two ways in a slide show. They can be used as backgrounds or as photographic illustrations on a plain background.

If you plan to use a photograph as a background for text slides, select images that are simple, with an uncluttered area for text. Be sure that the typefaces you have chosen will be readable against the background color. Apart from selecting a contrasting typeface color, use a drop shadow or outline to separate the text from the photograph.

Next, plan a basic format for photographs to be used as illustrations within a slide. A simple outline or box with a drop shadow can add crispness to the image. If your presentation will be shown on a television screen, outlines should be at least two pixels wide.

When designing charts and graphs:

201

Photographs can be used in a variety of ways in your presentations.

- Try to use no more than three different styles in a single presentation.

- Choose a color scheme that blends with the color palette of your slide template.

- Limit the number of data items. If you are planning a column chart, for example, you'll find that using more than eight or so items will make your chart look like a picket fence. Similarly, pie charts with too many slices lose their value for visual comparison.

202

Persuasion's diverse charting functions are provided through a separate, data-linked application, accessed from the presentation program.

- Sans serif typefaces usually work best for chart elements such as numbers and data names.

Organizations that use presentations on a regular basis find that standardizing particular templates for specific needs helps authors get started quickly. Carefully thought out standard designs also ensure that the company image is visually clear and well maintained. To aid in the standardizing process, you should prepare a style guide that covers chart styles, specs for handling of photographs and illustrations, and additional color choices.

It is also helpful to include libraries of selected clip art, logos, and so on designed to accompany these templates. Frequently used photographs can be stored on Photo CD discs as part of an image and archive library. Robert Hall, at Design Solutions of AT&T, notes that presentations are often put together under very tight deadlines, and being able to lift content and graphics from existing material and to draw on photo archives can be a real lifesaver.

USING PHOTO CD IN YOUR PRESENTATIONS

You can incorporate photographs into your presentation either by the traditional method of scanning the desired images or by accessing Photo CD files.

Copying photos to a slide application as TIFF or PICT files is a highly memory-intensive solution. You'll need loads of RAM, as much as 32 MB, to run a computer presentation that contains many photographic images—apart from enough disk space on which to load it. You can avert this problem by converting a photograph-laden computer-driven slide show to Photo CD format, keeping the images in Base resolution.

Some presentation graphics software such as Persuasion and PowerPoint include a basic no-frills import filter that can read Photo CD formats directly. Images will come in as-is, with no changes in their proportions. If you are using presentation software that does not yet have a Photo CD import filter, Kodak's low-cost Photo CD Access for both Mac and Windows provides this ability (see Chapter 6). Access also provides crop, zoom, and rotate functions not included in presentation software.

Remember, photographs in 35mm format are not cropped to the correct 3:4 ratio for television screen viewing. If your images need more extensive twiddling and manipulating than Access permits, use Adobe Photoshop (Mac and Windows) or Aldus PhotoStyler (Windows).

Image acquisition from Photo CD to the presentation program is accomplished through this dialog box after choosing "import" from the menu.

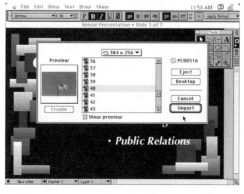

To import a photograph from a Photo CD disc, first make sure that you have the disc inserted in your CD-ROM drive. Choose the Import Graphic or Import Picture function from your presentation software, and a dialog box will appear. Choose the Photo CD file that includes the image(s) you want to import to your presentation. The Photo CD dialog box will appear with several file formats to choose from. OVERVIEW.PCD:1 is a catalog file for browsing for an individual image. The IMAGES folder contains the files for each individual image.

For on-screen display, select 512 x 768 (Base resolution) and 32-bit color from the

203

Import menu dialog box. Select Rotate if you want to change a horizontal slide to a vertical position.

Access works similarly to built-in import filters but also includes a Player emulation. You can view the contents of the disc as they would appear on a Photo CD player. Double-clicking on an image will select and show it full screen.

If you need to crop the image to the 3:4 proportion full-screen television format, it can be done in the Access environment. You may find that you need to add an extra-wide margin to the image to ensure that nothing important will be cropped when viewing the show. If this additional manipulation is needed, it will have to be done in Photoshop or PhotoStyler.

Some of your photographs may come from collections in TIFF or PICT format. These can be imported by any presentation software package. The same restrictions as those given for Photo CD discs apply—cropping and other manipulations may need to be done first in other software before the image is imported to the presentation program of your choice.

OUTPUT CONSIDERATIONS

What delivery platform will you be using for your presentation? Output choices include 35mm slides, overhead transparencies, or presentation on a computer or television screen. Since each output format is a somewhat different overall size, you will need to select the output format before starting to design your slides. Some applications group their templates selections for a particular output platform. Others allow you to choose a template design and then select the output device from the menu.

If you change your mind about the output format midway through the design process, you will need to rearrange the content to account for a different set of dimensions. If you are planning to use more than one final output platform for your slide presentation, you may need to redo the presentation for each different output device.

The part of the screen that is guaranteed not to be cut off by an output device is called the *safe area*. The safe area on a television screen, called the STA (safe titling area), is different from that of a computer screen or of 35mm slides. The STA is the part of the screen that is 80 percent inside of the total viewable television area.

If your presentation software doesn't provide a grid for television presentation, you can make one on acetate and place it over your computer screen. The television screen is in the same proportion as a 640 x 480 computer monitor—3:4.

TIP: *If you are designing your presentation for several output formats and want to avoid redoing the show for each different platform, you might want to try this workaround. Select the 35mm slide format and center all your text and relevant graphics well within the smallest recommended safe area, leaving extra-large margins. Test the format to verify that all the pertinent information falls within the safe area. Be sure to proof each presentation format as you work to ensure that nothing of importance will be cut.*

Colors, too, will look different depending on whether they will be shown on a television or computer screen or as 35mm slides. In particular, the color variations between those seen on a computer screen and those viewed on a television screen are quite pronounced. Desktop publishers have long known the difference between computer RGB (red, green, blue) formulation and CMYK (cyan, magenta, yellow, black) used for printing press inks. A similar difference holds for RGB and NTSC, the television color formulation. In this instance, NTSC does not stand for TV colors, which are also RGB, but for another naming convention. The color gamut, which is the range of viewable colors available to a particular platform, is much smaller on a television than on a computer monitor.

Persuasion allows you to choose the correct color for television screen viewing from Color Systems in the Show pull-down menu. If you are planning a TV presentation, choose NTSC color. You will notice that the allowable palette colors are not quite as bright as those for computer screen viewing, which are in RGB format.

If you intend to write your presentation to a Photo CD Portfolio disc, this menu choice will not be needed. When a Portfolio disc is accessed, it smart-selects the right palette, depending on whether you are viewing the images on an RGB computer or an NTSC television screen via a Photo CD player.

For presentations intended for viewing on an NTSC television screen, keep in mind the following guidelines:

- Make lines and dots at least 2 pixels thick especially along the horizontal, or else they will (appear to) flicker on the television screen.

- An alternative to thickening lines to avoid flicker is to apply antialiasing to your images. Antialiasing is a process that color blends the edges of an object with the background. This technique is widely used to smooth out "jaggies," the stair-stepping effect often seen on computer-rendered line drawings. Applications such as Photoshop, Fractal Design Painter, and Jag II can be used to apply antialiasing to presentation slides.

• Some color combinations will cause flickering and rainbowing at edges where they touch. Reds, in general, cause problems, especially when combined with green or blue. This effect is most noticeable when inappropriate color combinations are selected for type and background. Safe color combinations include white colors on a blue background, or pastel letters on a blackish or dark gray ground.

• As a rule of thumb, the more saturated the colors you have chosen, the more likely the color will appear to crawl on the screen. Very highly saturated colors are not supported by the NTSC standard and will appear pastel and washed out when viewed on a television screen.

Outputting Your Presentation

Once you've created a presentation using a software package such as Persuasion or PowerPoint, you have several options for outputting the results, depending on how you plan to display or show the presentation. If you simply want to show the presentation on your computer or on other computers, the least expensive route is to output the files to a disc. Short presentations can fit on a floppy or two, but larger ones may require a SyQuest or other type of removable media. You can then show the presentation on any compatible computer equipped with your presentation software.

If you want to show your presentation with projection equipment or on a TV screen, or if you want to have the program duplicated for distribution, you'll need to choose from among the other output options, which include having slides made, having the program put on a CD-ROM disc, or writing the program to a Photo CD Master disc.

CONVERTING YOUR DIGITAL PRESENTATION TO 35MM SLIDES

The advantage of 35mm slides is that they are available at a reasonable cost, and most people or companies have slide projectors avail-

Jeff Brice's poster for Newton's Apple. *For an explanation of how this poster was created using* Photo CD *images, see pages 102–103.*

These images all started from one Photo CD image pac. Each was opened using a different technique and converted to CMYK either directly by the acquiring software or, when opened as RGB, separated in Photoshop. The separation was accomplished by converting from RGB to CMYK using EfiColor profiles for Photoshop, SWOP with 75% GCR. These same color separations are available in Electronics For Imaging's Cachet program and from other applications that use EfiColor separation profiles, including QuarkXPress. No special modifications were made to any image, except to adjust each one similarly for the dot gains expected in printing the book.

St. Basil's Cathedral, Moscow, acquired from Photo CD in RGB mode, using the Kodak Photo CD Acquire Module for Adobe Photoshop.

C2

St Basil's Cathedral opened directly in CMYK using Purup PhotoImpress software. Purup software is capable of batch-processing a number of images in CMYK unattended.

St. Basil's Cathedral acquired (left) with the Kodak Acquire Module using a "flat" metric for the Acquire module part of the PhotoStep software. The image is opened twice, once to measure the dynamic range and a second time to actually acquire the image. The second pass (right) has brighter whites and blacker blacks, filling the reproduction range possible with Photo CD images.

St. Basil's Cathedral acquired with the Kodak Photo CD Acquire Module for Adobe Photoshop. Included with this plug-in are 21 metrics, which control the color, brightness, and contrast of acquired images. These examples show three of these metrics in use: (top left) Gamma 2.2 5000°K, (above) Gamma 1.8 5000°K, and (left) Gamma 1.4 5000°K.

St. Basil's Cathedral, acquired with the Human Software CD-Q plug-in in Adobe Photoshop. In the first example, the image is opened flat; the second example uses several of CD-Q's color correction options for a fuller range of colors.

Images recorded on film cannot help but visually degrade over successive generations and enlargements. You can see how the same image, duplicated as second- and third-generation slides, not only loses sharpness and gains contrast but shows a significant color shift from the original. Digitized images don't suffer these afflictions, because digital "dupes" are identical to the original in every way. (see page 27)

Data from a Kodak PCD scan of a 35mm slide can be recorded in scene space color (top) or universal film terms (bottom). Scene space color, which is also used for making prints from negative film, compensates for film type and lighting conditions to produce an image that recreates the scene in "memory" colors, with blue sky, gray pavement, and so on. Universal film terms maintain the "look and feel" of the particular type of film, to produce colors that look like the original slide, such as "warm" or "cool," for example. (see page 30)

In order to be written to Photo CD, images are converted from the RGB mode to the Photo YCC format, which takes advantage of human color perception by employing one luminance (Y) and two chrominance (C^1 and C^2) channels for each image. Since much of the color information contained in an RGB image is superfluous, the Photo YCC format eliminates such data, so that high-resolution images can be stored and reconstructed as efficiently and as accurately as possible. (see page 31)

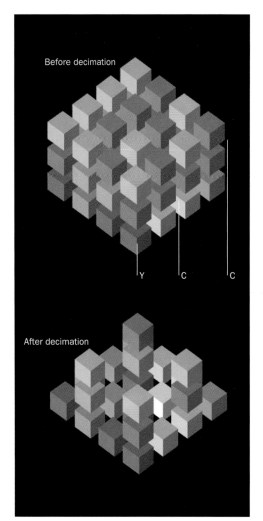

Before decimation

After decimation

C6

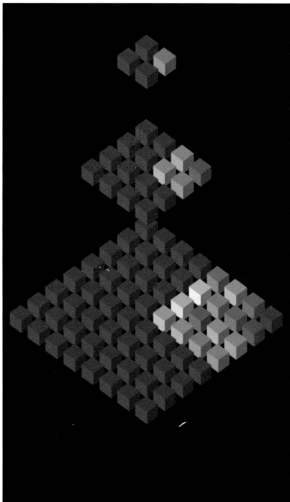

In chroma decimation, the first step in image pac compression, the chroma values for three-fourths of the pixels in the image are removed. This process retains all of the original luminance information but reduces the amount of data in the file to half. (see page 32)

A sophisticated averaging and subsampling program averages the color values in the 9 MB file to produce a Base version. At each of the two stages, the residual information (the difference between the averaged and the original data) is saved in a compressed format so that it can later be added to the Base data to reconstitute two higher-resolution versions of the image (4XBase and 16XBase). (see page 32)

Should you shoot negatives or transparencies if you plan to have your images scanned to Photo CD? Color negative film (top) produces very different results than transparency film. For a discussion of this issue, see page 69.

C7

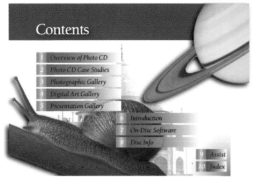

The Official Photo CD Handbook's *companion Photo CD Portfolio disc is an example of interactive multimedia created with Kodak's Arrange-It software. With custom music, narration, an inviting interface, and striking screen graphics, it offers a variety of informative material. Shown here (clockwise from top left) is the Contents screen; a photo of Robert De Niro from photographer Greg Gorman's presentation in the Photography Gallery; one of San Francisco artist Diane Fenster's works from her "exhibit" in the Digital Art Gallery; and a space shuttle photo from San Diego astronomer Dennis Mammana's Hubble Space Telescope show in the Presentation Gallery.*

C8

able for viewing them. The disadvantages are that slides need to be loaded into a carousel in the correct orientation and in the desired order, and they need to be projected onto a screen in a darkened room. If your presentation is to be part of a small group meeting, you may really prefer a well-lit room for discussion and note taking.

To create a 35mm photographic slide show, you will need to choose that format as you start to design a presentation. Selections for presentation formats are usually found under the File menu in both Windows and Mac software.

When your slide show is complete, save it to disk to take to your service bureau. You will need to include all the art files that were part of the presentation. Your service bureau will also want to know what typefaces you used (including the manufacturer) and what presentation software you used. The bureau will convert the digital information to 35mm transparencies and mount them.

If you need quantities of slides or if you make many presentations throughout the year, your company may want to invest in in-house equipment that's available at a relatively low cost.

CONVERTING A DIGITAL PRESENTATION TO CD-ROM

If you want to distribute your slide show to a number of presenters, the CD-ROM format is becoming a reasonable alternative, now available at a fairly low cost per disc.

CD-ROM is nothing more than a computer storage medium whose format offers the advantages of mammoth capacity and data that cannot be erased or altered. All the transitions and effects present in the original presentation will still be included, along with any sound, videos, or animations supported by the presentation software. If the Player file that comes with your software is included, the presentation can be viewed without the presence of the authoring software. However, playing the slide show in this format requires not only a computer but a CD-ROM drive.

CONVERTING A PRESENTATION TO PHOTO CD

To avoid many of the problems associated with traditional slide projection equipment, you can go an additional step and have your output presentation slides written to a Photo CD Master disc, then show them on a TV monitor or a video projection system using a Photo CD or other compatible player. With your slides written to Photo CD, you have one handy disc to carry around instead of a carousel full of slides. And with Kodak's portable player, all you need is a TV set to show your presentation, rather than a projection system. A further advantage is that you can change the order of the slides or leave some out, which is difficult with the traditional carousel slide show. And you know the slides will never be upside down or backward.

To have your slide show put on a Photo CD Master disc, simply provide your service bureau with the slides you plan to include, along with the sequence you want to follow.

Marcia Reed, a photographer who prepares traditional and multimedia press kits for television and motion pictures, uses Photo CDs to show her portfolio to prospective clients. She selects transparencies or negatives of the images she wants to show and has them put on a Pro Photo CD. Since she has worked as a photographer for over 25 years, her images are a mixed bag of photographic media, including Ektachrome, Kodachrome, and dupes. She has found that putting them on Pro Photo CD has improved the quality of older slides and that the entire presentation is visually better balanced than showing the images as individual slides. Marcia shows her Photo CD discs to prospective clients on a portable Philips CD-I player.

Another approach to using Photo CD as an output medium is to have your presentation written to a Portfolio disc at a service bureau. You'll need to provide your slides and a "script." As with the Master and Pro discs, a Portfolio disc can be shown on a TV or projection system with an appropriate player or it can be shown

on a computer with a CD-ROM XA drive. The advantage of Portfolio is that it will hold as many as 700 images in Base resolution, which is all you need for TV or computer viewing.

Portfolio supports noncontinuous sound. It also allows for attaching different sounds to basically the same slide show. For example, you can have the same slide show in English, Japanese, and Spanish, if you need to. The viewer merely selects the desired language track before running the program. A Portfolio disc showing scenes of Japanese culture was produced for 3,000 members of the press attending an Economic Summit in Tokyo. Viewers had the choice of playing it in Japanese or English. Keep in mind, though, that sound is very memory-intensive. If you are not thrifty in its use, it will eat up your disc space. (For more on the use of Portfolio discs for presentations, see Chapter 13.)

COMBINING DIGITAL FORMATS FOR PHOTO CD OUTPUT

Suppose you have a slide show in digital format on presentation software, along with many slides in Photo CD format. You do not want to bring the photographs into the presentation because of limited memory requirements. And you have no reason to crop or otherwise manipulate the Photo CD images. In this instance, you could use Kodak's Arrange-It software to sequence all your material, slide by slide. Arrange-It controls file allocation and sequencing prior to producing a Portfolio disc. Arrange-It accepts PICT, TIFF, and Photo CD YFF files, and AIFF sound. You can either import

209

These photos of Japanese life are part of a presentation on Photo CD Portfolio discs given to journalists visiting an economic summit in Tokyo. The disc, produced by Kodak, was commissioned by the International Society for Education Information (ISEI), which is affiliated with Japan's Ministry of Foreign Affairs. A goal of the ISEI is to ensure that Japan's traditions, culture, and contemporary development are accurately portrayed abroad.

each slide file into Arrange-It and indicate the desired sequence, or you can have a service bureau do it for you (see Chapter 15).

If you want to manipulate Photo CD images and design the entire slide show in a presentation application, follow Panfilio & Company's procedure, described in the case study. P&C converts their product slides to Photo CD format and imports them into Persuasion for television image cropping and any other needed manipulation. They then import each image into Persuasion, where the final presentation is authored. It is then written to a Photo CD Master disc for presentation on a player.

Corporations that make many slide and multimedia presentations throughout the year may be interested in setting up an in-house CD-ROM or Portfolio production facility. The cost for setting up an in-house CD-ROM unit is as low as $4,000. The cost for a workstation for producing Portfolio discs is about $30,000 if the platform is a Sun SPARCstation, but it is closer to the $4,000 figure for Macintosh or Windows II setups (see Chapter 15 for more on Portfolio disc production).

Showing Your Presentation

When it comes to showing your presentation, you have three main options: projecting it on a screen, showing it on a television, or showing it on a computer.

Obviously, if your final output is actual slides, you will need to use a projection system. If your output is a computer file or a CD-ROM, you'll need to show it on a computer or a video projection system connected to the computer. But if you've put everything on a Photo CD Master or Portfolio disc, then you can display it on a video projection system, a television screen, or a computer monitor. Here are some guidelines to follow for each situation.

PROJECTING YOUR PRESENTATION

If your audience is large, and the hall is spacious, you will need to project the slide show onto a large screen or on several connected monitors spaced around the hall using a video system. Display requirements are similar whether your slide show will be running from a computer or a Photo CD player. A video or computer projector will alter and distort color substantially, while color television monitors will display color with better fidelity. If color is important to your presentation, use large-screen monitors that can

FOCUS ON PANFILIO & COMPANY

Panfilio & Company (P&C) in Portland, Oregon, a producer of business meetings and presentations, has created a variety of presentations using Photo CD. One of P&C's clients is adidas America, for which they have produced several Photo CD training presentations for showing at the athletic shoe company's annual sales/marketing conference.

The initial content for a typical training presentation is supplied by adidas marketing executives, along with samples of the actual products. Each business unit manager develops a script for his or her division—running, basketball, adventure, soccer, and so on. Using Aldus Persuasion, the producers at P&C design the slide show based on the supplied scripts.

P&C shoots all the product photographs and has them processed as 35mm transparencies. They then select the ones to be used in the presentation and have them written to Photo CDs. The digitized images are then available to be manipulated. Quite likely, they will be cropped, retouched, or stored temporarily on the hard drive.

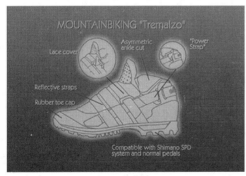

Next, the P&C designer imports the edited photographs into Persuasion, where text and other graphics will be added as needed. The designer pays particular attention to maintaining the TV safe area and the way colors will reproduce on a television screen. However, since the final output will be projected in Photo CD format, NTSC color needn't be selected in Persuasion—the Photo CD player will sense and automatically balance colors to the television environment.

The slide show in computer format is then reviewed by adidas. When the approval cycle is completed, the Persuasion presentation is converted to 35mm slides using an in-house film recorder. P&C then sends the slides to a service bureau to be written to Photo CD Master discs.

At the adidas sales meeting, the presentation is projected onto a large screen with a video projection system. P&C finds that, although the video resolution and colors are not equal to actual 35mm slides, the audience's impression that this is not just another slide show more than makes up for the difference. The panning, zooming, and random access features built into the player are also helpful to the presenter.

The adidas presenter supplies the narrative and controls the Photo CD player. Most presenters find the remote easy to use. However, the lagtime between pushing the Next button and seeing the next slide appear on the screen can create problems. For example, if the presenter pushes the button, gets momentarily distracted, and looks back to the screen and notices that the slide hasn't changed, his or her tendency is to press the button a second time, causing the player to skip an image. Forewarning the presenter about this problem usually helps.

211

display in both RGB and NTSC mode, such as Sony Trinitrons, as part of the presentation display platform.

DISPLAYING YOUR PRESENTATION ON A COMPUTER

The slide shows you develop in presentation programs can be run on a computer as an onscreen electronic slide show. QuickTime movies, sound, and any special effects and builds that you've included will remain part of the slide show. You will need to select computer screen format when starting your design. You can prepare the presentation to run as a completely automated show, with preset timing for each slide, or to be shown manually by a live presenter who advances each slide with a mouse click. Your presentation can be stored on the hard drive, on a CD-ROM, or on a Photo CD disc. To display Photo CDs, you'll need CD-ROM XA drive and appropriate Player simulation software (see Chapter 6).

If your presentation is intended for viewing by no more than two or three people, you can use a 14-inch monitor with a computer supporting 256 colors, although a 16-inch monitor would be preferable. If your audience will be sitting around a conference table, use at least a 19-inch screen. In a large conference room, use a 25- to 27-inch screen, or a computer color screen projector.

DISPLAYING YOUR PRESENTATION ON A TELEVISION SCREEN

In addition to display on a computer, Photo CD presentations can be shown on a television screen with a Kodak Photo CD player, a Philips CD-I player, a Panasonic 3DO player, or some other compatible device. Features such as time sequencing, panning, and zooming are available when a player is used as the display platform. (Chapter 6 provides more information on which players are compatible and the capabilities of each.)

To show images on a Photo CD disc manually, use the Next and Previous buttons on the remote to present the screens. To select a specific picture, use the numeric keys. You can also present the show automatically by pressing AutoPlay.

Printed Presentation Components

Most slide presentation packages will allow you to print out your presentation in a variety of formats. You can select a printout style to hand out to your audience. You can usually select from more than one format—one, three, or six images to a page. Handouts can usually be embellished with a name and address or other text and a company logo. A style designed for speaker notes is also included as one of the format options.

Check your software to find out where their selection options are kept for printing handouts and other slide formats. You will usually find it under the File menu.

213

13

Authoring Presentations with Kodak's Create-It

If you want to develop a slide show that includes sound and perhaps an element of interactivity, you'll need to use a multimedia authoring system. Kodak has developed its own presentation/multimedia authoring software and hardware designed to best present Photo CD images or to combine them with sound, text, and graphics. Kodak calls this authoring system Portfolio.

Portfolio: An Overview

A portfolio is a flat portable case for carrying a collection of loose papers, documents, or drawings. Kodak has adapted the term to describe its format for presenting collections of digital images—organized as a linear slide show or as an interactive multimedia presentation.

Kodak's Photo CD Portfolio authoring system consists of three separate software products and a hardware setup for writing the resulting programs to a special type of Photo CD disc.

The software packages are called Create-It, Arrange-It, and Build-It. Create-It Photo CD Presentation Software allows you to create image-intensive linear presentations. Arrange-It Photo CD Portfolio Layout Software helps you organize presentation screens (in PICT format), images, graphics, and sound files into a branching, interactive multimedia program. Build-It Photo CD Portfolio Disc Production Software writes the presentation to Portfolio discs.

Portfolio discs differ from Photo CD Master or Pro discs in two ways. First, the stored images are limited to Base view only, allowing for a total of about 700 single images to be stored on a disc (recall that only 100 images in multiple resolutions are stored on a Photo CD Master disc). Second, the Portfolio format allows the use of sound. A disc can contain a half-hour of sound along with 350 images. The combination of images and sound can vary, as long as the total space of the presentation is limited to 600 MB.

Kodak offers a family of software products for creating Photo CD Portfolio discs. Create-It and Arrange-It software let users design interactive presentations on the desktop. Both of these packages output a script language that enables Build-It software to structure the images, text, sound clips, and other content on a Portfolio disc.

Portfolio discs can be viewed on a computer with a CD-ROM XA drive, or on a television screen with a Photo CD player or compatible multimedia player (such as CD-I or 3DO). Because of their portability and potential for interactivity, these discs are ideal for doing business presentations, conducting training and educational seminars, and presenting product information at point-of-purchase kiosks.

Create-It and Arrange-It are both available as consumer products. If your main need is to produce uncomplicated presentations with a simple design, sound, and some branching, Create-It should fit your needs. If you want to do something a bit more complex, especially if you need to design some complicated interactive branching, you'll want to use Arrange-It to sequence images that have been put together in Create-It or other software. Arrange-It is described in detail in Chapter 15, "Advanced Portfolio CD Production." In this chapter, we'll fill you in on how to use Create-It.

Create-It: An Overview

Create-It is similar to existing presentation software products such as Aldus Persuasion and Microsoft PowerPoint. You can design content screens, building your frames from scratch or using templates. You can add text and graphics. Create-It lets you import "palettes" of low-resolution PCD images from discs in your CD-ROM drive. You can edit individual images for brightness and

PCD FORMAT 5
PHOTO CD PORTFOLIO II FOR MULTIMEDIA

Image source: Photo CD or other digital image files

Playback: Photo CD players, CD-I players, 3DO players, Photo CD–compatible CD-ROM with Photo CD Player software

Authoring system: Kodak Create-It presentation software; Kodak Arrange-It Photo CD Portfolio layout software; Kodak Build-It Photo CD Portfolio disc production software and PCD Writer

Storage capacity: 700 images, one hour of sound, or some combination of the two

Optional features: Audio; text; graphics; programmed access (branching); incorporation of QuickTime movies (for computer replay only); output to 35mm slides

Description: The Portfolio CD disc is designed to carry sound, graphics, text, and other files in addition to base-resolution Photo CD files. The disc can hold about 700 images with no sound, and about 350 images with a half-hour of sound.

Kodak has developed its own authoring software for preparing multimedia programs to write to Portfolio discs. The software is available in three modules: Create-It, Arrange-It, and Build-It.

Create-It is a presentation-authoring program that allows you to prepare a slide show. You can design content screens that incorporate text and graphics, add audio, and set the sequence of images. You can also bring in QuickTime movies if the intended output is for the computer and not TV. Create-It can be used to make a straight linear slide presentation or an interactive program with limited branching. To get your presentation put on a Portfolio disc, you take the Create-It script files and accompanying graphics and Photo CD files to a service bureau.

Arrange-It is authoring software that allows you to develop a multimedia presentation that incorporates photos, text, sound, graphics, and interactivity. You can design branches, menus, and a user interface and can incorporate screens and images created in other application programs. You then turn the script and all accompanying files over to a service bureau that assembles them using the Build-It software module. The resulting files are written to a Portfolio disc.

Portfolio discs can be played on a television with appropriate players or on a computer equipped with a CD-ROM XA drive and the Kodak Player software.

217

contrast, crop them, and adjust the color. You can also bring in PICT and TIFF files and even QuickTime movies (if your program will be for computer viewing only).

After creating the screens and selecting and editing your photos, you can sort them in any order you want. At this point you can also insert sound files to accompany specific slides. Create-It also enables you to introduce a limited amount of branching and to designate "hot button" areas. You can, for example, create an introductory screen with six "hot buttons" for choosing from among six branched sequences.

Once you have designed your presentation, you can preview it and even play it for others on your computer screen. Most likely, however, you will want to take it to a service bureau to have it written to a Portfolio disc. You can then play the disc on appropriately equipped computers or TV sets with PCD players. You can also have the disc duplicated or mass-produced (see Chapter 16 for more on disc duplication). Alternatively, you can output your Create-It screens as traditional slides, transparencies, or laser-printed pages. You can also import Create-It files to Arrange-It to add a greater degree of interactivity and more sophisticated transitions (see Chapter 15).

Building a Create-It File

Create-It offers you three desktop views for developing your presentation. In the Edit view, you can create frames or import them from templates, import image files and PCD palettes, create and edit text and graphics, and create buttons. In the Sort Frames view, you can add or delete frames, assign names to frames, and rearrange the order. In the Presentation view, you can add hot spots and branching and indicate how you want the show to play back (order and timing).

DESIGNING FRAMES

To develop a presentation in Create-It, choose New from the File menu, and a frame in Edit view will appear. If you plan to import images into your portfolio from a Photo CD, load it into your CD-ROM drive and choose Load Photo CD Palette from the File menu. On the screen, you will see an empty frame, and to the right, the Photo CD palette in a floating window. The window can be resized, scrolled through, and moved to other locations on the

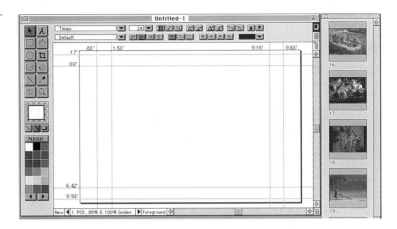

The Photo CD palette appears in a floating window. You can drag and drop any image onto the frame.

screen. Any Create-It portfolio stored on your hard drive can also be opened as a palette if you want to reuse the images in a new presentation.

To begin, you will want to design the basic look of your screens. You have the option of using one of Create-It's available templates or developing your own from scratch. To import a template, you open the Templates folder (under File, Open) and click on the name of your chosen template. (A spiral notebook showing the various templates comes in the software package.) You can use several templates in a single presentation and modify them to meet your particular needs.

You can also design your own frames in Create-It. You begin by opening the Frame Setup dialog box under Preferences, where you can specify your frame size. You can then use Create-It's tools to pick a background color, create graphics, and design text blocks.

219

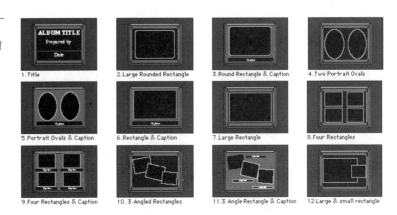

These are some of the frame templates provided with Create-It.

Whether using existing templates or your own frames, you can also design a Master Frame that will place the same items (such as a company logo) in the same place on all frames of the presentation.

IMPORTING IMAGES

Importing an image from a Photo CD is as simple as opening the CD from the file menu and dragging the image you want right onto the desktop. You can choose the resolution you wish to import, but normally the default is set to the Base resolution (the standard one Kodak developed to be displayed on a TV set).

The File menu also allows you to import PICT and TIFF files, which is also a good way to bring in Persuasion and PowerPoint documents that have previously been created. This importing methodology allows you to cross platforms as well, since both Persuasion and PowerPoint run on both the Macintosh as well as the PC.

QuickTime movies can be imported and played within the Create-It environment on a computer, using the Slide Show command in the File menu. However, these movies will not export to a Photo CD Portfolio disc. When you play the Portfolio presentation on a television, you will see only the first frame from the movie.

EDITING IMAGES

In the Edit view, images can be cropped, enlarged, straightened, and panned within their individual containers. Photographs can be placed within a graphic element such as an oval, using the eyedropper tool. In addition, photographic editing to adjust color, contrast, and brightness is supported (although it is preferable for you to use a more sophisticated image-editing application, such as Photoshop, before importing images to Create-It).

The ominous red eye, resulting from flash photography, can be removed with the software. A Brightness/Contrast selection is provided to alter overall tonal quality; color balance can be adjusted in the Color Adjust window. Using the Defect Removal option, defects such as dust spots and scratches can be removed or minimized.

The color palette includes a set of professionally developed color schemes, or you can create your own. Elements can be colored with an opaque paint, or with one that is transparent. When a transparent color is chosen, the selected object will be redrawn at 50% opacity. Any element positioned underneath a transparent object will then show through.

SIDEBAR

THE NTSC SAFE AREA

When Kodak originally developed Photo CD to be viewed on the home television, they took into consideration the fact that many people still own older TVs that have a somewhat smaller viewing area then the newer ones. If you use Create-It's "85% NTSC safe area" template to create your images, and size any imported images to be within the inner-most rectangle, the data and images you want the audience to see will be visible on all TV sets.

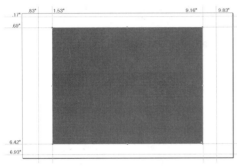

You should "bleed" your backgrounds to at least the second template rectangle or even to the edge of the template to ensure that your background is showing all the way to the edge of the TV screen and is not cut off at the sides or the top or bottom.

In Create-It you can choose the Frame PCD 85% NTSC template to provide the safe image area for playback on any television screen. All important and relevant material should be placed in the area within the "safe rectangle." Be sure that you fill the area outside the safe rectangle with background color or image, in case the presentation will be shown on television sets that can display a larger area.

Note: The Create-It template folder includes TV Colors, a template with a color scheme designed for display on television monitors. The NTSC "safe area" guides are included as part of the template.

In the Edit view you can use Create-It's drawing tools to produce graphics and Create-It's text tools to add all the text to your frames.

ORGANIZING SEQUENCES

The Sort Frames window in the View menu is used to organize or change the frame sequence. To create a sequence, you simply drag and drop frames into the Sort Frames window, in any preferred sequence.

Audio files can be added to individual frames in the presentation at any time. These files must first be created elsewhere and saved in AIFF format. To import a sound file, choose Acquire from the Audio menu, and locate it when the dialog box appears. Click the sound to hear it. Click the Acquire button and the sound file will appear in the Audio pane on the screen. The sound will attach to any selected frame when you drag it onto its window.

In the Sort Frame window you can attach sound to frames and create a sequence for your slide show.

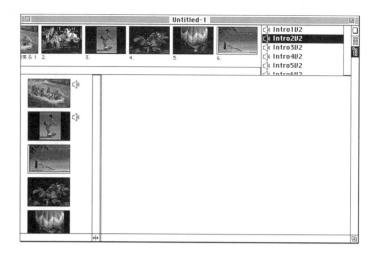

ADDING BRANCHES

If you plan to have branching in your Create-It slide show, you will need to first create menus and hot spots, then indicate the desired branched sequences. You begin in the Edit view, laying out the menu frame. You can place your menu items anywhere on the frame. You may want to use actual graphics "buttons," draw boxes, or simply provide numbers or labels that the user can click on.

You add hot spots in the presentations view, then indicate branching order in the Sort Frame window.

You can customize the playback of your sequence in the Presentation view.

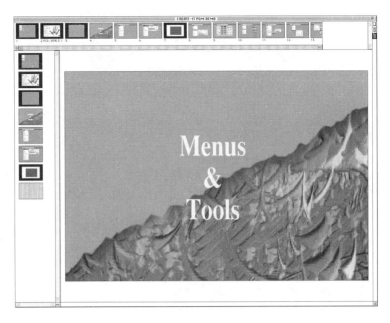

You next go to the Presentation view, where you can add "hot spots" by simply using the pointer tool to drag and click diagonally across the designated "hot" areas.

Finally, you go to the Sort Frames window to specify which frames go with which branches. To associate a sequence of frames with a menu branch, you simply drag the frames into the hot spot for a branch.

PREVIEWING YOUR PRESENTATION

The Presentation view is used to create a customized playback of your frame sequence. This view allows you to set slide show options, including automatic frame timing. A Sequence panel (a "windoid" in Macintosh terms) shows you the playback sequence for frames in the slide show.

Output Options

Screens developed in Create-It can be output to

- 35mm slides

- hard copy as high-resolution paper positives, paper handouts, or overhead transparencies

- a Portfolio disc

223

If you plan to export frames to have them converted into 35mm slides, they must have a 3:2 aspect ratio for the film recorder. Make sure that you have selected the 35mm Slide option and have set the resolution to 1536 x 1024 pixels for the resulting PICT files. (If you choose the standard PICT command, the resolution will be set at 72 dots per inch and cannot be changed.)

Create-It provides a number of options for hard copy output in the Print dialog box. Click the appropriate items for the output you want.

Output can also be exported in PICT format to Arrange-It, for further manipulation. A completed Create-It presentation can also be exported directly to Build-It for processing and writing to a Portfolio disc.

To create a Photo CD Portfolio disc from a Create-It script file, observe the Photo CD script export process. A folder will be

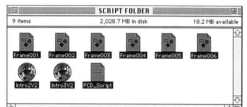

created containing a PICT file for every frame in the portfolio and any audio files that you attached to frames in the presentation. The folder will also include a Photo CD script file with instructions for your service provider.

To have Create-It files written to a Portfolio disc, you place all the elements in a PCD script folder.

It is a good idea to check with your service bureau when you first plan your project for any suggestions they may have. They will also let you know how they would like your final material delivered. Some providers prefer to work from your original files, instead of those created during the PCD export process. To find out which are your original files, choose Reference List from the Export submenu and print it out. The Reference List will itemize all the files you will need to send to the service provider.

Showing Your Portfolio Presentation

To show your Portfolio presentation on a television screen, you will need a Kodak Photo CD player, a Philips CD-I player, or other compatible device.

To show a Portfolio presentation using a Kodak Photo CD player, just load the disc and press the Play button to start the show. Press AutoPlay if you want to view the pictures automatically, slide by slide. You can set the time interval for each slide for automatic viewing, or use the default setting. If you want to run the show manually, press the Next and Previous buttons to move

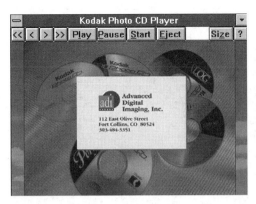

Player software is needed for playing a Portfolio disc on computer. This software is somewhat different for Windows (left) and Macintosh (right).

forward or back. You can select a specific picture by punching in its number in the sequence, using the 0 to 9 keys. If you want to zoom in to any detail in an image, press the TELE button. You can also change the composition of a picture: Enlarge the picture with TELE, and reposition the image within its container by using the Pan buttons to move it up, down, left, or right.

If you want to change the viewing sequence of the slide show, the player identifies the sequence you have selected, slide by slide, in a Favorite Picture Selection (FPS) list. This list is held in player memory until you choose to reorganize it. (For more detailed information on playback, see Chapter 6, or check the instructions that come with your player.)

For a self-contained presentation platform, you can use a portable Photo CD player. These players include a 6-inch color screen and built-in stereo speakers. The compact CD-I player by Philips can operate as a stand-alone unit or can be connected to projection systems or a large screen monitor for group presentations.

Portfolio slide presentations can also be run on a CD-ROM XA player on a computer. You can prepare the presentation to run as a completely automated show, with preset timing for each slide. It can be configured to run in a loop, if you want it to be shown on a store counter or at a trade show. The slide show can also be narrated by a live presenter who advances each slide with a mouse click. The presentation software files can be stored on the hard drive, on a CD-ROM, or on a Portfolio disc. (If the presentation is run on a computer, the player zoom feature will not be available.)

If your presentation is to take place in a large auditorium, you will need a video projector or a number of television monitors placed around the room. In a large conference room, a 27-inch or larger screen works well as a viewing platform.

FOCUS ON VEDCO

Vedco, a national veterinary supply company based in St. Joseph, Missouri, used Create-It and Kodak Portfolio CD technology to develop a presentation for its annual sales meeting. The presentation consists of 350 screens, containing images of new products, information on features and benefits of the products, and sales tips and techniques.

This simple linear presentation was developed entirely with Create-It. All images were imported into Create-It from Master Photo CD discs. Screens were designed using Create-It's graphics tools, and other graphics, text, and sound were added. The files were then sent to Advanced Digital Imaging in Fort Collins, Colorado, which used Build-It software to write the Portfolio disc. It took only a day to produce the disc and get it to Vedco's general manager, Craig Campbell, in time for him to have it for the sales meeting.

Campbell used a portable Photo CD player

hooked to a large-screen television to make the presentation. He was impressed with the portability of the system—he had previously used a traditional slide projector and had to lug the unit plus several carousels to his meetings. "The Photo CD format is extremely convenient," says Campbell, "I travel extensively, and the player and my entire presentation fit into one briefcase."

The Portfolio disc contains no narration, since Campbell prefers to provide his own commentary. The disc does contain sound effects, though—breaking glass, crashing cars—to punctuate the presentation.

In addition to the sales meeting, the disc has been used for distributor sales training and in-house training of telemarketing staff members. And because the product images have all been scanned to Photo CD, Vedco's publications department is able to access the higher-resolution versions for the company's catalog and other printed materials.

226

Kiosk Presentations

Portfolio presentations can be specifically designed for accessing in a kiosk. They can be run from a computer with a CD-ROM drive or from a player connected to a television monitor.

One of the first Portfolio-based kiosks was done for the Information Age exhibit at the American History Museum, part of the Smithsonian Institution in Washington D.C. The curators saw Portfolio as a medium that would help them produce high-quality presentations quickly, and at reasonable cost.

The first kiosk featured an interactive slide show of segments from the Annual Festival of American Folk Life. David Allison, the exhibit director, wanted the presentation to capture the music and spirit of the festival. Photography director Jim Wallace selected still photos taken at the festival, as well as photos from the museum's collection. The final images were combined with a narrative track and music on a Photo CD Portfolio disc. Viewers could choose from a menu of New Mexico–related topics that included American Indians, Spanish Colonial, and On the Range. Each choice brought up a brief slide show of images with accompanying sound.

In another Information Age project, a series of Portfolio discs were created for kiosk viewing during the Clinton inauguration. Dane Penland, who was in charge of the project, described Portfolio as a tremendous tool both for photographers and the mu-

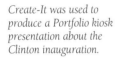

Create-It was used to produce a Portfolio kiosk presentation about the Clinton inauguration.

seum. Twenty-one photographers donated their time over a four-day period, amassing 15,000 images. The color film they shot during the day was processed and edited each evening. After editing, the selected images were transferred to Photo CD by Digix Imaging that same night, at a special facility set up at the Smithsonian's Office of Printing and Photographic services. The Portfolio disc made each night was available for viewing the next morning at the Information Age kiosk. Later, Digix produced a disc containing 100 of the best images taken during the inaugural week. Penland views this technology as extremely successful in getting world events to the public in a timely manner.

Those involved in the Information Age exhibits are excited by the popularity of the kiosk presentations and the immediacy that the technology allows. When budgets permit, they would like to convert the museum's collection of over 3 million photographs to digital images and use them to create a variety of Portfolio multimedia projects.

A popular use of Portfolio discs for kiosk presentations has been for point-of-purchase information in stores and malls. A group of Chicago department stores was one early user of the kiosk format for visual merchandising. Dayton, Hudson's and Marshall Field coordinated a Christmas gift idea Portfolio disc to be used in kiosks at the stores. Prism Studio of Minneapolis, working with Kodak, produced the disc for them. The kiosk consisted of a Photo CD player and a television monitor. A custom keypad was provided for selection purposes. The main menu allowed shoppers to first select a store. A second menu gave them a choice of four price categories from which to choose. Succeeding frames displayed a group of gift suggestions available at the chosen price as text and images. The stores found that although the use of kiosk technology was new to their customers, they were pleased with the final product.

There is apparently enough interest in using Portfolio for kiosk presentations that support industries are already springing up. Video Messenger Company, for example, offers a system for generating text messages to overprint on a presentation while it is playing. These messages scroll or crawl across the screen, can be programmed to change at various times or on different days, and can be changed from a remote location (via satellite, modem, or computer network). The system can also be used to combine Photo CD presentations with video delivery systems.

228

Photo Factory for Windows

If you are a Windows user who wants to do very simple slide shows using only Photo CD images, as an alternative to Create-It you might want to try Photo Factory for Windows.

This inexpensive product comes on a CD-ROM and is bundled with 50 stock Photo CD images, 50 original MIDI songs, and several demonstration slide shows.

Photo Factory is designed specifically for importing and editing Photo CD images. Editing features include cropping, zooming, flipping, rotating, resizing, gamma correction, color balance, mirror imaging, brightening, softening, embossing, and more. After you've edited your images, you drag and drop them to create a sequence. Although frame-building tools are minimal, you can add borders, a background color, and text overlays. Both WAV and MIDI audio are supported, so you can add voiceovers and music.

You can output your files (in compressed form) to diskettes and show your slide show on any Windows computer. You can also use your final show as a screen saver.

According to The Multimedia Store, which produces Photo Factory, future releases will support Photo CD Portfolio Script Producer and Player software, allowing users to create multimedia and interactive shows and have them written to Portfolio discs.

Producers of all sorts of presentations who want to dazzle viewers with more than a straight slide show are turning to multimedia authoring systems, which allow them to incorporate video, animation, and sophisticated interactivity. How does Photo CD fit in with multimedia production? We'll see in the next two chapters.

Part V

USING PHOTO CD IN MULTIMEDIA PRODUCTION

14

Photo CD and Multimedia Production

It's a word that glitters, mysterious and filled with promise—*multimedia*. Hyped from coast to coast and around the world as the Next Big Thing, multimedia has spawned an entire new industry, one powered by ambitious computer programmers and creative professionals, fueled by venture capitalists. But what exactly is it?

At face value, multimedia is a new medium that combines pictures, sound, and the latest computer technology to produce entertainment, education, and information products. It encompasses interactive games, entertainment extravaganzas, school curricula, research and training projects, documentaries, voluminous reference titles, and more. Multimedia is causing big companies and disparate industries to converge, pooling technologies, talent, and resources in hopes of capitalizing on a market that has yet to materialize.

Media conglomerates and garage producers alike have great expectations for sales of multimedia "titles" for home computers and—the big bonanza—home entertainment centers featuring multimedia-equipped TVs. Incompatible systems so far include CD-I, 3DO, Sega Genesis, Nintendo, and Sony. In spite of all this attempted consumer-market development, CD-ROM has been the only real market to date, made up primarily of business and professional users such as graphic designers, photographers, videographers, and multimedia producers, extending to the consumer market in the form of reference works, clip art collections, educational software, "edutainment," and games for all ages.

Integrated Media

In any discussion of multimedia production, the key word is *integration*. From the multiprojector photographic slide shows of the 1970s to the full-blown productions lighting up monitors everywhere today, the common thread is a *combining of elements*.

Multimedia interfaces take a wide variety of forms, but all are designed to help users navigate through the production. (left) Media Band, from Canter Technology, is an "interactive music video" consisting of six rooms. Each room provides a different type of interactive experience; moving the mouse over hot spots triggers solos within a musical theme. (right) Salt of the Earth is a CD-ROM containing the entire film Salt of the Earth (in QuickTime video), made by blacklisted filmmakers during the McCarthy era. The disc also contains background information on the movie, the filmmakers, and the topic (a strike by zinc miners in 1950); the original screenplay in four languages; and hundreds of photos.

Multimedia productions bring together digital images, sound, text, animation, and video to create a synergy that transcends each individual medium.

Multimedia producers "author" such productions using digital tools in a complex process that involves extensive planning and a variety of preproduction procedures. Their three primary considerations are content, architecture (how the information is organized and accessed), and interface (how the information is made available to the user). Because multimedia users must "navigate" through large amounts of material, it's the designer's job to create a program that's streamlined and unintimidating in its appearance— hence the importance of an elegant and responsive interface and functional program architecture.

Inventive multimedia producers today are creating programs designed to run on computers, public kiosks, and television screens. Content can range from training, on-line help, or documentation and customer-service support to entertainment, interactive advertising, catalogs, "magazines," and educational programming. Whatever its purpose, however, every well-designed multimedia product gives the user the illusion of direct control and constant feedback from the system. Interface design always depends on the content and the intended use of each specific title.

Multimedia programs can vary dramatically in the degree and type of choices users must make as they travel through the content. Some are largely passive presentations, but most are more interactive, requiring continual user input to direct a path through the application. While games in multimedia format usually appear to offer unlimited choices to players, the navigation is actually highly controlled in many cases, offering a limited number of new contexts at each decision point.

Whatever the type and purpose of the multimedia production, the quality of its screen graphics plays a major role in its success with users. In this context, photography is increasingly recognized as a useful, viable form of imagery.

How Does Photo CD Fit In?

As more and more titles hit the market and competition heats up among the various publishers, one clear trend points toward increasing use of photographic imagery in multimedia productions. It's a fact that, whether the content is games, storybooks, recipes, or an entire encyclopedia, beautiful graphics in your presentation can make all the difference in its appeal.

As an avenue for digitizing the multitude of photographs to be incorporated into multimedia applications, Photo CD technology offers several advantages:

1. *Cost effectiveness.* As we've seen, it's much less expensive to get images written directly to Photo CD discs than to have all the individual images commercially scanned. As a result, multimedia developers have greater flexibility in using large numbers of photos in their productions.

2. *Time savings.* The turnaround time for having Photo CD files written is significantly faster than having dozens to hundreds of individual scans done. Also, ease of access to the images (especially by using Shoebox or another image-management application) reduces much of the tedious time spent organizing, hunting for, and accessing traditional image files.

2. *Consistency.* Scans produced as Pro Photo CD files balance and unify the overall color for all the images on a disc.

3. *Storage savings.* The storage requirements for a multimedia product can be daunting. Although the size of the finished product may be a few hundred megabytes, the raw media materials used in its creation can easily require up four to ten times that much space. Still photography imagery consumes less memory than video, while offering higher resolution. With still photography, the illusion of motion can be created by skillfully focusing on different parts of individual images— panning, zooming, wiping, focusing first on one and then on another segment of a complex scene.

235

4. *Multiple resolutions.* The Photo CD image pac stores five resolutions of each image, offering ready-to-use screen-resolution versions or higher-resolution versions for image manipulation. In short, one scan fits all.

5. *Cross-platform flexibility.* Photo CD discs can be read by any CD-ROM XA drive for desktop computers, where most multimedia authoring is done today.

6. *Digital archiving.* Photo CD discs offer real economy of space and easy file management—both important factors when you consider that it's not uncommon for a multimedia presentation to use thousands of still photo images. The hundreds of images that can be stored on a handful of Photo CD Master discs would otherwise require several removable discs or storage on tape, both of which are less convenient, more costly, and often less reliable.

One project in which Photo CD was used extensively is *Haight-Ashbury in the Sixties,* a CD-ROM title for the Macintosh and Windows platforms published by Rockument, Inc. The production is an interactive documentary and adventure experience that lets the user explore a vast collection of images, text, graphics, animation, video clips, narration, and music from the 1960s.

Producers Tony Bove and Cheryl Rhodes, and writer/editor Allen Cohen, began by gathering some 800 slides from 20 photographers and having them written to Photo CD discs. No color correction or special processing was specified. The printed color thumbnails supplied with each Photo CD disc were copied on a Canon color laser copier, and copies were given to various members of the production team. The Base versions of the images were copied to various hard disks for production. Since the goal was to produce images for the RGB computer screen at standard screen resolution, the higher resolutions were not needed for most images. However, higher-resolution versions of some images were used for packaging and printed materials.

Because different color corrections were needed for print than for RGB screen usage, it was highly efficient to simply scan the slides with no correction and later perform whatever color corrections were necessary for the particular usage. As Bove notes, "The flexibility of Photo CD is particularly important in situations where different production teams are used for different projects using the same images."

In addition to being incorporated into CD-ROM products, the Photo CD format can function as a limited multimedia authoring system in its own right. As we noted in Chapter 13, Kodak's Create-It software allows you to create a presentation with sound and limited branching, which you can have written to a Photo CD Portfolio disc. Kodak also offers Arrange-It multimedia authoring software for developing Portfolio discs. Arrange-It can accommodate a wider variety of files than Create-It and permits more extensive branching and interactivity (for more on Arrange-It, see Chapter 15).

The Multimedia Development Process

The first step in developing a multimedia project is to plan the content, keeping in mind the target audience, the platform for which the product is being produced, and the budget and schedule. Brainstorming the content will supply you with a usable outline of the major content areas. At this point, you will want to start developing a content branching map showing major screens and how they link with others in the user interaction. Without a coherent plan, it is easy for a user to get lost in multimedia hyperspace.

A content map usually looks like a corporate organization chart with connections showing who reports to whom. You will need to indicate the individual screens where the viewer can make choices, and the screen(s) that each choice will lead to. Organizing the content areas will help you to provide visualizations for them. The content can be organized as a simplistic table of contents, or it can provide pathways that enable users to view the inherent data in mind-stretching, unexpected alternatives.

STORYBOARDING

Some people prefer to go from the content map directly to a rough software prototype, while others prefer to work out the design in *storyboard* form first.

A storyboard is made up of a series of drawings of the screen areas in a presentation. Each major screen area is defined and sketched, and the subsidiary screens in the sequence are defined, if not sketched in any detail. The required navigation schemes are included, but not necessarily designed. Narrative, if any, is written below the screen frame it is attached to. If Photo CD images are

CASE STUDY

FOCUS ON STAR TREK: THE NEXT GENERATION
INTERACTIVE TECHNICAL MANUAL

The *Star Trek: The Next Generation*® *Interactive Technical Manual* CD-ROM title from Simon & Schuster provides an up-close look at the inner workings of the legendary starship *Enterprise*. In creating this cinematic 3D universe that players can explore and control, its creators used over 10,000 interwoven Photo CD images of the show's set, models, and props. The title is available for both Macintosh and Windows.

Imergy, a production company based in S. Norwalk, Connecticut and New York City, spent four days on the show's set shooting four different types of 35mm color photographs before constructing the interactive presentation. Panoramic shots were used for QuickTime videos; set details were photographed up close; stop-motion photography was used for moving down corridors and into rooms; and stop-motion shots were taken of various doors, boxes, and things opening.

All frames were scanned to Photo CD discs. The company sent a set of prints to Paramount Studios so technical consultant Michael Okuda could identify each frame and write the captions that appear on the CD-ROM.

The index prints provided with the Photo CDs came in handy as a record of each frame shot and helped track the images when rescanning or reshooting became necessary.

"When dealing with thousands of images, any enforcement of the identification system is crucial," points out Peter Mackey, Imergy's director of media integration. "Plus, we took advantage of being able to use the Photo CD player 'off-line'—if all the computers were busy, the archivist could use the Photo CD player and a normal television to view the images."

Once all the information was entered into a database, everything was handed off to the production teams, who could readily identify the images they needed. All Photo CD images were backed up via CD drives onto Macintoshes, where they could be opened in Photoshop.

"Recent versions of QuickTime have a processing scheme that builds a series of images you can open as PICT images, without any processing," explains Mackey. "Then in Photoshop you can color, crop and color-balance—I don't think there was a single image we didn't color-correct."

Imergy's team found that it was necessary to boost the black level in the images. Another revelation, which may have been a scanner peculiarity, was that in the Photo CD images, the details dropped out of all the *Enterprise* control-panel display screens. To regain those details, the original 35mm images were rescanned on a high-tech drum scanner. Mackey says that 95 percent of what appears in the released title is from Photo CD imagery,

while the remaining 5 percent is from the workaround process.

Imergy used Macromedia Director as the primary tool for assembling the production. Much of the coding was custom-built for assembling the images to Imergy's requirements, and DeBabelizer was used extensively to generate custom color palettes. Mackey says all images were kept in 32-bit color as long as possible for manipulation purposes, then were 256-color-dithered to a color palette customized for this project.

The key to the whole project was Apple's new QuickTime VR technology. QuickTime VR allows multimedia producers to use still images, captured in a sequence to develop panoramas, to create "real" spaces and objects in a three-dimensional world. The software provides correct perspective of every view in a scene in real time, giving the user the sense of being there, looking around. In addition, the object movie technology in the software allows users to examine objects close up and interactively. *Star Trek: The Next Generation Interactive Technical Manual* is the first commercially available product to be developed with QuickTime VR technology.

being used, thumbnail versions can be placed into applicable storyboard frames.

Special storyboard drawing pads are available. Sections can be torn apart along perforations and tacked to a large bulletin board as you develop the sequences. Storyboards can also be sketched on-screen in HyperCard or other applications and rearranged within the program. Storyboard screens can also be printed out and rearranged on a bulletin board. When working in this medium, you can use the completed storyboard to build your first rough prototype.

DESIGNING THE INTERFACE

Once you have pinned down the content and developed your storyboards, you can begin designing the program's interface.

The first step is to determine the visual style of your production. Will you be using illustrations or photographs? What kind of navigation devices are you planning? What are the interface requirements for your platform? (Both Macintosh and Windows follow a defined set of menu styles, screen descriptions, feedback requirements, and other interface parameters. Apple's publication, *Macintosh Human Interface Guidelines,* and its accompanying CD-ROM describe and illustrate Apple's interface guidelines in great precision. Interfaces for Windows applications are very similar.)

The screens define the context of any multimedia application. They should be designed to limit ambiguity and define the goals of the program. Most developers prefer to use a graphics program to design screens. Among the most popular applications for this purpose are paint programs (such as Fractal Design Painter, Electronic Arts's Studio/32, and TimeWorks's Color It!), drawing programs (such as Adobe Illustrator and CorelDraw!), or image-editing programs (such as Adobe Photoshop and Fractal Design's ColorStudio).

The age range of the target audience will, of course, affect the look, size, and behavior of control items that go on the screens. For example, a product targeted at the younger set should use large pictorial buttons, clear icons, and entertaining elements such as sounds and animations; it could use voice prompts instead of dialog boxes.

Navigating to and from the levels of depth that a user can potentially reach should be made as easy, rapid, and clutter-free as possible, using techniques such as smart window management, obvious hierarchies, fast ways to resurface from an unintended destination, and even a smidge of educated guesswork on the program's part so that similar future actions take the user more quickly to a destination.

You should be aware of memory requirements and the trade-offs you may need to make in your design. Fancy full-color graphics in complex motion, with sound, use a lot of disc space and take more time to load from disc and to render to the screen. You may find that using still images as a background, with simple animated foreground objects, will serve the visual interest while using less memory.

TIP: *If you are developing an application for cross-platform distribution, you will need to pay special attention to the target machine's color display capabilities, as well as to the specific color palette you use. Windows and Macintosh systems running in 256-color mode each use a different palette scheme. The best option is to capture the Windows color palette and use it on the Macintosh as well. A variety of applications such as Photoshop and DeBabelizer will allow the remapping of a graphic to a specific palette. Check the authoring program you are working with for its cross-platform requirements.*

While some design requirements are essential to all multimedia programs, products vary in their specific demands, depending on what they are designed to do. For example, products designed to

Menu screens should be easily understandable. This menu screen is from Taste Mate Video Selection System, a CD-ROM that contains information on 40,000 videos, categorized by title, star, director, and category. You tell Taste Mate what sort of video you're in the mood to see, and it makes recommendations.

access information require a completely unambiguous interface, while game players prefer a certain amount of paradox as a challenge to their skills and ingenuity. Regardless of the program, users like to have direct and immediate control over the environment they are in, and screens need to be designed with that in mind.

Main menu screens for information and education titles display the basic categories included in the program. You should design the navigation to allow viewers to move immediately to any main category they desire. In a catalog, for example, a main entry will move you to a screen with secondary selections. If your program will utilize a touch screen as a navigation device instead of a mouse (as with an informational kiosk), the menus should have large, clearly spaced buttons, and the design should take into account the fact that the user's hand will partially obscure the screen.

Multimedia games differ from other applications in that the activity has no intrinsic purpose other than the reward of fun, playing, and winning. Fast feedback is of utmost importance, along with animated graphics that are fun to look at. People are drawn to novelty but usually get bored when the novel aspect never changes, so successful games include hidden or ambiguous patterns to challenge the player or else become increasingly complex as the player increases his or her wins.

Graphically rich games are particularly challenging to engineer so that they respond quickly to context changes, because the same graphics that enrich the game also take time to access and load from the CD-ROM. Some experimentation with techniques, such as preloading a graphic into memory or onto hard disk during user inactivity, can shift the loading delay to a game phase where it's not as noticeable—or at least, more easily forgiven.

TESTING THE PROTOTYPE

A computer prototype is a highly simplified version of the final interactive application. At the start, it may include only the major screens with text titles only. Each menu screen contains the navigation schematics that link it to secondary topics. Storyboard sketches can be scanned to be placed on major screens.

HyperCard has been the old standby for a first quick, rough prototype. SuperCard is a good alternative to HyperCard when more power is needed to prototype the interface or a special program behavior. Another alternative, which isn't an authoring tool at all, is using a drawing program, such as MacDraw, Canvas, IntelliDraw, or CorelDraw, which has a rich object-oriented and layered environment in which an interface can be constructed from imported bitmaps, photos, and drawn objects. Some developers prefer to use their full-fledged authoring program such as Director, AuthorWare, or Apple Media Tool for prototyping, because it is easier to accommodate color and grayscale PICT images.

> **TIP:** *A sign that an interface item or context isn't working is when you find yourself explaining it repeatedly to users, making excuses, and thinking of perfectly good reasons why it's best to do it that way. The bottom line is, no matter how consistent, elegant, entertaining, slick, fast, or cutting edge it is, and regardless of how much work you put into an item, if it doesn't work with the user, let it go. Go back to basics. Consider the user's intent and natural train of thought, and you'll create a better solution.*

Producing a Multimedia Product

When you've finally worked out your content and interface through the prototyping process, you can proceed with actually producing the multimedia product. Among the elements that all need to come together are icons and buttons, type, images, animation/video, and sound. They can then be combined in a multimedia authoring program.

ICONS AND BUTTONS

Buttons, which can be any shape or size, trigger a media event or provide a link to another screen within the application when clicked. Such button "hot spots" can be represented by photographs, graphics, or text menus. Whatever their appearance, it should be clear to the user not only that the object is a button but also what its function is in the application. When selected, buttons should always offer feedback to the user with highlighting or a sound. Color is one way to maintain unity to a set of button hot spots, especially text buttons. Another unifier, especially for photographic hot spots, is using the same outline style and color for each. If the popular drop-shadow format is used, the convention to be followed is to have the light coming from the upper left of the screen. Games, differing from informational products, often maintain their sense of fun by letting the user guess which screen object is "hot" and what its function is.

243

TYPE

Typography will need to be rendered for titles, buttons, and descriptive text if it is included. If the text is initially written in a word-processing program, make sure that the program is compatible with the text importation capabilities of your authoring software and that imported text comes in cleanly and doesn't have to be fixed up or modified in any way. Many producers format text in a word processor exactly as it will be used onscreen before bringing it into the authoring program.

In designing the use of text, you will need to make legibility your top priority. Choose a font, type size, and spacing that will enable users to comfortably read your screens. As with any good print design, try to keep the number of fonts to a minimum, and be consistent in your typographic treatment of like elements.

PHOTOGRAPHS

Proper organization and preparation of photographic imagery will make your production process run more smoothly. Your preproduction storyboard should indicate the topic, content, and orientation of each image. Maintaining a list of all required images will help you during the selection process, whether you have them shot to order, have them supplied by a client, or have them provided as stock. Slides and negatives can all be digitized by having them scanned onto Photo CD discs. In addition, many stock photo and clip photo houses now supply images in Photo CD form (see Chapter 9).

By its very nature, most multimedia material is presented on screen at screen resolution, which is rather coarse compared to printed resolution. A typical screen size for a multimedia product or presentation is 640 x 480 pixels, on both Macintosh and Windows platforms. Although this is a relatively small screen size by today's standards, most LCD projection panels and computer-to-video converters use this display size. Anything larger than that will be lost off the edges of the display. What this limited size means is that the resolution of the photos you use in your multimedia product generally needs to be no better than the display resolution.

The digitized images will often need color correction, sharpening, retouching, cropping, and other manipulation. You can do as little as just cropping the photograph and saving it for import by the authoring program of your choice. The important sequence to remember is to do all your retouching and editing on the high-resolution version of the image, within the limitations of your authoring platform, and then resample it to screen resolution—and while you're at it, apply a custom palette if necessary.

Photographs can be incorporated into multimedia in a variety of ways. The photographs of Pedro Meyer are the main content of Voyager's I Photograph to Remember. *This documentary of nearly 100 still photographs of Meyer's parents in the last few years of their lives is narrated by the photographer in both English and Spanish.*

Photographs are often used as a screen background. Buttons and other menu items generally show up better against a photograph background when brightness and contrast levels are toned down. One formula suggests that you reduce brightness by 50 percent and increase contrast by 25 percent to make the photo dark enough so that objects on it will stand out. Choose a photograph that will not have a "busy" area where you plan to place a button panel.

ANIMATION AND VIDEO

Animation segments are storyboarded and assigned to an animator for rendering. Logos and opening titles are often animated, even if there is no animation in other parts of the program.

Video is added to multimedia products by digitizing standard video frames using built-in or add-on video capture hardware and software. The source of video can be a recorded broadcast (copyright laws apply here), camcorder video, or professionally recorded work. Generally speaking, the horsepower for converting live video to full-motion, full-screen (640 x 480 pixels) digital video is still not readily available or accessible. There are reasonable substitutes and compromises, such as a smaller image (320 x 240 pixels), and fewer frames per second. These alternatives can look pretty good, and the live-motion alternative to still images often compensates for the reduced resolution and frame rate.

The tools for splicing and editing multiple digital movies are

Adobe Premiere is the program of choice for editing QuickTime video.

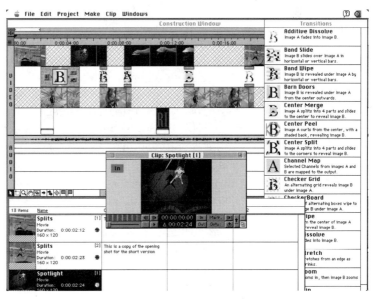

245

not necessarily growing in number, but they are growing in capabilities. Adobe Premiere, available for both Macintosh and Windows, can satisfy most editing and special-effects needs. On the Macintosh digital video is saved in QuickTime format, which is Apple's "native" movie format. On Windows systems, it can be in QuickTime format (if the target machine is equipped with Apple's QuickTime for Windows software), or it can be in AVI format, which is Windows' native movie format.

Authoring tools are able to import and play, at minimum, the platform's native movie format and even control playback and frame access to a high degree.

SOUND

With all the attention given to graphics in multimedia, sound is the most often overlooked and yet essential element. As any film director knows, properly produced sound and music have everything to do with the mood and with the pacing and impact of visuals. In multimedia, key sound components include (1) sound effects—for button clicks, wipes, transitions, and load times; (2) music—a continuous music bed for a presentation, or brief loops for certain screens or events; and (3) narration—for presentations, on-line help, or "guided tours." In all cases, carefully chosen sound elements, professionally produced, are of utmost importance for successful multimedia products.

To add sounds to your production, you will need appropriate recording equipment. Since your final product will be digital, the best way to go is to record sounds digitally, using either a 16-bit hard disk recording system (such as Digidesign's SoundTools, ProTools, or Audiomedia, Mark of the Unicorn's Digital Waveboard, or MediaVision's PAS16) or an 8-bit system (such as Articulate Systems's Voice Impact or Voice Impact Pro, Macromedia's MacRecorder, or the built-in hardware of the Macintosh). For 16-bit sound, you may need to have a sound card added to your computer if it does not already accommodate 16-bit.

A number of audio formats are available, including AIFF, snd, and native system formats for Windows and Macintosh. The most universal is AIFF, used for CD-ROM and Photo CD Portfolio formats..

You will also need sound editing software. Some popular packages include Macromedia's SoundEdit Pro, Opcode's Audioshop, Digidesign's Sound Tools, Passport's Master Tracks Pro, and Steinberg's CueBase.

AUTHORING

Final authoring consists of putting all the elements of the project together with the authoring application of your choice. These elements include completed backgrounds, menu screens, sound, text, graphics, and animation and video clips. All the navigation devices and links between screens are programmed, based on concept tests done earlier. Narration and music tracks often need to be completed before the final animation is rendered, if timing to sound is important.

Although most of these elements must be prepared in other applications, some authoring packages, such as Macromedia Director, allow you to do sophisticated graphic rendering directly in the application. Others, such as Kodak Arrange-It and Apple Media Tool, provide the shell for programming links and navigation but all text, graphics, images, and sound need to be developed elsewhere. If sound and timing are important, you will probably want to work with a program like Passport Producer Pro, which incorporates SMPTE time coding.

If your program is relatively linear, with uncomplicated branching screen to screen, you might want to work with Astound, a presentation program with simple multimedia features built in. Astound is described in Chapter 12.

TESTING AND DEBUGGING THE PROGRAM

Testing with potential users of the program can ensure that the documentation and the user interface are appropriate for the target audience. Here are a few of the questions to ask when testing a multimedia program, especially an informational one:

- Are the menus and icons clearly defined?

- Is the text readable?

- Are repetitive movements kept to a minimum, reducing user fatigue?

- Is the help system useful?

- Can the user reasonably remember how to work the program from one session to another?

Testing is critical, and yet, because it comes at the end of a long and complex production process, it often is not given proper attention. If testing in depth is beyond the capabilities of your production team, consider farming it out.

When you have completed all the debugging and platform testing procedures and made all the needed corrections, you will probably want to have some users work with the near-finished product. "Beta testing" almost always uncovers glitches that did not turn up during the initial testing process and can be a very involved process with many beta testers, depending on the product.

MASTERING

Mastering is the process of creating an original disc from which others are reproduced. The first step in the process is the creation of a master, either in CD-ROM or Portfolio CD format, depending on your need. Before producing a master disc for distribution, you will need to preview and test your multimedia title on a one-off—a relatively inexpensive single copy of your program. Only after you are satisfied with this version should you make the master. Always make two master discs—one to be saved as a backup and the other to go to the disc mastering company. For more information on disc mastering and duplication, see Chapter 16.

248 | *Multimedia Authoring Packages*

Authoring software allows you to streamline many of the development procedures involved in putting together a multimedia product. These packages differ in their strengths, ease of use, and basic cost.

MACROMEDIA DIRECTOR

Among Macintosh users, Director is the most commonly used software package for creating interactive multimedia presentations combining sound, images, and movies. The Windows version is code-compatible with the Mac, and cross-platform players are available for both Windows and Macintosh.

Movie is the term Director uses for a multimedia production. Five windows within the application are used to create a *movie*. The Cast window is a multimedia database, storing all the elements, called cast members, used in the movie. It includes any graphics and photographs, text, sound, buttons, special palettes, and QuickTime movies. Cast members can be created in the Paint window or imported. Photo CD images can be imported as PICT or Scrapbook files. Many developers prefer to work on images first in Photoshop, then export them to Director as PICT files.

A Paint window furnishes you with the basic tools you would find in a paint application such as Fractal Design Painter. When a Cast member is highlighted, it will also appear in the Paint window, where it can be edited. The window can also be used to create new Cast members, including graphics, buttons, and custom color palettes. Illustrations and photographs can be cropped and manipulated within the Paint window once they have been imported into the application as PICTs.

The Score window keeps track of the position of each cast member in the movie. Its display is a matrix format composed of individual cells similar to a spreadsheet. Each cell represents the contents of a frame at a specific point in time. A character from the Score window is displayed in a row made up of cells, called a channel, devoted to the action of the character in the movie. Parallel rows of cells unite the multiple tracks of images, sounds, and transitions. Overlapping actions between several characters are seen within a matrix column. A single column represents a single moment in a Director movie.

Your Director show can be viewed on the Stage window at any time during the creation process. A Playback window similar to the controls on a VCR is used to control the action.

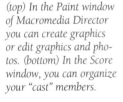

(top) In the Paint window of Macromedia Director you can create graphics or edit graphics and photos. (bottom) In the Score window, you can organize your "cast" members.

Branching and interactivity is supported, although complex branching may require some programming skills. Director includes an object-oriented programming language, called Lingo, that controls Cast behaviors and interactivity. Lingo will allow you to specify actions from simple to very complex. If your production uses complex interactivity, you will need to understand and program in Lingo or work with someone who has these skills. Lingo is essentially a superset of HyperTalk, the original HyperCard language. It does have the potential for looking and behaving very techy, but as programming languages go, it's fairly natural and conversational, and it isn't overly structured and rigid.

Director allows you to create animated sequences, select from a variety of transitions, and add narration, music, and sound effects. Sound cast members are limited to two channels set aside for sound use only. The Lingo programming language can be applied to sound, allowing you to control changes in volume. Digitized sound that can be imported include SoundEdit files, AIFF, snd (8-bit) resources, and MIDI. Sounds can be previewed before use and can be played as a looped repeat if desired.

MACROMEDIA AUTHORWARE

AuthorWare is a powerful program for both Mac and Windows, designed to reduce the time and effort needed to build a complex multimedia application for educational and training purposes. The program is geared to instructional designers who do not have the programming skills to author a complex production.

Programs are developed by arranging icons on a "flow line." Attributes for these flow-line icons are set through a series of dialog boxes. Flowline sequences designed for one project can be saved in a library and used for new projects. Graphics can be created directly within the program or imported from almost any source. Photo CD images can be imported as PICT files.

A full gamut of interaction capabilities is available, including on-screen pushbuttons, click/touch areas, movable objects, fill-in text entries, key presses, conditional responses, and time-limit responses. There is no limit as to the number of interactions you can have going at any one time. On-screen control is provided for interactive videodisc players.

Although AuthorWare is expensive and complex, it offers the functionality that nonprogrammer instructional designers need for creating educational projects in multimedia. However, this soft-

AuthorWare Professional is a complex, high-end program for multimedia production.

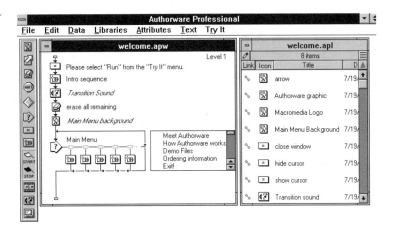

ware was not intended for programs that need fast, gamelike responses. Support for hypertext is limited, as is the ability to arrange multiple concurrent tracks for complex picture and sound sequences. Mac versions can be exported to Windows, but Windows versions cannot be exported to Macintosh.

PASSPORT PRODUCER PRO

Unlike most other multimedia products, Producer is built on the timing standards of SMPTE/EBU time code and Apple Quick-Time. This ensures that sound is always synchronous with visuals, locked in to run continuously at the same rate of speed, to produce presentations that are frame-accurate. Producer also takes advantage of Apple's Sound and Speech Managers and Apple-Script. The program integrates graphics, text, animation, Quick-Time, and sound, supporting PICT and TIFF files, AIFF, Sound Designer, and MIDI formats. It also allows you to control VCRs, laserdisc players, and MIDI players. Although Producer is a Macintosh-based authoring platform, it includes stand-alone players for both Windows and Macintosh.

Producer's working platform is the Cue Sheet—a timeline-based window that determines the order in which Cues (associated with media files) are played. A Cue Palette provides tools for working in the Cue Sheet window. The interface duplicates the metaphor of laying in video, film, and magnetic sound tracks when editing or mixing video or motion pictures. Tracks containing individual Cues are placed parallel to each other horizontally across the window.

The timeline indicator runs down the left side of the window. Cues are played according to their timeline position on the Cue

251

Passport Producer Pro's basic metaphor is the Cue Sheet.

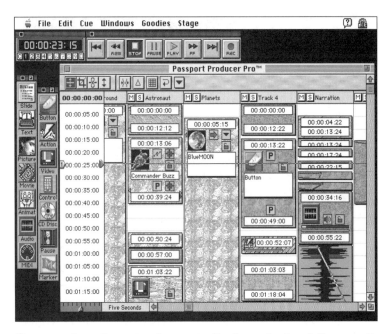

Sheet window. One nice feature in Producer is the ability to edit audio files easily, to fit music beats to Cue entrances. You can actually cut and paste a sound file to add to a segment or eliminate one.

Each Cue contains a Start and Stop time, a visual ID picture, a text field for making notes, and buttons defining motion in and out paths for the Cue. A sound Cue has a provision for volume control. Button Cues provide interactivity. Text labels can also be associated with any screen button.

Background graphics are placed in the program via a Picture Cue. Photo CD images, when cropped to size in Photoshop and converted to PICT or TIFF file format, can be used as a frame background. You can also create a still or blended color background within Producer. All elements other than buttons, text, and background color will need to be created in applications separate from Producer and imported as Cues.

KODAK PORTFOLIO

Kodak's Photo CD Portfolio authoring system provides Mac users with the means to create interactive, branching multimedia presentations on Photo CD Portfolio discs. For information on creating multimedia projects with Kodak's Arrange-It and Build-It Portfolio software, see Chapter 15.

APPLE MEDIA TOOL

The Apple Media Tool is a cross-platform multimedia authoring tool for integrating QuickTime movies, PICT, text, and sound files. Unlike some of the other authoring systems, you can't produce any of the media components within the Apple Media Tool—they must all be imported for assembly within the application. The Apple Media Tool keeps its memory usage down by using "pointers" to indicate the locations of the media that are used. A sound or picture can be used several times during a presentation, but the memory usage is for a single file only.

A separate package designed to work with AMT is the Apple Media Tool Programming Environment, in which programmers can customize a presentation and add other functions to it.

The program provides a map window showing all the screens and their linkage. Clicking on a single screen opens it up for work. Once in a screen, you can place buttons, layer pictures, indicate hot spots, and add sounds, each defined as an "object" in the program.

An "Actions" miniwindow displays the properties and actions that you may want to attach to a particular object on the screen. Terms for the actions are all listed within the window and are not at all difficult to define, once you understand what *properties, actions,* and *events* mean. You can define events before and after objects are displayed. You can play back any actions you have defined for an object just as soon as you have set them up.

To use Photo CD images, you need to first open them in Photoshop or another image-editing program, then save them as a PICT files for import into AMT. Sound files need to be in snd or AIFF format for Macintosh, and WAV format for Windows.

The only word processor that retains text style and color when brought into Apple Media Tool is MacWrite Pro, which includes a translation filter for AMT. Other word-processing files can only be imported as text. The program documentation suggests that you prepare text in a paint program, antialias it for higher quality, then save the file as a PICT for export.

KIDS STUDIO

Kids Studio by Storm Software is a family-oriented application with an easy-to-use interface. Kids can use it to produce their own stories, either as printed pages or as QuickTime movies. Kids

253

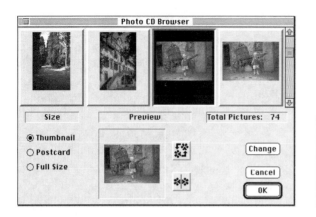
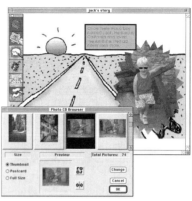

Kids of all ages can use Kids Studio to create multimedia presentations that incorporate Photo CD images.

Studio includes many of the features found in full-fledged authoring programs while still retaining an interface that even multimedia-illiterate parents will find user-friendly.

The program includes multiple drawing layers, sound, text, and a Photo CD filter capability. To write on a text page, select the writing tool and click on a page, anywhere, and start writing. You can format the type to any font in your system, color it, and even color its background. In addition, Treasure Chest clip art files containing cartoons and a variety of photographs are included with the application. For a more personal touch, you can have rolls of 35mm film processed directly to a Photo CD disc and include the digitized photographs as part of the story pages.

This low-priced program is available in both Macintosh and Windows versions.

HYPERCARD

HyperCard 2.2 is the latest version of the inexpensive Macintosh software that allows you to create and link screens without any programming experience. It is being used for interactive books, tutorials, and presentations in general. While HyperCard has been replaced by more complex software applications, its power, ease of use, and reasonable cost have made it a favorite for students and teachers from grade school on up.

HyperCard's metaphor is that of the index card, which can accept drawings, text, and navigation devices. Ready-to-paste buttons, fields, templates, and programming scripts are included. Hypertext links can be established between marked words and related information.

Color is part of the 2.2 release, but its use is still not full-fledged, without the use of ancillary tools. Portfolio Maker by Crit, Inc. is a HyperCard-based tool that can place up to 20 images on a single floppy disk for distribution. FastPitch Pro by Objective systems is an inexpensive HyperCard extension for making multimedia presentations. It allows you to include color and grayscale pictures and Photo CD images in reports and interactive programs.

ASYMETRIX MULTIMEDIA TOOLBOOK

The Asymetrix Multimedia ToolBook is a turnkey software application running on Windows. You can combine sound, video, and animation with text and graphics and run the program with pre-scripted cut-and-paste objects that are part of the application. The program applies links from one object to another through buttons and hypertext hot words.

LINKWAY LINE

LinkWay Line was developed by IBM for multimedia development on IBM and DVI platforms. It is a media management product designed especially for students and teachers who are new to multimedia. To support the ease-of-use concept, the LinkWay QuickStart documentation is produced in comic book format. The program is object-oriented and includes Buttons, Pictures, Fields, and Media. Sound files are supported, and text and simple graphics tools are provided. Resources such as digital audio files and video laser discs can be accessed through the Media object.

LinkWay Line was initially released as a DOS program, with Windows and Mac versions following.

Publishing on CD-ROM

CD-ROM PLAYERS

CD-ROM discs are designed to run from a CD-ROM drive connected to a computer. They hold far more content than floppy disks, using the same basic drive mechanisms and disc manufacturing processes as audio CDs. CD-ROM is an inherently flexible system that enables engineers to manipulate the data in many ways. Its open architecture permits CD drives to be attached to many different kinds of computers, players, and other data systems.

USEFUL SOFTWARE ADDITIONS FOR MULTIMEDIA PRODUCTION

DeBabelizer has become the program of choice for converting Macintosh graphics files. It not only works on a multitude of file formats but can be programmed to batch process an entire diskful of files overnight. DeBabelizer is especially useful for converting Mac files to Windows format.

TextureScape by Specular International is great software for producing interesting backgrounds for multimedia. Instead of buying expensive texture software, you can make your own backgrounds, customized to blend with photographs and other artwork. The program provides a set of EPS shapes that are easily manipulated by color, depth, lighting, grid arrangement for an infinite variety of innovative effects. Or you can make your own basic shapes and save them in the Library. Not only does TextureScape provide many ways in which you can produce still image textures, the software also provides routines for morphing from one background to another.

Morph, from Gryphon, is an excellent tool for creating special effects and transitions between two or more images. The effects can be used to make or reinforce a point or to serve as part of game-play. The finished product is a movie you can then play within your authoring environment. The setup for morphing one image into another is simple: you basically choose what point on one image will become what point on the other image. For example, the eye of a cat would morph to the eye of a human. The real trick is morphing graphics that don't have natural corresponding parts, such as a TV set into a baby bottle. For any morph, the more work you put into it, the better the results.

Pixar Typestry produces 3D animated type and logos.

Adobe Dimensions and Ray Dream AddDepth allow you to add a third dimension to two-dimensional graphic objects. AddDepth allows you to export files in PICT format.

Clip products can make life easier for multimedia developers. Clip photo collections are becoming popular sources of images. In the audio department, high-quality clip sounds are available on CD-ROM, including mechanical and everyday noises, animal sounds, long and short music clips, and cartoon-style sounds like crashing into walls, pratfalls, or a bee that's run out of breath.

The CD-ROM standard describes how to record 2048-byte sectors of data on a disc to a specific address for each sector. This type of address notation allows you to retrieve data either randomly throughout the entire disc, or serially, in chunks. The standard also provides for error correction.

CD publishers in increasing numbers are moving to a cross-platform format that can be played on both PC and Mac platforms. This hybrid standard places duplicate data on the CD-ROM. This does not mean, however, that the disc contains a duplicate of everything for each platform. In many cases, it's possible to store two versions of the executable logic—one for each platform—but have only one copy of the actual graphical and audio content. Works produced with Macromedia Director are capable of this feat. Producers need to press and package only one set of discs, suitable to both PC and Macintosh formats.

The ISO 9660 standard, required to play Photo CD discs, is pervasive in CD-ROM drives, making Photo CD an important cross-platform format.

MULTIMEDIA PLAYERS

Various video/CD player formats are available as well. These machines are sold as entertainment devices but are actually covert computers—with a CPU, memory, and a CD-ROM drive. These machines have one common denominator—they are designed to be connected to a television set. While most of these devices are devoted to playing games, Philips CD-I and Panasonic's 3DO are designed to play a more diverse mix of software, including Photo CD discs.

When producing products for these multimedia players, considerations for proprietary formats need to be taken into account. These formats include:

257

- *CD-I (compact disc-interactive).* This is an official standard for a completely self-contained delivery system first outlined by Sony and Philips in 1986. It consists of a highly specified format for both hardware and software. The CD-I system contains its own dedicated computer and is designed to run on a television set, using the screen as its output device. It also runs on self-contained players. The CD-I system can display 256 colors at a time out of a 24-bit palette. Product development is done on Mac and Sun systems with a variety of authoring programs, including Media Mogul, which optimizes the use of Macintosh production tools.

  CD-I differs from CD-ROM in that it can run full-motion video. It is capable of playing back as much as 72 minutes of compressed video from a CD, using a digital video cartridge which supports MPEG-1 full-motion video. More than 200 titles have been released so far, aimed at the upscale family market. Topics include games, sports, education, entertainment, and children's programming. The CD-I player can also play standard Photo CD and Portfolio discs.

FOCUS ON MULTICOM PUBLISHING, SEATTLE

Multicom Publishing Inc. of Seattle currently has eleven CD-ROM titles on the market, all of which use Photo CD imagery as a source of photographs for the presentations.

From documentaries such as *National Parks of America* and *Americans in Space*, to a series of *Better Homes and Gardens* titles, to *Warren Miller's Ski World*, Multicom's presentations use Photo CD images not only for communicating information—such as how a finished recipe should look or how to distinguish between different types of wine grapes—but as stylistic backgrounds behind an interface.

According to Therese Adlhoch, Multicom's director of marketing, all the CD-ROMs rely heavily on photography. *National Parks of America*, for example, features the works of renowned nature photographer David Muench. That CD-ROM uses nearly all of its 680 MB capacity as it tours the nation's 230-plus national parks and monuments via photographs and full-motion video.

For source material, Multicom partners with several major publishers, including Simon & Schuster and Better Homes and Gardens, as

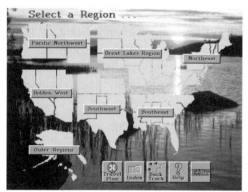

well as various third-party content-providers (such as Luna Corp., headed by ex-astronauts, for *Americans in Space*). The Multicom staff integrates audio, video, animation, and interac-

tive capabilities for the CD-ROM.

After outlining the program's contents and determining what kind of information will have the most consumer appeal, staff members organize transparencies and then send them

out to a color house for scanning to Photo CD discs. When digital files are needed in a rush, Adlhoch says, turnaround takes only 24 hours.

The Photo CD images are brought into Adobe Photoshop for enhancement, positioning, and cropping on Macintosh computers with plenty of RAM. Images are then written to the company's own CD-ROMs.

This development process is not without glitches. Unnatural skin tones is one problem Multicom has run into with Photo CD scans of images containing people. "That's not necessarily the fault of Photo CD," explains Adlhoch. "That's just the storage mechanism. But depending on the person doing the processing— if they're not color correcting or don't have their settings straight, you have a problem."

But Adlhoch says Photo CD technology saves Multicom time and money by greatly streamlining the development process. "For storage, as well as a means to preview images, Photo CD is very effective," she adds. "And you also get the advantage of durability in storage and handling."

258

• *3DO.* This consumer platform standard was introduced in 1991, and the first player, the Panasonic FZ-1 REAL, was shipped in late 1992. The 3DO player's CD-ROM drive is double-speed and can read video as well as audio CDs, plus Photo CD and Portfolio discs. The CPU supports a multitasking environment for interactive movies, games, and edutainment titles. The 3DO machine can display more than 16 million colors for graphics and animation, but there is a trade-off between colors and performance. Development is done primarily on Macs. AT&T and Sanyo have plans to release their player versions in the near future.

• *Sega Genesis CD system.* The Sega Genesis format was originally developed to compete with Nintendo. The CD drive, an add-on to the cartridge player, adds more speed and memory to the environment. Most of the software code required to run a title is accessed directly from the CD software. The system can display 16 colors at a time out of a palette of 512. About 80 animation sprites are available to a developer of Sega CDs.

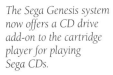

259

• *TTI.* An NEC subsidiary, Turbo Technology, Inc., developed the TTI machines. Like the Sega CD player, this platform also evolved from a game background. TurboGrafx was the first game machine designed with a built-in CD-ROM drive. The TurboDuo model can be used as an external CD-ROM drive for Macs and PCs with the appropriate cabling. The system can display 241 colors out of a possible 512. Titles are developed in Assembler and delivered on CD-ROM. The TTI format offers a good look and feel, but the machine has a small installed base of users and a limited selection of titles when compared to other game machines.

The Sega Genesis system now offers a CD drive add-on to the cartridge player for playing Sega CDs.

15

Advanced Portfolio
CD Production

As we noted in Chapter 13, Portfolio CD is an exciting presentation/multimedia technology that incorporates both sound and images and the capability for interactivity. In that chapter we took a close look at Create-It, Kodak's software for authoring simple slide presentations. Although Create-It allows for adding sound files and limited branching, it is not a "multimedia" authoring program on the level of what we talked about in Chapter 14. Kodak's more complex multimedia authoring software, Arrange-It, is used in tandem with a hardware setup that allows for writing Portfolio discs that can carry a wider variety of files and for greater amounts of branching and interactivity.

Arrange-It: An Overview

The Arrange-It software name speaks for itself. The product is designed to "arrange" your presentation in the order and sequence you desire. It is also designed to establish your branching requirements to tell the Photo CD player where to go after you have gone down a selected path and need to return to somewhere. The software looks complicated on the screen, but it is actually easy to use.

Arrange-It is meant to be used in combination with Create-It. It does not have tools for creating or designing screens. Rather, you first develop screens in Create-It, then export them as PICT files for use in Arrange-It. In addition to frames from Create-It, Arrange-It can import fully designed images from other software in TIFF, PICT, or PCD format. Sound is imported as AIFF files.

Once in Arrange-It, you import all your files into a "collection" that will then be seen at the top of the Arrange-It desktop. Through a simple drag and drop approach, you select items from the collection and drag them onto the desktop. You then link them all by dragging lines between them.

To lay out a presentation in Arrange-It:

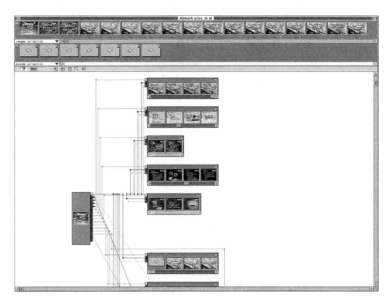

The basic Arrange-It Canvas displays your collection of images and sounds at the top. You drag and drop items from the collection onto the desktop, then link them by drawing lines between them.

262

1. Prepare a storyboard. What do you want to have on each slide? What kind of sound do you want to accompany each frame? What sequences and branching do you want to incorporate?

2. List all needed image and presentation files, and check their file formats. If conversions are needed, most software will allow you to resave an image as a PICT or TIFF. DeBabelizer is one software application dedicated to converting graphic formats in batch mode if you need to transform a large number of images.

3. Import all necessary image and sound files (what your service bureau will later refer to as "assets").

4. Lay out the presentation, incorporating branching and other flows.

5. Verify, test, and proof the final presentation, running the emulator.

6. Export the presentation as a PCD script, so that it can be processed by a service bureau and written to a Portfolio disc.

Arrange-It Versus Create-It

If you are confused as to which Kodak software you should choose for a particular project, you can consult the accompanying chart to see the main differences between the two packages.

Basically, if you need an application in which you can create your own screens, do a certain amount of image editing (adjust color, brightness, etc.), add type, create your own graphics, and design limited branching, you will want to use Create-It. But if you already have all the elements for your product—sound files, image files, graphics—and simply need an authoring program to put them all together and add interactive branching, you will want to use Arrange-It.

	Comparison of Create-It and Arrange-It	
	Create-It	**Arrange-It**
Purpose	Best used to design simple presentations; intended to be used in general office environment	Best used to lay out complex and sophisticated interactive presentations with intricate branching nodes and timeouts
Input	PCD, PICT, and TIFF files, audio files in AIFF format	PCD, PICT, and TIFF files, audio files in AIFF format
Features	Lets you choose templates and color schemes, draw your own graphics, enter text, create "hot spots," edit images (color correction, brightness, etc.); imported images can be edited and combined	Allows you to create complex links, looping, and branching sequences, timeouts, and transitions
Does *not* support	Timeouts, loops, complex branching, sophisticated transitions	Image editing (combining images), drawing your own graphics, entering text, creating frames
Output	Export as a script file for Build-It processing to create a Portfolio disc	Export as a script file for Build-It processing to create a Portfolio disc
	Export as one or more PICT files to Arrange-It	
	35mm slides	
	Print on standard laser printers for use as a transparency or hard copy presentation	

263

Create-It scripts can go directly to a service bureau for production of a Portfolio disc at a Build-It workstation, or Create-It files can be imported into Arrange-It for the addition of more sophisticated branching, organization, and transitions. Create-It can also be used to produce traditional presentations that are output to slides, transparencies, or hard copy prints. Arrange-It scripts plus accompanying files must go to a service bureau to produce a Portfolio disc.

Getting Started

To create a new Arrange-It document, choose New from the File menu. To open an existing one, choose Open. To open a second document, you will have to close the open one first, as Arrange-It can support only one open document at a time. An existing document will appear on the Canvas scrolling window as a visual schematic. When a New document is chosen, the Canvas work area is blank.

COLLECTIONS

The Collection Bar window above the Canvas displays the current collection of visual and audio files. An image or sound from this window can be selected and moved into the Canvas as you build a presentation document. A collection is an arbitrary arrangement of images and sounds that you can organize in any way you choose. Collections can be an arrangement of pictures related by subject, as in a People collection or a Transportation collection. Two collection bars can be shown at any one time. Collections can be switched by choosing a replacement from the Collections menu.

To make a new collection, all you need to do is import selected image files from your CD-ROM drive, your hard drive, or other source. Files from which to make your selections will be displayed in the Edit Collection—Import dialog box. Images can be previewed in this window, and sound files can be played before you import them into the new collection. When you have made all your selections, you will be asked to name the group as a new collection; the files you have chosen will be imported into the newly named collection. Any previously

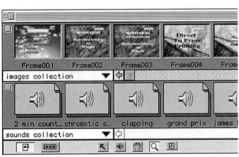

The Collection bar window has rows for both your images and your sounds.

You can add items to, drop items from, or re-order items in your collection by using the Edit Collection dialog box.

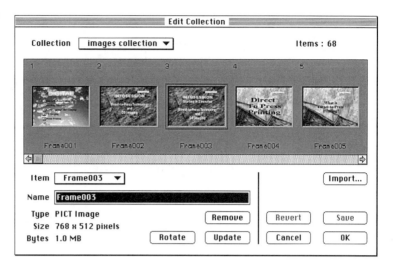

organized collection can be revised through the Edit Collection dialog box. Images can be renamed, reordered, or deleted. To add new images you will need to go to the Edit Collection—Import dialog box.

INCORPORATING SOUND FILES

It is easy to place the sound behind an image or over a menu item in Arrange-It. The sound file format must be Apple's AIFF (Audio Interface File Format). You import the sound and create the collection of sounds exactly the same way you do with images.

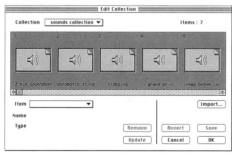

Sound collections are compiled and edited using the same process as that for image collections.

One of the existing limitations with the Portfolio CD is that the sound is noncontiguous. That is, when an image is displayed on the screen, the accompanying sound then plays. The sound then stops and the next image is displayed. The reason that the Portfolio CD currently only supports noncontiguous sound is that the original players that Kodak sold into the marketplace were incapable of supporting continuous sound while displaying images. To have this ability, the new generation of players will include memory buffers for the data so when the player has to seek through either the data or the audio track, the sound or the displaying of an image will not be interrupted. Additionally, some software has to be written by Kodak in order to create the continuous sound both for the creation as well as the production elements in the making of a Portfolio CD.

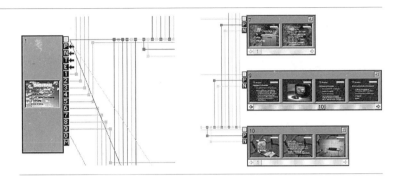

Branching in Arrange-It involves two kinds of nodes: menu nodes, with an array of path tabs down the side (left), and sequence nodes (right), which contain a linear sequence of any number of images and sounds.

266

NODES

The interactive branching in Arrange-It is viewed as a visual schematic made up of *nodes* and *paths*.

Nodes are connection points used to mark the image and button points at which branching paths start and end.

There are two types of nodes in Arrange-It:

- **Menu nodes**. These hold tab menu selections for a branch. A menu node must contain at least one image. It can also contain a sound file.

- **Sequence nodes**. These can contain any number of image and audio files, but no menu path tabs. A sequence node consists of a linear selection of images, connected to a menu node or nodes.

Each type of node has a set of tabs along the side for making path connections.

PATHS

Paths show the order in which nodes are connected. Node and Path menus provide commands for editing, grouping, and constructing nodes, and making paths between them. Paths and nodes can be color coded and aligned, and the origin and destination of a path between two nodes can be displayed. Paths begin with a numbered or lettered tab and end at a home tab.

Letters can indicate Previous (P) and Next (N) nodes, an Error (E) path, and numbered menu selections. The Home tab is the place to connect other nodes leading to the selected one. Paths can be selected by menu or by drag and drop using the mouse.

When your branching gets to look spaghetti-like and confusing, vertices can be added to clarify the scheme. Color coding helps as well. When the document starts to crowd up, you can hide and display selected paths as you work.

Paths on the menu node are used to connect it to sequence nodes. You can create a path simply by dragging a line from one tab to another.

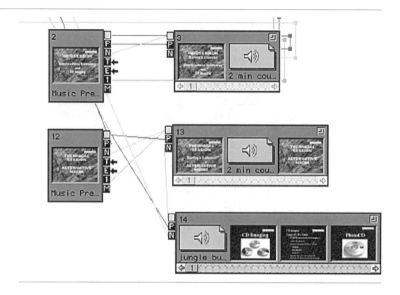

TRANSITIONS AND TIME DELAYS

In addition to nodes and paths, Arrange-It includes a ribbon bar with an assortment of tools to put the document together.

Transitions are the visual patterns by which one image replaces the next when the presentation is played. A specific transition style can be chosen for each individual frame in the show. Unfortunately, not all the transitions you can see when Arrange-It is shown on a computer can be displayed on a Photo CD player. At the present time, the player displays wide or landscape images in a top-to-bottom transition and long or portrait images moving from left to right.

You can choose the timing for your whole presentation or for individual slides using the Time Delay dialog box.

You can set slide *timing* in Arrange-It as an overall selection or for each slide separately. The time can be as little as the time it takes the Photo CD player to actually wipe the image onto the TV

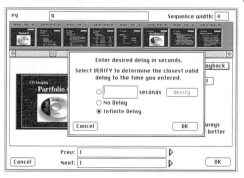

screen or the time can be set to Infinite (unlimited). Typically, you will use the time delay to establish the flow of the presentation. If you are the kind of person who likes to personally speak to each screen image, you will use the infinite setting. If you are creating a sequence that will be self-running, you may want to set the time delay to delay only as long as it takes the average person to read or look at your slides.

EMULATION

Once you have created your presentation, added the sound, and linked the menus to the sequence frames, you should emulate the presentation. What this does is put a small TV-like screen up on the desktop along with a visual of a Photo CD remote control hand unit. From the hand unit you click on the buttons to watch your presentation run. The emulation will allow you to see whether you have linked all of your presentation together correctly and to verify that the sound you placed is in the right spot.

The things to look for when you emulate are:

- Are the images in the right sequence?

- Is the sound that plays the right sound for the slide?

- Is what you see in the small screen the entire image you want to view?

- Does the presentation branch to the desired spot when you select the appropriate number from the menu?

- Does the presentation return to the right spot after the sequence has been viewed?

- Do all of the menu selections go where you thought they should go?

- Does the slide stay on the screen for the duration that you selected?

This step is extremely important prior to scripting the presentation, because once you've had the program written to a Portfolio CD, you can't change it.

268

In Emulation mode, you can run a simulation of your presentation to make sure all your sequences are in the intended order and that the sounds are in the right place.

CASE STUDY

FOCUS ON *TAKING REFUGE*

Since becoming full-time nature photographers in 1988, John and Karen Hollingsworth have built up a professional library of 100,000 images. Operating as Reflections of Nature, the Hollingsworths sell nature photos to such clients as *National Geographic, Audubon, National*

Wildlife, Field & Stream, Birder's Word, Ducks Unlimited. Under their publishing arm, Worm Press, they have produced a calendar on the National Wildlife Refuges for several years and published a 64-page book, *Seasons of the Wild: A Journey Through Our National Wildlife Refuges with John and Karen Hollingsworth,* which traces the seasons through 71 photographs taken at 47 refuges.

Working with Advanced Digital Imaging in Fort Collins, Colorado, the Hollingsworths have developed a Portfolio Photo CD disc, titled *Taking Refuge,* that features 120 of their photos of the National Wildlife Refuge System (there are 475 refuges in the U.S., Caribbean,

and South Pacific). The intent is for the disc to be available for viewing at Refuge visitors' centers across the country.

The disc, which is designed for viewing on a television equipped with a Kodak Photo CD player, educates refuge visitors about endangered species, preservation, the refuges themselves, and volunteer opportunities. The disc also contains a branch describing the Hollingsworths—how they had abandoned their "day jobs" (he had been an engineer, she a travel agent) to pursue their dream of becoming natural history photographers. A unique feature of the disc is an ever-changing "attract loop" without sound (to preserve the sanity of the refuge staff).

All the photographic work at the National Wildlife Refuges has been funded out of pocket by the Hollingsworths themselves. They have received no grants from the U.S. Fish and Wildlife Service, which runs the refuges—although they *have* received whole-hearted support.

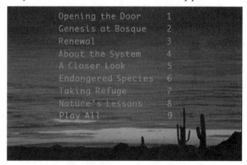

269

VERIFICATION

When your document is complete, you can locate errors you may have overlooked in a verification process. The Verify command finds unconnected paths, nodes with missing paths, sequences without images, overlapping hot spots, and any missing source files. It will also calculate the amount of space you will need to hold the required files for transfer to a Portfolio disc. This is a good step to

You can run a verification at any time to find problem areas in your presentation, such as unconnected paths or missing source files.

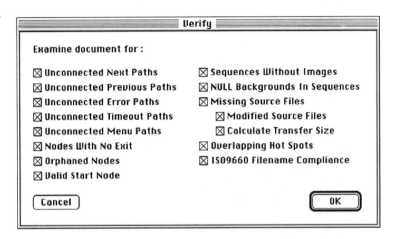

do along the way in creating the presentation, for it can let you know if you are missing links as you build the presentation. After Verification corrections are complete, run the document one more time in Emulator mode for a final check before building the script.

FINALIZING THE SCRIPT

When you are satisfied with your script, you will need to assemble the files to take to your service bureau to have a Photo CD Portfolio disc written. Select Build script from the script menu, and Arrange-It will create a script record and a "LOOR" record for each image you have used. It is the script record and all of the LOOR

Your script file should look like this: all images will be in the form of "LOOR" records.

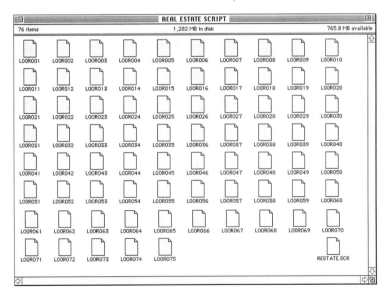

records that you put on removable media and send off to the service provider. In general, besides the script file and the LOOR records, you will need to send any Photo CD discs containing images you added to the presentation in Arrange-It. Your service bureau may also want copies of any PostScript type fonts you have included, just in case. Check with them early on for suggestions and details on their preferences. It is preferable to put all your files on a removable medium, such as a SyQuest cartridge.

Writing the Portfolio Disc

When you turn over your Arrange-It files and assets to your service bureau, they will move the records onto the Kodak Build-It workstation. A good reason to use the SyQuest method of sending your asset records to the service provider is that the Build-It workstation will have a SyQuest removable drive on it along with some conversion software to read Macintosh format over to the Sun SPARCstation format if the service bureau is using that platform.

Once the asset records are on the Build-It workstation, the operator will set the software to "Premaster" (which creates and writes the presentation to a hard disk, not the Portfolio CD) then ask the software to execute the script record you sent along with the LOOR asset records. The Build-It software then begins to convert the images to the Photo CD format (YCC). Once it has converted all of the images, it will work on the sounds and prepare them in a separate area. Finally, Build-It will add the CD-ROM Player software to the overall set of data. This is software from Kodak that can be used by either a Macintosh or a PC Windows computer to "play" the Portfolio CD by creating a TV screen window with buttons along the bottom. Users can then navigate through the presentation with these buttons and hear the sound through the computer's speakers.

After Build-It has successfully processed the asset records, the operator will use a utility to actually write the Portfolio CD from the premastered data. The operator will then view the finished Portfolio CD on a Photo CD player to ensure that all went well.

The Kodak Portfolio CD offers a great opportunity to use technology to its full advantage. A linear slide presentation can be effective, but a branchable presentation can be more flexible. A Portfolio disc is more expensive to produce than a slide presenta-

FOCUS ON THE ADVENTURE DISK

The Adventure Disk, developed for Mountain Travel•Sobek by Custom Process of Berkeley, California, has been described as a virtual travel catalog for high adventure travelers. Mountain Travel•Sobek in El Cerrito, California, is a company that features exotic trips worldwide, from trekking through Patagonia, to exploring Everest, through rafting the more rapid rivers of the world. Richard Bangs, President of MTS, wanted to describe and sell the excursions that his company offers in a more captivating, larger configuration than a catalog affords. Hence, Photo CD Portfolio, a format that can be viewed big on large television screens, with narrative and musical accompaniment.

Howard Brainen, of Custom Process, a professional photo laboratory and digital imaging service bureau, worked with Bangs to produce the Portfolio disc. Bangs supervised the creative, administrative, and legal elements of the project, while Brainen was involved with its technological aspects, from editing the initial slide selections through to mastering the discs and reproducing them in quantity. The joint project also involved the Eastman Kodak Company, who provided technical assistance.

Alaska / Canada
Tatshenshini

Bart Henderson

The Adventure Disc includes over 200 high-resolution photographs describing the ten trips offered by Mountain Travel•Sobek. An extra attraction is the segment "Forty Years of Everest," with images provided by the Royal Geographical Society of Great Britain. Kodak slides from both the famous 1953 climb of the mountain and the 1988 commemorative ascent are shown as PCD conversions.

The first step in putting the disc together was editing the more than 5,000 available slides down to a final 200. Bangs made the first overall edit, while Brainen did the next cut, with his understanding of the technology and knowledge of how a chrome image would translate to a digital one. The final cut was made segment by segment, to narrow an edited selection of about 25 images down to the final 15. This was done by scanning images onto a Photo CD Master and viewing them on a player.

Once final images had been confirmed, the task of obtaining permissions, usage rights, and model releases began. Not only were photographers contacted, but individuals participating in a trek as well.

Each sequence, with its finished narrative, was then recorded to videotape for Chip Harris at Timestream to use for composing the original music track. His task was made all the more difficult because the music had to be composed in sound bites—10- to 15-second bits of sound—because Portfolio does not support continuous sound at this time.

The interface was designed by Sandra Ragan, who started her design with a rough chart indicating the interactivity, accompanied by a storyboard. The overall design was developed as a collaboration between the folks at Custom Process and MTS. Screen designs were first modeled in Photoshop and converted to Photo CD using Build-It. Photographs were received as 35mm slides or as negatives and were also converted to Photo CD in Build-It. The sequencing was done in Arrange-It, prior to mastering the final disc.

MTS found that producing the disc in quantity was far less expensive than printing their catalog and mailing it. Printing 50,000 catalogs costs about $2.00 per unit, compared to $1.35 per individual disc. The real savings is in mailing—$.29 for the disc compared to $2.90 for a catalog. For the time being, TMS is inserting a

Skip Horner

copy of the disc in every catalog for customers who have a player or a CD-ROM drive. In addition, travel agents have been asking for customized versions.

tion, but if you add sound to a slide presentation, the costs can rise to the point where a Portfolio CD can seem economically attractive. On the other side of the economic scale, the videotape presentation is an effective way to communicate, but the costs to produce it range from $1,000 to over $6,000 per minute, well above what a Portfolio CD presentation might cost. And finally, how many of you have dropped a slide presentation and had to play 52 pickup just before having to do your presentation? All the Portfolio CD needs for "on the road" is a portable Photo CD player, your Portfolio CD, and a TV. Unless you roll over the Portfolio CD with your chair, it will most likely run.

16

Mass Production of Discs

In this chapter we will attempt to give you the tools necessary to be prepared to have your CD (whether Photo CD or other type of CD-ROM) duplicated, from 1 to 1 million+ copies. We will talk about the different ways of getting your data ready to be duplicated, define what is meant by a gold master, discuss the steps involved in making thousands of copies at a disc duplication house, and finally, give you some ideas about what all this will cost you.

Creating a Gold Master

The "gold master," or "one-off master," is created when data from a hard disk are written or "burned" into a compact disc, using a method termed compact disc recordable, or CD-R. Typically, a writable CD disc has a gold reflective layer—hence the term *gold* master.

Creating a gold master requires four components: (1) hardware in the form of a CD writer, (2) CD mastering software for simulating, testing, and creating your gold master, (3) a computer system that meets or exceeds the specifications of both the CD writer and the mastering software, and (4) quality blank writable CD media that are approved for the CD writer. Both the writer and the mastering software must support the CD format and the platform for which you want to write CDs. The CD platforms to choose from include CD DA (Redbook audio), CD-ROM Mode 1, CD-ROM Mode 2 (Forms 1 and 2), CD-ROM XA, CD-I, CD Video, Native HFS CD, and Kodak Photo CD.

CD-R SYSTEM COMPONENTS

A number of manufacturers make desktop CD-recordable hardware and software. The price of the hardware has dropped considerably in the past few years, and you can now get a complete system for under $3,000, although most of the better-known and reliable systems (including software) are in the $5,000–$7,000 range.

The hardware is available from Philips, Yamaha, Ricoh, JVC, Sony, Pinnacle Micro, Plamon Data Systems, Kodak, and numer-

The Kodak PCD Writer 600 is one of two models available from Kodak for writing compact discs. This higher-speed model is for users with high demand.

ous other manufacturers. Kodak's line of products for disc production include the PCD Writer (in 2X and 6X versions), which is compatible with CD-ROM, CD-ROM XA, CD-I, CD DA, CD Video, and Photo CD.

Macintosh, DOS, Windows, and UNIX systems are all supported with CD mastering software. Among the best-known software products are Easy-CD Pro, WinOn CD, SimpliCD, CD-Record, and Gear. Kodak CD mastering software (QuickTopix) is available for Macintosh and Windows. Kodak Build-It software for the Sun SPARCstation (and soon the Mac) allows you to write to Kodak Portfolio media.

As far as your computer system is concerned, if your Mac or Windows system meets the normal high-end requirements of a fast processor, has 8 MB or more of RAM, and has a fast, large hard disc, you are close to what you need. Hard disc drives must meet the specific requirements designated by the CD writer manufacturer and the CD mastering software. Normally a SCSI disc drive that is at least 1 GB in size with a minimum continuous data transfer rate of 600 KB is required. The Kodak PCD Writer 600 requires a 1.2 GB hard disk dedicated to the application with a continuous data transfer rate of 1.2 MB/sec and average access time of 15 msecs or less.

The final component you'll need is the writable media. Kodak's Writable CDs can be used for most CD formats. These discs are used for storing all types of data, including text, graphics, sound, video, and animation. They come in two sizes, 74 minute, which holds up to 682 MB of data (that's the equivalent of 500 floppy

Available as a supplement to the Kodak PCD Writer is the Kodak Disc Transporter, which sits in front of the CD writer and automatically selects a disc from a 75-disc input spindle and places it in the open drawer of the writer. When the writing process is complete, the disc is removed to an outside spindle and a new one is automatically loaded for continuous production flow.

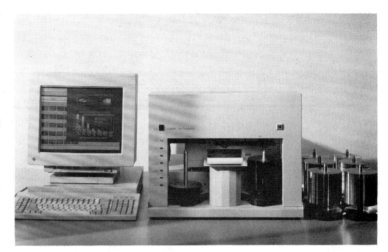

discs) and 63 minute, which hold up to 580 MB of data. Kodak's Writable CDs with Infoguard also have individual numbers and bar codes for identification, tracking, and security. If Writable CDs are written with the ISO 9660 formula plus HFS extensions, they can be cross-platform—that is, data can be accessed by numerous computer platforms, including Macintosh, Windows, DOS, and UNIX.

277

Writable CDs cannot be used for Photo CD or Portfolio discs. Kodak Photo CD Master discs, Pro Photo CD Master discs, Print Photo CD, and Catalog discs are all special media that may only be used by the appropriate Kodak Photo CD Imaging Workstation, while Portfolio discs must be written at a Portfolio workstation. Any disc produced at a PIW is a gold master, comparable to any other CD-ROM gold master or one-off master. Also, any Portfolio disc created with Build-It software is a gold master.

PREPARING THE DATA FOR REPLICATION

Considering the finality of a CD after it is written (another term for a CD being "burned" might be "cast in stone"), perhaps the single most important part of creating a gold master is preparing the data prior to the gold master creation. We advise you to check it, check it again, and check it a third time. The type of data being committed to the CD will obviously determine the kind of checks you will do, as will your time and budget.

In the case of presentations and multimedia, you should check the script, all the operations, the screens, the animation, the sound, and the speed. One of the final tests of a multimedia product is how well it plays once it has been written to a CD. It is advisable to run your test CD on a single-speed CD drive and on the types of computers the multimedia presentation was designed for. If all goes well, you can have copies made.

If the material being written to a CD is a manual, a catalog, or an archive of documents, you need to make sure the retrieval method will work from a CD and that the necessary database for the retrieval is created prior to burning the CD. A thorough test of the retrieval database is important, since the data written to the CD may later be lost, discarded, or corrupted, making it impossible to recreate the data files for the CD.

For Photo CD Portfolio projects, it is imperative that you emulate the presentation several times for review of branching, time outs, error branching, sound placement, and overall presentation feel. As we noted in Chapter 15, it is also important to "verify" the presentation. The verification process will check all the branch nodes and the available data and will ensure that a valid script can be written to the disc. If you skip the verification process and go ahead and build your script, you may see that you have all the LOOR asset records in the script file. This may lull you into a false sense of security. Errors can occur in the script writing process, such that no script is actually written. Using verification will ensure that a script record along with the LOOR asset records are both written before you send everything off for a Portfolio CD to be made.

If you want to make several copies of your Portfolio gold master, ask your service provide to *premaster* the information to a Writable CD. Currently you cannot make copies of one Portfolio disc from another. You must either have a premaster copy or the original assets and scripts to make another Portfolio disc. For help with this process, call your service provider or Kodak and request the current instructions: *Photo CD Portfolio Information on Disc Replication* and *Guidelines for Using the Photo CD Symbol.*

Note that there are actually two kinds of Portfolio discs, interactive and noninteractive. An interactive disc contains a Portfolio interactive presentation and Kodak Player software. A noninteractive disc is one that contains hundreds of PCD images and perhaps Kodak Browser software. To develop a noninteractive disc you begin by copying your PCD images at a given resolution to a Portfolio disc. This disc is then used along with Kodak Shoebox to create photo captions and indexes of keywords. Once the database is complete, the data may be exported from the Mac version of Shoebox and imported into the Windows version, or vice versa, creating a data catalog for both platforms. Once all catalog data are verified, the data files, Browser software, and the images are all written to a new Portfolio disc.

With all CDs, make sure you keep the files and procedures used to create them in a safe place. And be sure to get written permission to use all logos, trademarks, and software. In many cases there are fees and other requirements you must meet. For example, if you wish to put Kodak Browser software, Kodak Player software, or Kodak Access software on your Portfolio disc, you can do so at no charge. However, Kodak still requires that you sign a software distribution agreement and obtain a registration number. For more information, ask your service bureau or call Kodak (800-235-6325).

TRANSFERRING FILES TO A SERVICE PROVIDER

In all likelihood, you will not have your own CD-R production system for making a gold master, so you will need to get everything to a service provider to have a disc burned.

You will need to put all your data on a transfer disk of some kind. For Portfolio CD, most service bureaus prefer an 88 MB SyQuest cartridge for the data, because the Build-It workstation usually uses a SyQuest drive for removable disk transfer (both Mac- and PC-formatted SyQuest cartridges are acceptable). For Writable CD or CD-ROM, the types of transfer media can range from DAT to SyQuest to tape to optical disc to floppy. The service provider may even ask you to bring in your hard disk to be directly attached via a SCSI cable for the fastest transfer to the company's equipment.

You should provide on your transfer media all the necessary data to complete the CD. Review all the files to ensure that they have been copied to the transfer disk. Missing that one logo you put in your logo folder but forgot to copy to your transfer disk can foul up the whole production process.

One other factor to keep in mind when moving your data to the transfer disk is data paths. If your PC or Mac application has built, or if you have built, specific data paths to other files or applications, make sure that these paths can be maintained from the copy to the transfer media and then to the CD itself. A specific reference to a disk's name or location could mean trouble when trying to execute the final result from the CD.

HAVING THE DISC BURNED

When you hand over your transfer disk to the service provider, you should also include as much documentation as you think is necessary to explain what it is you are putting on the CD. After the CD is written, the service provider will typically "test run" the finished product to ensure that the disc was burned properly, and the documentation will help in this review. If you are going to need several copies of the disc, tell the service bureau to hold onto the data if possible. That way you can review the disc and make sure there are no problems before you give the okay to have additional copies made.

The cost of having a gold disc made varies among service providers, but generally you'll pay $100 to $200 for your first disc. The more you require of your service provider, the more it will cost.

Short-Run Duplication of Your Gold Master

You now have your gold master in hand. What do you do if you want multiple copies? The answer depends on how many copies you want, what kind of disc labeling you want, what kind of packaging, and so on. Prices will range from $15 to $100 each for additional copies of your gold master.

If your need fewer than 50 copies, you have several options to choose from:

1. Depending on the type of CD you are having reproduced, the place you had your gold master made may be in a position to continue to create "one-offs" for you up to the quantity you need.

2. Ask the company that made your gold master to have the copies "replicated" as opposed to having one-offs burned one at a time. (The company will act as a disc broker and probably send the job out to be done, since most such companies do not have their own stamping equipment.)

3. Take the disc to a duplication house.

The usual criteria for determining whether to have your service provider reproduce the copies as one-offs is the cost. If the cost for the number of copies you need exceeds about $1200, you should probably not go with one-offs and instead choose one of the replication options.

Each of the three types of CDs that can be burned by a desktop workstation (Photo CD, Portfolio CD, and Writable CD or CD-ROM) has its own short-run duplication requirements.

A Photo CD Master or Pro disc must be duplicated by a PIW. It is also possible to copy a Photo CD to a Portfolio CD on a Kodak Build-It workstation.

Because of the way a Portfolio CD is written, it is not possible to duplicate one in small numbers after the data have been re-moved from the Build-It workstation. So, if you need copies, ask your service provider to premaster your Portfolio and save the data to Writable CD so future duplicates can be made,

You may also want to keep all of your Portfolio assets together (SyQuests, Photo CDs, and so on) and use them to create new Portfolios as needed.

Writable CD discs can be duplicated in low quantities by any Writable CD workstation at any time after the original has been produced. Your service provider may have a low-volume CD publishing system whereby one CD may be written to a bank of CD writers.

281

PRINTING ON A GOLD MASTER DISC

Normally gold masters produced in low quantities are not screen printed. Exceptions are possible. Trace Corporation makes an ink-jet printer that will print on CDs. Some service providers also take discs to a replication facility to have them screen printed. Be careful about using labels—trying to remove them once they are attached to a disc will probably damage the disc and make it unreadable.

INSERTS FOR GOLD MASTER DISCS

Consider using a color printer to make inserts for the jewelcase in which you place your master disc. Dye sublimation prints give a photographic look that works well. The ink can come off some color prints, so be sure that the printed side does not face the disc.

Large-Quantity Disc Duplication

Disc duplication houses specialize in the mass replication of CD discs as well as packaging of the CDs once they have been stamped.

THE DISC DUPLICATION PROCESS

Here are the basic steps a disc duplication house goes through to make copies from your gold master:

1. The data from the gold master are used to create a *glass master.* The glass master can be created in one of two methods. The first is called the Photoresist method. In this process, an optically ground glass disc is coated with a layer of Photoresist. A laser then writes a pattern of pits on this layer, representing the data from the gold master. The second process is called NPR (non-Photoresist). This process starts with a glass disc that is coated with a layer of plastic, which is then vaporized in a pattern of pits and lands by a laser. A reading laser follows the cutting laser to check the integrity of the cut directly after it is made. This eliminates the chemicals used in the Photoresist process.

2. The glass master is then electroplated with nickel. This nickel layer, when removed from the glass master, is a negative of the master and is called the *father.*

3. Although the father could be used (like a printing plate) to stamp out the duplicate CDs, it would wear out too quickly, so a series of *mothers* are created from the father.

The disc duplication process is a fairly simple one.

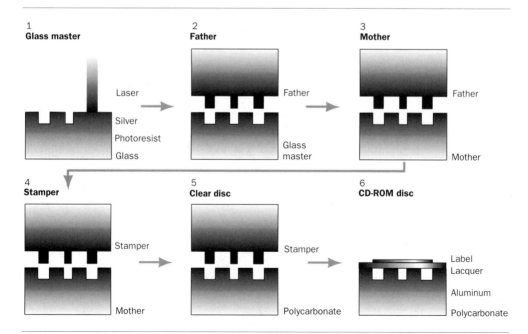

4. From each mother (which is a positive image of the glass master), several *stampers* are created. These (negative versions) are what are actually used to create the finished duplicates.

5. The stampers are placed in an injection molding machine, which applies both heat and pressure to a polycarbonate material that is injected into the stamper. An exact duplicate of the original (positive) disc is created from this process.

6. Since the finished product is clear, a coat of aluminum is put on the polycarbonate to give it a reflective surface for the laser. A clear coating is put over the aluminum to protect it.

Testing is the final process. You should have a clear understanding of the testing procedures that your replicator will use. CD-ROMs have a more stringent set of standards than audio CDs, for example.

After the manufacturing stage, the discs are sent to silk-screening equipment where up to four colors can be silk-screened onto the top of the CD. From silk-screening, the discs go to the packaging area, where they are inserted into jewelcases along with any printed material inserts and bottom inserts. The finished product is then either shrink wrapped and boxed, or just boxed ready for shipment back to you.

Obviously, this is a cursory overview of the manufacturing process, but it gives you a feel for how the process occurs. If you would like to know more about the overall process, you should contact Disk Manufacturing, Inc., which offers an excellent CD-ROM (for Macintosh only) titled DMI Interactive Gallery that presents the disc duplication process. The number to call is (800) 433-DISC.

PUTTING THE FINISHING TOUCHES ON YOUR DISC

To complete the process of disc publishing, you need to consider the artwork that goes directly on the disc, design and printing of an insert, packaging design, and any other elements that will accompany the disc.

First is the silk-screen artwork that goes directly on the disc. You will need to check with the disc duplication house or your service provider for the details on specs and finished artwork requirements for the silk-screen equipment. Typically, a two-color silk-screen is included in the price of the disc duplication, and the house will require either film positives or negatives of what you want on the discs. If necessary, work with a designer on getting

You have several options to choose from besides the jewelcase.

the artwork for both the silk-screen and the inserts. Many designers are familiar with the specification requirement terminology and can offer suggestions and design ideas to ensure a quality package.

If your finished disc is going into a jewelcase and will require printed inserts (like the ones you get when you buy an audio CD), you will need to have them printed ahead of time and have them delivered to the disc duplication house. Again, the duplication house or your service provider can supply you with the necessary printing specs (such as the finished size, thickness, and weight of paper to use). Make sure you follow these specs to the letter—the automated insertion equipment has little tolerance for out-of-specification inserts and may not work. This can be a major problem if you have thousands of inserts to put in.

One other thing to consider when it comes to packaging your CDs is having them placed in a Tyvek sleeve instead of a jewelcase. The sleeve is less expensive and can be printed ahead of time with your information on it. Again, check with the disc duplication house or your service provider for additional information on this alternative packaging.

COSTS OF MASS PRODUCTION

Several things go into the final cost of getting a CD mass duplicated. The basic costs of creating the glass master and its subsequent stampers is usually broken out as a separate cost, which varies depending on the turnaround time required by the customer. Another separate item is the actual cost per finished disc, followed by the costs for the packaging. An additional cost is any royalty and licensing fee. Here are some examples of what might be typical costs for mass replication of various project scenarios:

1,000 CD-ROM discs with 5-day turnaround, 2-color printing, and a jewelcase with inserts:

Mastering	$1,000 or more
Discs	$1.20 each or more
Jewelcases	$.30 each
Inserting	$.05 each
Shrinkwrapping	$.04 each
Serialization	$150.00
Artwork charge	$35.00

1,000 CD-ROM discs with 1-day turnaround, 2-color printing, and a jewelcase with inserts:

Mastering	$2,000 or more
Discs	$1.95 each or more
Jewelcases	$.30 each
Inserting	$.05 each
Shrinkwrapping	$.04 each
Serialization	$150.00
Artwork charge	$35.00

1,000 Kodak Portfolio discs with Player software, 5-day turnaround, 2-color printing, and a jewelcase with inserts:

Mastering	$1,000 or more
Discs	$1.20 each or more
Jewelcases	$.30 each
Inserting	$.05 each
Shrinkwrapping	$.04 each
Serialization	$150.00
Artwork charge	$35.00
Kodak "Player" license fee	$.00
Kodak royalty fee	$.10 per disc

Note that if you want to duplicate a Kodak Photo CD disc of any type, you must use a disc duplication house licensed by Kodak, you must pay a replication fee of $5,000, and you'll be charged a royalty of $.05 per disc.

Part VI
OTHER PHOTO CD APPLICATIONS

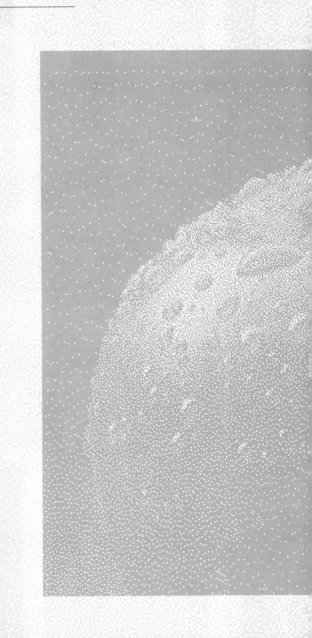

17

Photo CD at Libraries, Museums, and Universities

Photo CD and its allied technologies are being used not only for publishing, presentations, and multimedia but in highly specialized ways in many academic and scientific fields. Educators, museum curators, and librarians, for example, are exploring a wide variety of uses for Photo CD, from simple image storage and retrieval to on-line databases and interactive teaching materials.

University and museum libraries are home to tens of thousands (sometimes millions) of images—photographs, artwork, biomedical slides, maps, and other kinds of graphic information that has great value for instruction and scholarship. Unfortunately, these image archives are not always readily accessible to students, faculty, and other potential users. Their use normally requires permission, supervision, and special handling to ensure their preservation. Some materials may be decaying, such as books and journals printed on acid paper. The solution? High-resolution digital conversion of images to Photo CD makes valuable photos, art, and text available without damage to delicate or one-of-a-kind originals. The projects described in this chapter are making library and museum collections widely accessible for teaching and research.

The Kodak Library Image Consortium Project

The Kodak Library Image Consortium (KLIC) project (formed by Cornell University, the University of Southern California, Kodak, and the Commission of Preservation and Access in the fall of 1992) has been exploring ways in which libraries, museums, and universities can use Photo CD technology for storage and retrieval of materials. Their purpose is to preserve rare documents and artworks while making the images of these documents accessible both on site and via computer networks. The method that has been chosen for digitizing these images is Photo CD. This project is

The Leavey Information Commons, an electronic and work facility equipped with 100 Photo CD–capable workstations, is designed to encourage student collaboration. It is the heart of the University of Southern California's new Thomas and Dorothy Leavey Library.

Irene Fertik

290

part of an effort by universities and corporations to build a national electronic highway bringing a rich array of information—text, images, sound, and multimedia—into schools, colleges, corporate offices, medical facilities, and homes over the next two decades.

With the assistance of Photo CD technology, researchers, schools, museums, and libraries all over the world will be able to access an increasing number of materials formerly available only on site. In some cases, the digital file will replace the need to see an original. In others, researchers may conduct an on-line search to preview the holdings of one or more repositories and then determine exactly which originals they want to see in person.

The KLIC project has contributed to the use of common standards for document capture, storage, and transmission. Penn State, Yale, Harvard, and Tennessee are now using the system as a model for developing their own projects.

In this chapter we explore many of the projects being undertaken by KLIC members Cornell University and USC, and by other institutions as well.

Cornell University

Cornell University has been a pioneer in the application of digital technology. Since 1990 over a thousand books have been scanned, forming the first installment in Cornell's Digital Library. Desktop access across networks is now being implemented via Macintoshes,

IBM PCs, and Sun workstations, enabling students and faculty members to browse the digital library and request a printed copy of all or part of a book. In addition, Cornell has been testing the capabilities of Photo CD for capture, storage, and transmission of visual images.

Elaine Engst of the Rare and Manuscripts Collections explains that the first step in digitizing the collection's images is to photograph them onto 35mm film. They are then digitized onto PCD Master discs at a service bureau, proofed to be sure that the original image has been accurately and completely captured, and then cataloged.

DIGITIZING LIBRARY COLLECTIONS

So far Cornell has converted items from three of its major library collections: the Louis Agassiz Fuertes Papers, the John Nolen Papers, and the University Archives Photograph Collection. These collections include letters, student notes, notebooks, sketchbooks, diaries, articles, expedition journals, field notes, photographs, and architectural drawings.

Fuertes was an accomplished naturalist recognized by ornithologists as one of America's greatest painters of birds. Most notable in the Fuertes Papers is the artwork, including over 1,000 pencil, ink, and watercolor sketches and drawings. Fuertes's works from the collections of the Johnson Art Museum and the Laboratory of Ornithology are also being scanned.

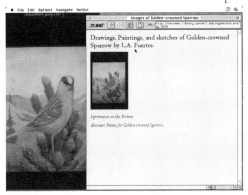

Cornell's other project devoted to the archives of a single person is digitizing the John Nolen Papers. One of the founding fathers of the urban planning profession, Nolen kept records of some 450 planning projects throughout the United States.

Finally, Cornell plans to scan a selection of photos drawn from the university's own archives, which document the 125 years of the school's existence. Besides research, these photos will be used for public relations purposes and in university publications.

Cornell University has scanned its collection of bird drawings and documents by naturalist Louis Agassiz Fuertes not only for archiving purposes but for several multimedia projects.

Searching for specific images is one of the primary problems in using large collections of visual materials. It is difficult and expensive to provide adequate information in textual form, and brows-

291

ing through original items endangers the materials. Cornell has catalogued images using Shoebox, Kodak's image-management software (see Chapter 8). The staff at Cornell finds Shoebox particularly useful because it allows the creation of customized databases for each type of collection.

Cornell has just installed a Kodak XLS 8300 dye sublimation printer so that researchers can output images in color. Previously, they had to make selections by previewing them on a computer screen, hand carry their requests to the photo department, and then wait two or three days for a print. Now they can obtain a glossy 8 x 10 copy in only a few minutes, and much more economically.

"As far as high-resolution conversion of color images goes, we're pleased with the quality of Photo CD," says Tom Hickerson, Director of the Cornell Libraries Division of Rare and Manuscript Collections. "This capacity to browse, select, and print at a reasonable cost is just what we wanted."

While exploring the use of digital technology, Hickerson says that Cornell will carefully examine the ways in which digitized images can specifically meet the traditional uses of classroom materials as well as the ways in which these technologies can expand their educational use.

MULTIMEDIA ON THE INTERNET

Cornell staff are also exploring multimedia uses for traditional sources. Mark Handel, a Cornell senior student/employee, worked with Engst to create a World-Wide Web (WWW) site relating to the work of Louis Agassiz Fuertes. The WWW is an Internet service that can show not only the actual text of documents but graphics, sounds, and movies as well.

The platform for Cornell's Web site is a Power Macintosh 8100/80 with 32 MB of memory and a I GB hard drive. The primary software used was Mac HTTP 1.3, Microsoft Word 5.1 to write hypertext markup language documents (HTML), HyperCard, and Adobe Photoshop to transfer images from Photo CD. The thumbnails are PCD Base/16 images in GIF format in 8-bit color. Larger images are PCD Base resolution in JPEG format, in 24-bit color. The WWW site is available on the Internet at the Uniform Resource Locator (URL): **http://rmc-www.library.cornell.edu** between 9 and 5 Eastern time Monday through Friday.

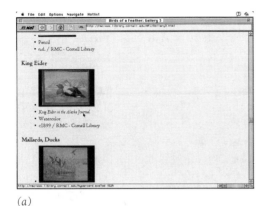

(a)

(b)

Cornell's "Of a Feather" on-line exhibit can be accessed on a World-Wide Web site on the Internet. It is set up as a walk through several galleries, each being a "page" on the server. (a) Here the pointer is on a hot link that will take the user to pages in Fuertes's Alaska journal. These hot links allow the user to not only find out about the work itself but the context in which it was created. (b) This is an example of the hot links (italicized text) in the journal pages to pictures of the bird mentioned. Here the user has clicked on the phrase "mallard" and a large image of Fuertes's water color of a mallard has been retrieved from the server.

One segment of the project is a transcription of Fuertes's journal. Kept on an expedition to Alaska, sponsored by Edward Harriman in 1899. Within each journal entry, the names of specific birds are highlighted to provide "hot links." Clicking on the highlighted text will provide thumbnail images of the bird. Bird sounds, acquired from the Library of Natural Sounds at Cornell (a unit of the Laboratory of Ornithology), are coupled with the images. The user simply clicks on "Listen to it" to hear the bird. Users can also click on a map depicting the expedition's route to go directly to the journal entry for that area.

Also available on the Internet is an electronic version of an exhibit held at Cornell's art museum in the summer of 1994. The "Of a Feather: Audubon and Fuertes" exploration allows the user to wander through a virtual gallery of the original exhibit. By clicking on a particular "gallery" on the screen, the user is able to see a PCD thumbnail version of the artworks and to access information about each image.

WORKS IN PROGRESS

The Digital Access Coalition Project (nicknamed "Eutopia") is an attempt to bring members from all aspects of Cornell's academic community together to look at new ways of using digital technology at the university. "We feel that for large collections we really need an underlying database. That's one of the questions we have to answer soon. I've talked to a number of software developers to give them our criteria but I haven't seen the ideal product yet," says Hickerson. "I have particular hope for a local network version of the Kodak Picture Exchange. Some of the access criteria they incorporated into that software is really very imaginative and interesting. . . . At this point there isn't a great variety in image databases out there. They all use the same approach, and I don't think we know enough yet."

Cornell is also looking at Photo CD as a publishing medium for particular bodies of material. "While we see some of the access of the published materials via networks, we also want to test their publication in CD form," says Hickerson.

The underlying goals for digital technology at Cornell are (1) to create virtual collections of materials housed in different sites, and (2) to use the technology effectively in an educational environment.

The University of Southern California

The James Irvine Foundation Center for Scholarly Technology of the University Library at USC is using Photo CD technology to scan thousands of photographs and is exploring the use of Photo CD for both classroom presentations and studying outside the classroom.

For USC's Regional History Project, photographs that document the history and development of Southern California and the Southwest are being scanned for an on-line database. About 1,000 black-and-white images (dating back to 1860) have been scanned.

"There are somewhere between three and four million photographs in our archives that we would like to be able to access more efficiently," says Michael McHugh, manager of USC Electronic Publishing. So far his lab has scanned several thousand of these images onto Photo CD Master discs to make the pictures more accessible to students, who view them using CD players and televisions. The next step is to make the images available for viewing on personal computers and UNIX workstations as a part of USC's planned on-line image database.

Now that images can be so much more easily accessed, there is greater demand for them. Faculty members have asked for scans of images for use in multimedia projects and for presentations in classes such as art history, religion, anthropology, and molecular biology. For example, 400 slides have been scanned for students' use in an art history survey class on Renaissance art. The availability of digital images and the software to manipulate them is changing the way that teachers think of presenting information in the classroom.

These are some images from the "Dick" Whittington Collection, Regional History Collection, Department of Special Collections, University Library, University of Southern California. The Whittington Collection contains over 500,000 negatives documenting the commercial development of the Southern California area from 1925 to 1960. The USC Library is in the process of having the collection scanned to Photo CD Master discs at the university's Center for Scholarly Technology.

295

The University of Michigan

The University of Michigan's Digital Media Initiative allows for the PCD conversion of thousands of images for placement on networked servers at the university. The images are accessed by a variety of methods, often by faculty who present the images in class lectures.

Instructors are excited about this new technology and are using it increasingly to help them teach in the classroom. For example, some art history slide-shows have been replaced by Photo CD images, a professor of anthropology has created a multimedia presentation describing the Mexican landscape and people, and a zoology instructor has put together a digital presentation of hundreds of animals.

The Office of Instructional Technology (OIT) provides assistance for faculty interested in pursuing multimedia in the classroom. Resources include a staff of instructional designers and technical experts, a well-equipped "hands-on" laboratory workspace, and a large collection of software in support of instructional technology projects. The OIT staff also work in partnership with other university units, including the Center for Research on Learning and Teaching, the Learning Resource Center, the College of Literature, Science, and the Arts, and many others.

The OIT staff finds Photo CD to be an inexpensive and efficient way to digitize and archive high-quality images and make them available on-line. As they work with faculty to create classroom materials, they are finding that the availability of images is increasing their use of multimedia authoring tools.

"Photo CD is the holy grail for most applications," says Ed Saunders, Director of the OIT. "It allows us to easily digitize and retain archival-quality images, as well as allowing us to use appropriate resolutions for things like network distribution and screen viewing."

ACCESSING IMAGE DATABASES

The university's image databases are being accessed in a number of ways. GET, the Generic Exploration Tool, is a popular retrieval method for viewing digital images and other multimedia resources that reside on a networked server.

As well as allowing standard searching methods, the Generic Exploration Tool (GET) browser lets users find items by traversing various faculty-created categories called perspectives. Here, a faculty member has included perspectives related to the appearance and content of art works, as well as more traditional fields such as the artist's name and country of origin.

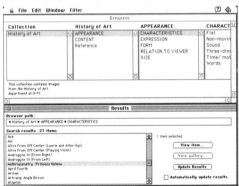

GET combines hierarchical exploration with Boolean and free-string searches (see Chapter 8), allowing the user to select information in a variety of ways. The database is designed to allow for the inclusion of multimedia resources, with an emphasis on clarity, comparison, and ease of use.

Faculty members can import, edit, and create multiple perspectives for viewing the data, as well as store and display information in the format that best suits their discipline. Multimedia data such as sound, still video images, MIDI music, and motion sequences are also accessible.

ART HISTORY CLASSES

Art History students use GET via Macintosh computers connected to a VIDS server to access the History of Art Database for 20th Century Art, which displays one or more of the 1,300 available

In the History of Art Database, students can bring up a "gallery" of thumbnail images in addition to viewing textual information about specific pieces of art. The gallery allows them to compare images by an artist or a group of artists. Clicking on an individual image expands to fill the screen, while clicking on the title brings up textual information about the image.

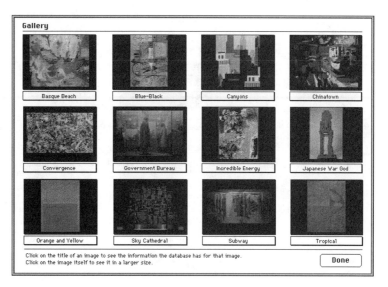

works along with information such as the artist's name, the media and technique used, and the year the work was created. Students can compare several works at the same time or study individual works to consider style, form, content, and other characteristics.

THE CALLIOPE'S SISTERS PROJECT

The Calliope's Sisters project provides a simple but flexible software tool to access a library of high-quality still and motion images, text, and audio files. Students in English literature courses can access classical music, text such as poetry and plays, and art images to study the relationships among literature, sciences, and the arts in a particular era. Subsets of these media files can be custom grouped to create slide shows to supplement traditional lectures.

Students access the library using Macintosh computers running QuickTime. This project has established standard procedures and hardware specifications that other faculty will use as a model to create libraries of digitized materials for in-class presentations.

ANTHROPOLOGY

Early New World Civilizations presents students with still images of various archaeological sites and artifacts from early American civilizations. Designed for an upcoming course, the database application will enable students to view the images and related text in the classroom, as well as study them at their own pace outside

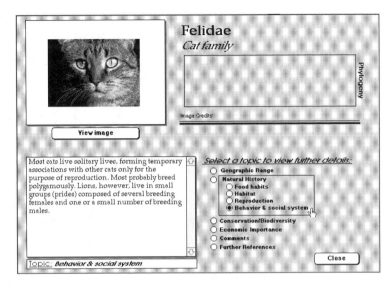

After traversing the phylogenetic tree in the Animal Diversity Database, students can view a description of a particular species, family order, or class. In this example, the student sees detailed information about the behavior and social systems of the cat family (Felidae).

298

of class. The images, organized by features such as topic, location, theme, and time period, are accessible from any Macintosh computer connected to the campus AppleTalk network.

NATURAL SCIENCES

The Animal Diversity Database will allow biology students to explore a collection of over 1,000 animal images. Some of these images were transferred from original 35mm slides to Photo CD; others were acquired from the new Photo CD collection at the university's Film and Video Library. Students access the database on Macintosh computers with Oracle SQL*Net software, MacTP, and an ORACLE server with GET data tables. The database contains a variety of authentic sound resources as well as images allowing students to see and hear animals from all over the globe.

Students can traverse the phylogenetic tree or can search by selecting such characteristics as food habits and geographic range. In addition to standard textbook information about the structure and classification of animals, students are introduced to basic concepts in ecology and evolutionary biology. The designers of the database hope that the images and accompanying rich description of particular species will encourage students to explore many issues concerning conservation and biodiversity.

THE LAST DEADLY DISEASE

Also at the University of Michigan, two staffers have developed *The Last Deadly Disease*, a Portfolio disc that incorporates still images, narration, sound, and branching to compare and contrast the history, research, and treatment of two diseases: polio and AIDS. Designed for audiences from high school seniors to college freshmen and sophomores, the program was meant to show that archival and historical sources can be used in a manner that conveys a timely message even while communicating technical or specialized subject matter, according to Dennis Moser, co-producer of the project.

Moser, a photo archivist, developed the project with Ann Gilliland-Swetland, who is director of the SourceLINK project at the

This is the main menu screen for The Last Deadly disease, a Portfolio disc produced at the University of Michigan that compares the history, research, and treatment for polio and AIDS.

university's Historical Center for Health Sciences and adjunct faculty member of the School of Information and Library Studies, where Moser is a doctoral student. They scanned source material from a number of archives using a HP Scanjet. On Macintosh computers they sized and edited the pictures in Photoshop and then imported them to Persuasion to lay out text and images. The narration, recorded on a Teac digital tape recorder, was processed through Sound Designer II to balance and equalize the files. A beta version of Kodak's Portfolio software was used for the final assembly of sound and images and for output to a Photo CD Portfolio disc.

The source material for this project was drawn from Public Health records in the State Archives of Michigan, historical photographs from numerous historical repositories in both Michigan and Ohio, and materials from various federally funded agencies.

WHISTLER PROJECT

In another University of Michigan Portfolio project, Moser examines the artist James McNeill Whistler. Based on an exhibit that Moser curated, the project explores Whistler's work in Italy, Holland, Paris, and London.

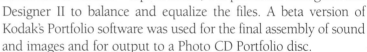

Moser first had all the images shot on 35mm slides and then digitized to PCD discs. The PCD files were brought into Kodak's Create-It in order to design the background screens and to add audio (see Chapter 13). Arrange-It was used to develop the branching structures. Both the Create-It and Arrange-It files, along with the audio and image files, were put on an Apple HFS CD-ROM, using TOPIX software and a Kodak CD Writer. This CD-ROM was then used to transfer the complete set of combined assets to a Sun SPARCstation, where Build-It was used to write the Portfolio Photo CD (see Chapter 15 for more on Portfolio disc production).

The Henry Ford Museum

Photo CD has also been used extensively at the Henry Ford Museum in Dearborn, Michigan, often in conjunction with the University of Michigan at Ann Arbor.

The museum's Mack Truck historical photograph collection contains some 63,000 items, covering the history of the Mack Truck Company from about 1907 to 1947. A large percentage of the photographs were done for advertising purposes, but a number of them reveal interesting insights into American industrial history.

Dennis Moser, working this time as a project photo archivist with the Henry Ford Museum, found that these photos were mostly 8 x 10's: black-and-white prints, negatives, or glass plates. There were a few 4 x 5 and 5 x 7 images as well. The fact that there were numerous negatives and plates without corresponding

300

The Henry Ford Museum is in the process of converting thousands of photos from its Mack Truck historical collection to Photo CD. Several of these images are being used to create interactive Portfolio discs.

prints presented some technical problems in Photo CD production. First, modern prints had to be made. Then, 35mm color slides were shot of all the prints. In this way, the tonalities and hues of the originals were retained and the Photo CD production was greatly facilitated. Moser is putting together a Portfolio interactive disc, complete with sound files and branching, for accessing a number of these photos.

"Moving Axles on Pixels" is a Photo CD Portfolio disc developed for the Henry Ford Museum and Greenfield Village to showcase the breadth and depth of the museum's collections and to demonstrate the museum's commitment to use of digital resources.

Another project under way is development of a Portfolio Photo CD that will provide an overview of the Ford museum's collections and activities. The project is a collaboration between the museum's Historical Resources Business Unit, the University of Michigan Historical Center for the Health Sciences SourceLINK Project, and the Commission on Preservation and Access.

In addition, scholars, collectors, restorers, and educators will be able to gain direct access to the museum's artifact database and OPAC, to copies of archival and manuscript-finding aids, bibliographies, and other research aids, on-line reference assistance, museum program information, educational and curricular materials, pre- and post-school tour, or research materials. Even a virtual tour or visit to the museum will be possible.

Publication quality copies of images will be ordered and supplied on line with the benefits of short turn-around time and preservation of the physical integrity of the originals.

A large collection of Model-A Ford parts drawings will be the first to be scanned for this project.

301

18

Medical Applications of Photo CD

The high resolution of images made possible with Photo CD technology has proven particularly useful for medical imaging, where display of subtle detail is particularly important. As we will see in this chapter, Photo CD's unique qualities both for scanning and as a storage medium make it ideal for a number of medical uses.

Indiana University School of Optometry

At the Indiana University School of Optometry, 8,000 photos of the human eye have been collected to be converted to Photo CD. Students previously had to hunt through volumes of slides stored in three-ring binders, then set up a projector to study them. After struggling for years to find a way to make clinic and research images more accessible, the staff finally found the solution with Photo CD. "We were amazed at the resolution quality of the images," says research associate Susan Doherty.

"It took a leap of faith for faculty to give up their 35mm slides for this project," says Doherty. "These are their original copies, and they're used to guarding them with their lives!"

Now the Photo CD images are used in the Optometry School's databases, for case studies, and for good old-fashioned lectures, which have been converted to Portfolio presentations combining images, graphics, text, video, and sound. These Portfolio discs are available for viewing in the library or can be purchased with course materials.

The new focus on multimedia has had a profound effect on the way faculty thinks about presenting materials in the classroom. For small classes there is a multimedia presentation resource room of Quadra 660 AVSs with CD-ROM slots. The lecture hall, which seats around 200 students, has RGB overheads, a full computer workstation, and a projection system. A portable Quadra cart, equipped for showing multimedia presentations, is available to wheel into classrooms.

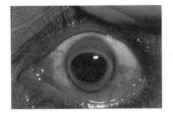 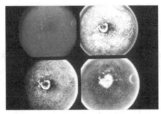 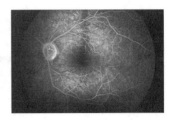

Thousands of 35mm slides of eye diseases are being stored on Photo CD Master discs at Indiana University's School of Optometry. The photos range from facial shots to close-ups of retinas. Faculty at the School of Optometry found that the PCD scans are so good that enlarging corneal images on a monitor actually allows them to count individual cells.

According to Doherty, with the more sophisticated teaching resources, the students are better prepared when they come to class, and there's more time for question-and-answer sessions.

THE EYE PROJECT

Selected cases from the clinical database are being used in an innovative training program called the EYE Project, an important study and testing tool in helping optometry students prepare for their licensing exam.

To create the training program, Doherty worked with Firehouse Image Center in Indianapolis, which prepared the Photo CDs. "Half the battle is collecting your resources," says Doherty. Bill Rainey served as the consulting expert for the optometry school.

Doherty used Kodak's PhotoEdge software to enhance the images. She created the interactive and text portions of the program in AuthorWare Professional, with the assistance of students in the School of Education's Instructional Systems Technology program.

The result is an interactive program that presents the student with patient information and an image of the patient's eye; the

In the past, students studying eye disorders had to hunt through volumes of slides stored in three-ring binders, then use a projector to study the slides. With PCD technology, not only are the images more accessible, they are integrated with practical study and research.

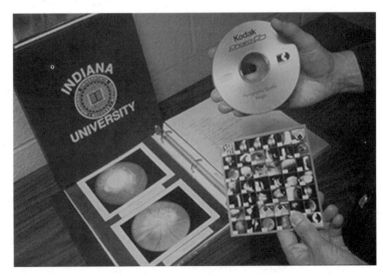

 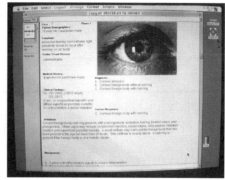

Susan Doherty demonstrates how students use the EYE Project test simulation for preparing for their licensing exam. Shown is a sample screen from the project, which was created with AuthorWare Professional, incorporating PCD images from the school's vast database.

student must then select the correct diagnosis. An incorrect choice triggers an explanation of why it is incorrect, and the student selects again.

This learning model has become extremely popular with students and has become a catalyst for other projects, such as a database of patient case studies, an electronic patient records system, and a national Task Force of Optometry Schools to share electronic research.

PATIENT RECORDS PROJECT AND SEMOR PROJECT

Under Rainey's direction, the IU Optometry clinic's Patient Records Project is investigating and prototyping an electronic format to replace paper records. High-resolution PCD images are integral to these records, along with video and voice annotation.

Running concurrent to the local project is a national project called SEMOR, formed to develop Standards for Electronic Management of Optometric Records. This project is sponsored by the Association of Schools and Colleges of Optometry (ASCO) and is under the direction of IU-Optometry's Larry Thibos. A 1993 ASCO task force established standards that will become guidelines for the design of a national database with text, graphics, and image components for the storage and retrieval of patient data. The goal of the SEMOR project is to use electronic communication technology to shrink the world, making distant competitors into close colleagues.

OTHER PROJECTS

Photo CD authoring and distribution of contact lens information and training is another area being explored at the School of Optometry. Douglas Horner, Sarita Soni, and Carolyn Begley have concurrent projects that address these needs on a global scale.

305

Photo CD delivery via television seems to be a universal answer to the perpetual question of how to deliver contact lens education to people in third world countries, where computer delivery is out of the question. CD authoring and PCD delivery via TV have also created a new opportunity for continuing education among optometrists who must earn credits for license renewal.

"Our projects are further reaching than the field of optometry itself," Doherty reports enthusiastically. "People in other fields, such as veterinary medicine, have seen our presentations. They're amazed at the pictures and are excited about developing similar applications for their field."

Demand for the tools used at IU-Optometry has provided funding for a digital camera and a CD Writer to make the school's applications available to others. The applications are also available on-line, via Mosaic on the Internet.

For more information on any of the IU-Optometry applications, you can contact Susan Doherty via E-mail at **sdoherty@indiana.edu.**

St. Louis University Biomedical Communications

Kirsten Ellis, a medical imager in the department of biomedical communications at St. Louis University's Health Sciences Center, has developed an interactive multimedia program for teaching nurses and other medical staff how to operate an intensive care monitor critical to patient care. She imported PCD images of open-heart surgery, heart specimens, catheter placement, and monitor readings into AuthorWare Professional on an IBM system. The resulting CD-ROM program is being used to train nurses in the operation of the Baxter Swan-Ganz catheter monitor. According to Ellis, this training method provides greater access and a higher learning curve for ever-changing hospital personnel.

IN-CLASS PRESENTATIONS

Another Health Science Center project is to transfer images to PCD for use by professors in in-class presentations. The transfer to Photo CD has not yet started, but among the images the center plans to include are patient photos and information, photomicrographs, pathological images, and medical curriculum for study. These images will be on a network for in-house use. "We would hope to share these images on the Internet eventually, but we're not sure how far it needs to go at this point," says Ellis.

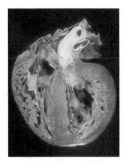

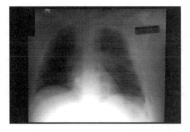

PHOTO IMAGING STATION WITH PORTFOLIO

Images such as these of the Baxter Swan-Ganz catheter monitor, heart tissue, and X-rays have been scanned to PCD and incorporated into a multimedia program for teaching hospital personnel about the monitor.

A Photo CD imaging station with Portfolio has been proposed to provide a multitude of functions. The Departments of Pathology and Radiology would like to store patient images and data and to replace microscopes and histological specimens with images on Photo CD. The Portfolio service will allow creation of in-house tutorials for residents, students, and patients. In addition, the medical library will have access to a greater storage medium. The audiovisual services will also offer video projection for PCD users. In essence, Photo CD will be universally used in as many areas of the medical arena as possible.

307

NEUROSURGERY

Soon, 3D images of brain tissue will be available in the operating room. These images are photographed at different angles to give them depth, a method called cross-polarization. This helps the surgeon visualize the ventral and dorsal (front and back) anatomy of particular areas of brain tissue.

A stereo device called an OR scope is used to aid the surgeon during the operation. Two cameras on either port of the scope take photos of the brain tissue. The film images, correctly set for stereo imaging, are transferred to Photo CD and later will be shown during microsurgery on a TV or computer screen.

The University of Michigan

The University of Michigan is also using Photo CD for a number of medical projects. Professor of Anatomy Brian Athey is working with the School of Information and Library Studies to develop systems that facilitate medical practices and research capabilities.

Athey and his group are currently focused on developing a large repository of medical imagery in PCD file format. Later on, the focus will shift to full multimedia implementation of the image repository, including integration of voice records and selected portions of patient records. "For the initial phase, however, the key is to adequately store the numerous microscope and other nonradiological medical imagery in a stable and accessible form," says Athey. "For some of our purposes we like to have the image pac capability where you can look at the images with different resolutions, from high-resolution for HDTV viewing, to conventional video, to thumbnail pictures for browsing and search."

All of the medical applications are UNIX-based. The school is working with Kodak to bring Photo CD into the UNIX world to run on HP workstations. Once in the database, these images will be brought up by students, doctors, and researchers for study and evaluation.

ARPA TELEPATHOLOGY PROJECT

In conjunction with Department of Defense's Advanced Research Project Agency (ARPA), Athey and a colleague at the Environmental Research Institute of Michigan are leading a consortium of over ten companies, including Eastman Kodak and Hewlett-Packard, to develop a system that stores and retrieves images of pathological specimens. These images will be sent and received over long distances and from remote areas, including rural settings and battlefield medical units. This system will be used in conjunction with DOD hospitals and their flagship Armed Forces Institute of Pathology (AFIP) in Washington, D.C.

Doctors in remote sites will send images to centralized reference laboratory facilities where images are stored and evaluated. In addition to using Photo CD discs to store work performed locally at a "pathologist's workstation," large-format Kodak optical disc media and jukeboxes will be used at the larger central sites. Pathology images will be evaluated and returned to the doctor, providing a long-distance second opinion.

INNER EAR IMAGE REPOSITORY

An internationally and freely accessible image repository of 3D photomicrographs of the inner ear is being developed by the University of Michigan's Kresge Hearing Research Institute and the School of Information and Library Studies. Photo CDs will be arranged with an appropriate database on a Kodak Professional Image Library system. These images will be retrieved and viewed with a 3D effect to study the molecular structure of the inner ear. The 3D effect is possible because the laser scanning confocal microscope collects a full 3D image and produces results similar to those of magnetic resonance imaging (MRI) and computerized axial tomography (CAT) scans for whole-body medical imaging—on a microscopic scale. "We're still in the planning stages," says Professor Miranda Pao of the School of Information and Library Studies, "but we are looking into many different uses for this product. For instance, the next project might be an image library of lung X-rays."

As we have seen, Photo CD, originally designed as a consumer product, has been embraced by professionals in dozens of fields, including medicine.

Some of the many areas being explored by medical researchers and educators include using digital cameras to capture medical and scientific images to be stored on PCD media, storing X-rays and other radiological data on Photo CDs, keeping patient records on Writable CD, disseminating PCD images via on-line databases, and using Portfolio to create tutorials and multimedia incorporating scientific and medical images.

As this technology comes into wider use, we can expect to see many more yet unconceived applications of this highly useful and flexible digitizing approach.

APPENDIX I

Using the Official Photo CD Handbook Portfolio Disc and CD-ROM

You will find bound into the back of this book two discs, a Photo CD Portfolio disc and a CD-ROM disc. The Portfolio disc is an example of Kodak's multimedia production format described in Chapter 15. The CD-ROM disc contains demo software and usable Photo CD and sound files. Both discs can be accessed with a CD-ROM drive on Macintosh or Windows systems.

About the Photo CD Portfolio Disc

The Official Photo CD Handbook disc was created by the Verbum team with the goal of offering a compelling example of this new cross-platform, easy-to-produce format. Like any successful multimedia publication, it has a thoughtfully designed interface, uses sound effectively, and includes high-quality graphics (see color section page C8 for examples of the disc screens).

The disc contains a variety of Portfolio presentations, which are basically "slide shows" of screen images, each with an accompanying sound file. A Portfolio disc can contain several of these sequential presentations, accessed via menu screens with buttons, similar to standard multimedia presentations. A Portfolio disc will play on both Macintosh and Windows computers, as well as on Photo CD players (and other Photo CD–compatible multiplayers, such as CD-I and 3DO) connected to a standard television set.

The disc contents include an overview of the five Photo CD formats; Case Studies of actual Portfolio products; Photography and Digital Art galleries featuring narrated presentations of the artists' works; and a Presentation Gallery with three examples of Portfolio presentations for both professional and personal use. The disc also includes an Introduction, a brief listing of the software included on the companion CD-ROM, and Disc Information about the publication itself. Useful features of the disc include Assist information, accessible from any menu screen, and the Index, a master menu screen that allows you to view and access any of the menu screens or presentations on the disc.

Viewing the Portfolio Disc on a Macintosh or Windows Computer

The Portfolio disc will play on a Photo CD–compatible CD-ROM drive attached to any Mac with System 6.05 or higher and Quick-Draw software, or any IBM-PC AT–compatible 80386 or 80486 with VGA display or better (minimum 256 colors), running DOS 3.3 or higher and Windows 3.0 or higher.

Insert the disc in a CD-ROM drive attached to your Macintosh or Windows computer. Click on the disc icon to open it, then open the Player folder/directory. Open the Mac or Win folder/directory. Double click on the Player icon. You will see the "Portfolio Player" at the bottom of the screen. Click on the Size button to enlarge the screen (it takes a minute to adjust the resolution on the larger screen image).

To go to a section on the disc, or to begin a presentation, click on the appropriate button (note that each button is numbered—you can also press the appropriate number on your keyboard). To move through presentations, click on the Portfolio Player Next and Previous buttons. A few of these presentations are self-running, so when you come to the last screen, clicking on the Next button will take you back to the menu. You can return to the menu while in a presentation on Windows systems by clicking on the Super-Previous button—the one with two arrows. On the Mac, hold down the Option key while clicking on the Previous button.

The Pause button will pause any screen's sound or any self-running presentation. The Restart button will take you back to the Welcome screen at the beginning of the disc. To quit, hit Q on Macs or ALT-F-X on PCs.

VIEWING THE PORTFOLIO DISC ON A TELEVISION

Insert the disc into a Kodak Photo CD player or a compatible multimedia player, such as Panasonic 3DO or Philips CD-I. To go to a section on the disc, or to begin a presentation, press the appropriate number on the remote, then the Play button. (For a diagram of the remote control and all its functions, see page 76.) Give the disc a moment before you press again. Use the Next and Previous buttons to move through presentations. A few of the presentations are self-running. When you come to the last screen, pressing the Next button will return you to the menu. If you want to return to the menu in the middle of a presentation, press the Previous button twice. The Pause button will pause any screen's sound or any self-running presentation. Finally, the Stop button will take you back to the Welcome screen. To quit, simply eject the disc.

HOW THE DISC WAS PRODUCED

Content for *The Official Photo CD Handbook* disc was developed by Michael Gosney. He worked with art director John Odam and authoring expert Ray Baggarley on the disc design. Ray authored the disc using Kodak's Arrange-It software on a Macintosh computer, then premastered it with Kodak's Build-It program on a Sun workstation. Carol Whaley at Eastman Kodak produced the final master on a 74-minute Photo CD Portfolio disc using Build-It. John Odam and Janet Ashford developed the interface and screen graphics using Photoshop 2.5. Most of the photographic images were scanned onto Photo CD or Pro Photo CD discs; a few were scanned with a Nikon desktop scanner.

Sound files were prepared by Jack Lampl using both a Media 100 system and SoundEdit Pro software on Mac systems. In some cases Ray Baggarley tweaked the final sound using Sound Designer II on a Mac system. Original music for this disc was composed, performed, and recorded by Janet Ashford on a Fostex Multi-tracker recorder, using a variety of acoustic instruments and an electric guitar. The master tape was mixed by Eric Thompson, who also recorded actress Reegan Ray's narration. Much of the audio content for this disc—the Introduction and About Photo CD sections, for example—was done by direct digital recording. The Case Studies section, including the narration, was created by Kathy Bauer and her team at Advanced Digital Imaging in Colorado.

313

DISC CONTENTS

The Contents screen is the main menu of the disc. From the Contents screen, you can reach the various sections of the disc. Button number 1 offers an overview of the five Photo CD formats.

Number 2 takes you to the Case Study section, with a selection of Photo CD Portfolio examples. Number 3, the Photography Gallery, features narrated photography presentations by Kurt Jafay, Greg Gorman, Graham Nash, and Craig McClain. Button 4 will take you to the Digital Art Gallery, with artists Dana Atchley, Mike Swartzbeck, Diane Fenster, and Frank Tycer. Button 5 leads to the Presentation Gallery, featuring the work of visionary architect Paolo Soleri, astronomer Dennis Mammana's Hubble Space Telescope show, and Amy and David Jacobs' San Francisco wedding. Button 6 is the Introduction. Button 7 offers information about the On-Disc Software contained on the companion CD-ROM you can use on your PC or Mac. Button 8 tells the who, what, and how of this disc. Finally, the Index screen, button 10, provides quick access to everything on the disc. If you need help at any time, select Assist from any menu screen.

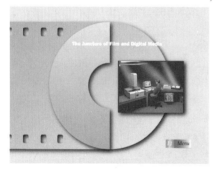

INTRODUCTION

In Michael Gosney's introduction to the disc, he touches briefly on the overall concept of Photo CD, its current applications, and some of the possibilities for this exciting new medium. It concludes with images of the all-star *Official Photo CD Handbook* team—not to be missed!

OVERVIEW OF PHOTO CD

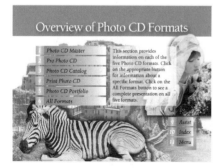

This section offers brief overviews of the five Photo CD formats. For each format, a screen lists key features, accompanied by a narration. You may select formats individually, or hit button 6 to review all formats. Hitting the menu button will get you back to the main menu screen, or you can call up the Index

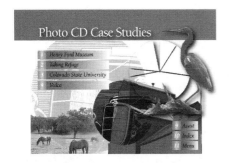

screen with button 10. You can select the Assist button from any menu. For navigation instructions, select buttons 1 or 2 on this screen. Button 11 will return you to the menu screen.

PHOTO CD CASE STUDIES

Select any of the buttons to view excerpted material from exemplary real-world Photo CD Portfolio presentations.

PHOTOGRAPHY GALLERY

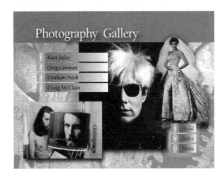

The photography gallery features narrated presentations from four outstanding photographers. Kurt Jafay is an innovative portrait photographer, now living in Denver, whose work in the 1950s set standards for official presidential and Miss America portraits, as well as classic Hollywood publicity photos. Los Angeles–based Greg Gorman is one of today's top photographers specializing in personality portraits of such figures as Robert DeNiro, Bette Davis, and Kim Basinger. Rock legend Graham Nash, long-time photographer and fine-art photography collector, shares his photos from the early days of Crosby, Stills and Nash. San Diegan Craig McClain's works exemplify the new wave of photography combining traditional and digital tools.

DIGITAL ART GALLERY

The Digital Art Gallery presents the work of four adventurous artists experimenting in the digital domain. Dana Atchley, based in San Francisco, is a well-known multimedia performance artist.

Big Drive, a tour of roadside attractions, was assembled by the artist as a branching Portfolio presentation. Mike Swartzbeck's collage techniques have inspired many digital artists. Diane Fenster, an instructor at San Francisco State University, has made waves in both fine art and commercial illustration circles with her thoughtful photo montage compositions. Frank Tycer, aka "Nar," combines a wide variety of programs in producing his "blendo" works.

315

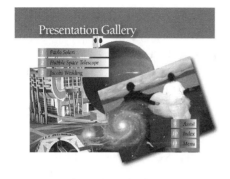

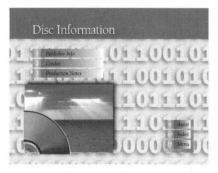

316

Frank accompanied his visuals with unique audio pieces produced on the Macintosh.

PRESENTATION GALLERY

We assembled the Presentation Gallery to showcase interesting subject matter presented as narrated slide shows. Visionary architect Paolo Soleri proposes ecological city designs. This is a concise presentation of his ideas and work, including the Arcosanti model city project in Arizona. The Hubble Space Telescope takes photography to revolutionary heights in this presentation by San Diego astronomer Dennis Mammana. Multimedia mavens Amy and David Jacobs captured their wedding in pictures and sound and put together their own Portfolio presentation.

ON-DISC SOFTWARE

This is a listing of the software available on the CD-ROM that accompanies this book. To use any of this software, or the images and clip media, just copy it onto your hard disk.

DISC INFORMATION

Choose Publisher Info, for ordering information, copyright, legalese and the like; select Credits to find out who made this disc; and click on Production Notes for info on how we did it.

ASSIST

If you need help at any time, just select Assist from any menu screen. Listen to the brief narration, then select button 1, 2, or 3 for more detailed narrations, or the menu button to return.

INDEX

Use the Index screen for instant access to any menu or presentation on the disc. Just make a selection and you're there! Hit the menu button to return.

MENU

Select this button any time to return to the menu screen from which you started.

That's it—we packed a lot of stimulating material into this Portfolio disc to provide an enjoyable and informative experience. We hope we've succeeded and that the disc inspires you in your own work with Photo CD!

About the CD-ROM Disc

This disc is a hybrid CD-ROM that will play on either Macintosh or Windows systems. It contains demo software you can use, as well as Photo CD images and clip-media files. To use any of the software, images, or clip media, just copy them onto your hard disk.

We've divided the disc into three sections: Windows, Macintosh, and Photo CD/clip media files.

WINDOWS APPLICATIONS

1. **Microsoft PowerPoint** is a popular presentation authoring application that allows you to develop slide shows with text, graphics, sound, and images.

2. **ImagePals 2** catalogs Photo CD images into visual thumbnail "albums." You can search and sort through these albums by description, subject, keyword, file name, data type and more.

3. **LEADVIEW** is a Photo CD–supported image-management system that lets you convert image files among many popular formats, with background modem communications capabilities.

4. **Photo Factory for Windows** is a multifunction image-editing and presentation program, with a focus on the Photo CD format (it also works with seven other popular formats). You can create slide shows and screen savers directly from Photo CD images.

5. **Image AXS** is an application for cataloging, retrieving, and displaying still and moving pictures. With unlimited projects, "smart" keywords, a 32,000-character text field, seven user-definable alphanumeric fields, and a dozen file information fields, you can organize your visual media any way you want.

6. **AuthorWare** boasts the broadest range of capabilities among current multimedia authoring tools. Unsurpassed in its ability to incorporate video into a project, it supports 24-bit graphics and stereo sound, as well as Macromedia Director animation files.

7. **Kudo Image Browser** creates self-contained catalogs so you can distribute your images for viewing by people who don't have the program. It offers extensive search capabilities and supports multiple file formats.

MACINTOSH APPLICATIONS

1. **Adobe Acrobat** is a Reader program that lets you view and print any document in the Portable Document Format (PDF). Virtually any document created on a Macintosh, DOS, Windows, UNIX, or other computer can be converted into the Portable Document Format—regardless of the application and fonts used to create the document. PDF files retain all the graphics, formatting, and fonts of the original document.

2. **Adobe Dimensions** is designed to take PostScript art from programs such as Illustrator and FreeHand and give it a 3D look. Unlike other programs that convert outline type to bit-map format, Dimensions works on type in its native vector format.

3. **Adobe Illustrator** is a powerful design tool with an elegant interface. It includes superb text-handling capabilities and handy automatic graphing, and it saves files in an EPS format that is fully compatible with Photoshop and Premiere.

4. **Adobe Photoshop** is the leading image-editing program, allowing you to create original artwork, retouch and composite scanned photographs, and prepare high-quality separations and output with maximum flexibility.

5. **Adobe Premiere** brings the world of digital movie-making to the desktop. Premiere works with Apple QuickTime software to let you record, create, and play movies from video, sound, animations, photographs, drawings, text, and other materials.

6. **DeBabelizer** from Equilibrium Technologies is an "image-operating system" that simplifies many repetitive image-processing tasks. It translates to and from over 40 graphics file formats and lets you automate, or "batch," tedious manipulation and editing operations.

7. **Kudo Image Browser** creates self-contained catalogs so you can distribute your images for viewing by people who don't have the program. It offers extensive search capabilities and supports multiple file formats for the Macintosh.

8. **Kodak Create-It** is presentation authoring software that is specifically designed to develop slide shows of Photo CD images. In addition to incorporating text, graphics, and sound, it allows for limited branching. Create-It presentations can be published in Kodak's Photo CD Portfolio format using Kodak Build-It software.

9. **Kodak Arrange-It** is a more advanced multimedia authoring application that provides greater flexibility and power in developing interactive presentations for publication in Kodak's Photo CD Portfolio format using Kodak Build-It software.

10. **Kodak Picture Exchange** is a worldwide on-line image service. You use search utilities to sort through Photo CD images online. Then you can call to order or download the "real" image.

11. **Cumulus PowerPro** is software for cataloging and managing images, sounds, animations, and documents. Its networking features let you build your database and manage its files across a range of client and server machines, and it's exceptionally fast for finding and retrieving documents.

12. **Apple PhotoFlash** is a page-layout companion that lets you quickly and easily acquire photos, enhance them, and place them in your documents. An integrated browser simplifies image selection, and automatic photo-enhancement tools let you remove dust and scratches, balance exposures, and otherwise tweak your images the way you want them.

13. **AuthorWare Professional** boasts the broadest range of capabilities among current multimedia authoring tools. Unsurpassed in its ability to incorporate video into a project, it supports 24-bit graphics and stereo sound, as well as Macromedia Director animation files.

14. **SoundEdit Pro** is sound-editing software from Farallon that supports 8-bit stereo sampling at 22kHz, 11kHz, 7.3 kHz, and 5.5 kHz. In addition to 6:1 and 3:1 compression, SoundEdit offers proprietary 4:1 and 8:1 compression options.

15. **KPT Bryce** is a powerful image-generation tool for creating backgrounds, 3D textures, and landscapes.

16. **Aldus Fetch** lets you catalog clip art, digitized photos, presentations, QuickTime movies, sounds, and more in a common visual database for fast browsing and retrieval. Items can be copied, previewed, played, printed, placed, or opened by the editing application of your choice.

17. **Image AXS** is an application for cataloging, retrieving, and displaying still and moving pictures. With unlimited projects, "smart" keywords, a 32,000-character text field, seven user-definable alphanumeric fields, and a dozen file information fields, you can organize your visual media any way you want.

PHOTO CD IMAGES AND CLIP MEDIA

1. **Corel Professional Photos** contains 100 photographs of people, famous cities, nature, and more. All images are completely royalty-free, with no additional fees.

2. **Gazelle Technologies Professional Photo Collection** features several different EduCorp collections, each containing 100 royalty-free Photo CD images.

3. **Digital Stock Professional Photos Signature Series** is professional stock photography collection that includes Western Scenics, Undersea Textures, and Food. Each disc contains the work of one world-class photographer shooting his/her special area of photographic interest.

4. **DiAMAR Portfolios** includes six volumes of clip photos, all avaiable in Photo CD, CMYK TIFF, and b&w TIFF formats.

5. **CMCD, Inc. Visual Symbol Sampler** is representative of CMCD's growing library of CD-ROMs. each containing over 100 Photo CD images.

6. **HiRez Audio** from Presto Studios offers several volumes of digitized music. Styles run the gamut from classical to R&B.

APPENDIX II

Photo CD Service Providers

U.S. PIW Service Providers by State

There are 30,000 places worldwide where Photo CD disc orders can be dropped off. As with other types of photofinishing, these orders are passed along to main processing sites. The following list is of main Photo CD processing sites (for either Master or Pro discs) in the United States, listed alphabetically by state.

Capital Film Works
909 Forest Avenue
Montgomery AL 36106
205-263-9718

Praxis Digital Imaging
2632 East Thomas
Phoenix AZ 85016
602-956-0529

Newell Colour Lab
221 North Westmoreland
Los Angeles CA 90004
213-380-2980

Zzyzx (A&I Photo)
1011 N. Orange Drive
Hollywood CA 90038
213-886-5260

Visual Creations
222 Standard Street
El Segundo CA 90245

LUNA Imaging
1315 Innes Place
Venice CA 90291
310-452-8370

Miller Imaging Center
2718 Wilshire Blvd.
Santa Monica CA 90403
310-264-4711

Finley Holiday Film Corp.
12607 East Philadelphia
Whittier CA 90601
310-945-3325

Dan Wolfe Productions
45 East Walnut
Pasadena CA 91103
818-584-4000

Photomation
2551 West La Palma
Anaheim CA 92801
714-236-2121

Alpha CA Imaging
675 Menlo Avenue
Menlo Park CA 94025
415-325-4877

Color 2000
570 Jessie Street
San Francisco CA 94103
415-861-5151

Zap Photography (ITS CD)
1588 Noriega Street
San Francisco CA 94122
415-731-3251

Custom Process
1700 Fifth Street
Berkeley CA 94710
510-6527-6900

Photo Drive Up
1900 Camden Drive
San Jose CA 95124
408-559-0400

Palmer Photographic
2313 C Street
Sacramento CA 95816
916-441-3305

Camillia Color
2010 Alahambra Blvd.
Sacramento CA 95817
916-454-3807

Robert Waxman, Inc.
1514 Curtis Street
Denver CO 80202
303-623-1200

Werner's Mile High Lab
1641 California Street
Denver CO 80202
303-446-0633

Amaranth
2540 Frontier Avenue
Boulder CO 80301
303-443-2550

Advanced Digital Imaging
230 South College Avenue
Fort Collins CO 80524
303-484-0188

Slide Effects
143 Myrtle Avenue
Stamford CT 06902
203-324-6000

Best Photo
143 Federal Road
Brookfield CT 06804
203-775-2377

Foto One
280 Connecticut Avenue
Norwalk CT 06850
203-855-0330

Data World Service
111 High Ridge Road
Stamford CT 06905
203-329-8926

Horizon Technical
122 Boone Street
Pensacola FL 32505
904-477-3770

Ross Ehlert Photo Labs
505 Lake Destiny Drive
Orlando FL 32810
407-660-0606

Dale Laboratories
2960 Simms Street
Hollywood FL 33020
305-920-3648

Thomson Photo Lab
4210 Ponce de Leon Blvd.
Coral Gable FL 33146
305-443-0669

Slide Imagers
(Presentation Services)
22 7th Street NE
Atlanta GA 30308
404-873-5353

Meteor Photo Imaging
680 14th Street NW
Atlanta GA 30318
404-892-1688

Wolf Camera Lab
3036 Commerce Way
Hapeville GA 30354
404-768-6419

Alto Services
46-056 Kamehameha
Highway
Kaneohe HI 96744
808-247-6737

CD Factory I
1526 Walnut Street
Des Moines IA 50309
515-244-9231

Boyd Fitzgerald
5001 B Tremont
Davenport IA 52807
319-386-6722

Crest Photo Lab
955 Brandt Drive
Elgin IL 60120
708-697-0700

Imageland (CPI)
333 North Michigan
Chicago IL 60601
312-984-1003

Helix
310 South Racine
Chicago IL 60607
312-421-6000

Imperial Color
219 North Carpenter
Chicago IL 60607
312-421-3338

Ross Ehlert
225 West Illinois
Chicago IL 60610
312-644-0244

Caterpillar Imaging
1335 SW Washington
Peoria IL 61612
309-675-8989

Firehouse Color Lab
1030 East Washington
Indianapolis IN 46202
317-236-1747

Mossberg & Company
301 East Maple Street
South Bend IN 46624
219-289-9253

Digital Imaging System
Center
1117 1/2 N. College
Avenue
Bloomington IN 47404
812-334-3420

CD Factory
128 Abbie Street
Kansas City KS 66202

CD Factory
6811 West 63rd Street
Shawnee Mission KS
66202
913-451-8811

Publishing Systems, Inc.
3500 West 75th Street
Suite 324
Prairie Village KS 66208
316-235-2216

Hanson Graphics
1500 L&A Road
Metairle LA 70001
504-834-4864

Boston Photo Lab
20 Newbury Street
Boston MA 20116
617-267-4086

Nobles Camera Shop
65 South Street
Hingham MA 20432
617-749-0588

Ritz Camera Shop
6711 Ritz Way
Beltsville MD 20705

Bara-King Photographic
4805 Frolich Lane
Hyattsville MD 20781
301-322-7900

Digix
1 Choke Cherry Road
Rockville MD 20850
301/977-0519

Regester Photo
50 Kane Street
Baltimore MD 21224
410-633-7600

Kibby Laboratories, Inc.
25235 Dequindre
Madison Heights MI
48071
313-544-3231

Color Perfect
3522 Rochester Road
Troy MI 48083
313-872-5115

Meteor Photo Imaging
1099 Chicago Road
Troy MI 48083
313-583-3090

Pro Color
909 Hennepin Ave South
Minneapolis MN 55403
612-673-8900

Prism Studios
25412 Nicollet Avenue
Minneapolis MN 55404
612-872-1060

Creative Visuals
731 Harding Street NE
Minneapolis MN 55413
612-378-1621

Art-Tech Photo
36 North Central
Clayton MO 63105
314-721-4888

Allied Photocolor
3218 Olive
St. Louis MO 63130
314-652-4000

McNab Inc.
16 East Main Street
Bozeman MT 59715
406-587-1300

Robin Matthews
2015 Ivy Road
Suite 311
Charlottesville NC 22903
804-295-3332

Applied CD Technologies
5600 Seventy-Seven Drive
Charlotte NC 28217
704-334-6766

Holigraphics
8311 Spring Plaza
Omaha NE 68124
402-391-2961

Advanced Photographics
2456-A Route 22
Union NJ 07083

PRO-SET
86 Lakawana Avenue
West Patterson NJ -7424
201-256-6626

QPL
1 East Main Street
Ramsey NJ 07446
201-825-7777

Applied Graphics
Technologies
50 West 23rd Street
New York NY 10010
212-627-4111

Colorite Film Processing
115 East 31st Street
New York NY 10016
212-532-2116

K&L Custom
Photographics
222 East 44th Street
New York NY 10017
212-661-5600

Showbran Inc.
1347 1/2 Broadway
New York NY 10018
212-947-9151

Raffi Custom Color
21 West 46th Street
New York NY 10036
212-302-5700

Speed Graphics
342 Madison Avenue
New York NY 10123
212-682-6520

Calev's Photo Store
21-20 45th Road
Long Island City NY
11101
718-361-1513

Campos Photography
Center
1016 Niagara Falls Blvd.
Tonawanda NY 14150
716-837-1016

Images, Images
(American Color Labs)
30 Corporate Woods
#350
Rochester NY 14623
716-273-1600

Wegmans Markets
3131 Winton Road South
Rochester NY 14623
716-272-4790

Chroma Studios
2300 Marilyn Lane
Columbus OH 44319
614-471-1191

AC Color Labs
2310 Superior Avenue
Cleveland OH 44114
216-621-4575

KSK Color Lab
32300 Aurora Road
Solon OH 44139
216-248-0208

Prism Photo
1256 Park Ave West
Mansfield OH 44906
419-529-4444

Robin Color Lab
2106 Central Parkway
Cincinnati OH 45214
513-381-5116

Lazerquick
2959 SW Cedar Hills
Beaverton OR 97005
503-644-9196

WY East Color Inc.
4200 SW Corbett Ave
Portland OR 97201
503-228-7307

Filmet Color Lab
7436 Washington
Pittsburgh PA 15218
412-351-3510

Fidelity Digital
620C East Oregon Road
Lititz PA 17543
717-581-8182

Camera Shop
485 Parkway South
Broomall PA 19008
215-690-1377

Centennial Printing
875 First Avenue
King of Prussia PA 19406
215-992-9700

Chromatics
625 Fogg Street
Nashville TN 37203
615-254-0063

Wal Mart Photo
331 West Lincoln
Tullahoma TN 37388
404-455-0099

Coupralux
2607 Caroline Street
Dallas TX 75201
214-220-0078

Color Place
1330 Conant
Dallas TX 75207
214-631-7174

Meisel Photographic
9645 Webb Chapel Road
Dallas TX 75220
214-352-6711

Barry's Corporate Lab
11171 Harry Hins Blvd.
Dallas TX 75229
214-241-0582

City Color
7300 Ambassador Row
Dallas TX 75247
214-951-9696

Dallas PhotoImaging
3942 Irving Blvd.
Dallas TX 75247
214-630-4351

NPL Inc.
1926 West Gray
Houston TX 77019
713-527-9300

Image Output
19 Briar Hollow #120
Houston TX 77027
713-621-3770

Fox Imaging Center (CPI)
1813 S- Post Oak Blvd.
Houston TX 77056
713-965-0971

Houston Photolab
5250 Gulfton #3-D
Houston TX 77081
713-666-0282

Photo Tech
675 Easy 2100 S
Suite O
Salt Lake City UT 84106
801-466-7039

Borge Anderson
234 South 200 East
Salt lake City UT 84111
801-359-7703

Bailey's Photographic
Center
5819 Leesburg Pike
Bailey's Crossroads VA
22041
703-941-9100

Publisher's Service Bureau
(Murad)
4300 King Street
Suite 105
Alexandria VA 22302
703-824-8022

Photo Link
(Photography, Inc.)
4544 Eisenhower Avenue
Alexandria VA 22304
703-370-3701

Pacific Color
7107 Woodlawn Ace NE
Seattle WA 98115
206-524-7200

Argentum Photo & Digital
Imaging
2001 4th Avenue
Seattle WA 98121
206-448-9027

Crivello Camera Center
18110 W. Bluemound
Road
Brookfield WI 53045
414-782-4303

Image Systems, Inc.
N94 W14530 Garwin
Mace
Menomonee Falls WI
53501
414-255-3300

Reimers Photo
300 East Bay Street
Milwaukee WI 53207
414-744-4471

Northwoods Personally
Yours
Highway 51 North
Woodruff WI 54568
715-356-4663

324

U.S. Portfolio Service Providers

All Sir Speedy "Team CD" sites are dropoff points for having your Portfolio discs written. In addition, the following U.S. service bureaus offer Portfolio services.

Copies Now Ctr
159 Dauphin St
Mobile AL 36602
205-483-COPY

Praxis Digital Imaging
2632 E Thomas Ave
Phoenix AZ 85016
602-956-0529

Alpha CD Imaging
675 Menlo Ave
Menlo Park CA 94025
415-325-4877

Custom Process
1700 Fifth St
Berkeley CA 94710
510-527-6900

Lazerquick Copies
17815 Newhope St
Ste O
Fountain Valley CA 92708
714-241-1962

Copies Now Ctr
575 Anton Blvd Plaza
Level
Costa Mesa CA 92626
714-966-9056

Copies Now Ctr
2540 Main St
Ste P
Irvine CA 92714
714-476-8606

Copies Now Ctr
1292 E Colorado Blvd
Pasadena CA 91106
818-793-2150

Copies Now Ctr
509 L St
Sacramento CA 95814
916-443-7565

Copies Now Ctr
5722 Telephone Rd 12
Ventura Village Shopping
Center
Ventura CA 93003
805-339-0800

Finley Holiday Film Corp
12607 E Philadelphia St
Whittier CA 90601
800-345-6707

Miller Imaging Inc
2718 Wilshire Blvd
Santa Monica CA 90403
310-264-4711

Camellia Color Corp
2010 Alhambra Blvd
Sacramento CA 95817
916-454-3801

Corporate Images, Inc.
10 Jackson St.
San Francisco CA 94111
415-421-9900

Advanced Digital Imaging
230 S College Ave
Ft Collins CO 80524
303-484-0188

Advanced Digital Imaging
112 E Olive St
Fort Collins CO 80524
800-888-3686

Copies Now Ctr
147 Williams St
Middletown CT 06457
203-346-2679

Copies Now Ctr
1960 Silas Deane Hwy
Rocky Hill CT 06067
203-257-3170

Copies Now Ctr
34 Midgeon Ave
Torrington CT 06790
203-496-0930

Copies Now Ctr
218 S Palafox
Pensacola FL 32501
904-438-3308

Franklins
135 Internatinal Blvd NW
Atlanta GA 30303
404-525-0406

Slide Imagers
22 7th St
Atlanta GA 30308
404-873-5353

Disc Maker
627 South St
Ste 101A
Honolulu HI 96813
808-521-3472

Rand McNally
8255 N Central Pk
Skokie IL 60076
708-329-2107

Copies Now Ctr
111 W Washington St
Chicago IL 60602
312-236-5587

Copies Now Ctr
209 S LaSalle St
Chicago IL 60604
312-541-1948

Copies Now Ctr
6111 N River Rd
Des Plaines IL 60018
708-292-2679

Copies Now Ctr
4010 Dupont Cir
Ste L7
Louisville KY 40207
502-899-1111

325

Copies Now Ctr
911 S Lewis St
Ste 1
New Iberia LA 70560
318-364-8714

Boston Photo Lab
20 Newbury St
Boston MA 02116
617-267-4086

Copies Now Ctr
7700 Wisconsin Ave
Bethesda MD 20814
301-907-0101

Meteor Photo
Imaging
1099 Chicago Rd
Troy MI 48007
810-583-3090

Prism Studios
2412 Nicollet Ave
Minneapolis MN 55404
612-872-1060

Copies Now Ctr
574 Prairie Center Dr
Eden Prairie MN 55344
612-943-2679

Copies Now Ctr
12 S Sixth St
Ste 225
Minneapolis MN 55402
612-338-2679

Copies Now Ctr
701 Fourth Ave S
Skyway Level
Minneapolis MN 55415
612-334-5679

Copies Now Ctr
1254 Hennepin Ave
Laurel Village
Minneapolis MN 55403
612-376-0888

Copies Now Ctr
101 E 5th St
Ste 295
Saint Paul MN 55101
612-291-0800

Holigraphic Inc
8311 Spring Pl
Omaha NE 68124
402-391-2961

Advanced Photographic
2456 Rt 22
Union NJ 07083
800-PHO-TOCD

Campos Photography Ctr
1016 Niagara Falls Blvd
Tonawanda NY 14150
716-837-1016

Images Images Inc
30 Corporate Woods
Ste 350
Rochester NY 14623
716-273-8100

Copies Now Center
930 Allerton Ave
Bronx NY 10469
718-798-8300

Copies Now Ctr
349 W Commercial St
East Rochester NY 14445
716-248-2840

Copies Now Ctr
199 North Ave
New Rochelle NY 10801
914-633-8551

Visual In Seitz Inc
225 Oak St
Rochester NY 146081702
716-454-4350

Digifilm Svcs Inc
119 W 57th St
New York NY 10019
800-943-3444

Coloright Film Processing
Inc
115 E 31st St
New York, NY 10016

KSK Color Lab
32300 Aurora Rd
Solon OH 44139
216-248-0208

Copies Now Ctr
426 Walnut St
Cincinnati OH 45202
513-421-8232

Lazerquick Copies
all Oregon locations

Copies Now Ctr
1206 SW 6th Ave
Pacwest Center
Portland OR 97204
503-243-3555

Copies Now Ctr
One World Trade Ctr
903 SW 1st Ave
Portland OR 97204
503-243-2234

Filmet
7436 Washington St
Pittsburgh PA 15218
412-351-3510

Quick Photo
1459 Sumter St.
Columbia SC 29201
803-254-9329

Copies Now Ctr
17 College St
Ste A
Greenville SC 29601
803-233-0870

NEC Inc
1504 Elmhill Pike
Nashville TN 37210
615-367-9110

Copies Now Ctr
124 Ridgeway Center
Oak Ridge TN 37830
615-482-3700

The Color Place
1330 Conant
Dallas TX 75207
214-631-7174

Kwik Kopy Corp Copy
Club
One Kwik Kopy Ln
Cypress TX 77429
800-231-1304

326

Dallas Photo Imaging
3942 Irving Blvd
Dallas TX 75247
214-630-4351

Copies Now Ctr
811 Rusk
Ste B-111
Houston TX 77002
713-222-2669

Copies Now Ctr
215 S State St
Ste 150
Salt Lake City UT 84111
801-328-1010

Picture Conversion Inc
5134 Leesburg Pike
Alexandria VA 22302
703-998-5777

Action Graphics of VA
Inc
2317 Westwood Ave
#101
Richmond VA 23230
809-359-2118

Lazerquick Copies
All Washington locations

Copies Now Ctr
1300 N State St
Ste 205
Bellingham WA 98225
206-647-7565

Copies Now Ctr
22121 17th St SE
Ste 114
Bothell WA 98021
206-483-4567

Copies Now Ctr
1111 Main St.
Ste 110
Vancouver WA 98660
206-695-4645

APPENDIX III

Technical Information

Hardware and Software Requirements for Portfolio Components

CREATE-IT HARDWARE AND SOFTWARE REQUIREMENTS

- Macintosh II or later computer with at least 3 MB of RAM. Additional RAM is recommended if you will be using photographs or creating large presentations.

- 12 MB of hard disk space (required for installing Create-It). Additional hard disk space is recommended if you will be using photographs or creating large presentations.

- Color monitor and 8- or 24-bit color video display card.

- CD-ROM XA mode 2 drive—CD-ROM drives with the Photo CD logo have been certified by Kodak as capable of reading multisession Photo CDs.

- Operating system 7.01 or higher.

- Optional Apple QuickTime System extension Version 1.5 or later.

- Device and media for carrying script files to the Build-It site. Check with your Build-It service provider in advance to find out what devices and media they support. For example:

    SCSI removable hard disk, any capacity
    SyQuest cartridge (44 MB or 88 MB)
    Magneto-optical (MO) 3.5 inch,128 MB disc

Any sound application that you can use to create AIFF audio files. You can also capture voice annotation using the Create-It application and a microphone connected to your Macintosh.

ARRANGE-IT HARDWARE AND SOFTWARE REQUIREMENTS

- Macintosh II or later computer with at least 8 MB of RAM (4MB if virtual memory will be used) and a hard disk drive.

- Operating system 7.01 or higher.

- CD-ROM drive required if images will be imported from CDs; if, on the other hand, you plan to use Arrange-It for other reasons (for example, to link TIFF files together) you do not need a CD-ROM drive.

- If you plan to do any photo editing or to create and edit text in images, one or more applications such as Create-It or Adobe Photoshop.

- Device and media for carrying files to the Build-It service provider. For example:

  > SCSI removable hard disk, any capacity
  > SyQuest cartridge (44 MB or 88 MB)
  > Magneto-optical (MO) 3.5 inch,128 MB disc

329

BUILD-IT HARDWARE REQUIREMENTS

- SUN SPARCstation, Power Macintosh, or Windows NT computer (486/50-based processor) with at least 64 MB of RAM

- A minimum of one 2-GB hard disk or two 1-GB hard disks recommended

- 16-inch color monitor

- 8- or 24-bit color board

- Three-button mouse

- One or more multisession CD-ROM drives

- Kodak PCD Writer 200 and a dedicated SCSI host adapter

CD-ROM Drive Speeds for Accessing Photo CD Images

	Technique of opening Photo CD*	Computer Platform	Processor /Speed	CD ROM Drive 1X Speed	CD ROM Drive 2X Speed	Internal Hard Disk
Photoshop Plug-ins	Photo CD Acquire Module/Photoshop v 2.0.1 (RGB)	Mac	68040/40	2:00	2:00	2:00
	Photo CD Acquire Module/Photoshop v 2.2 (RGB)[1]	Mac	68040/40	1:05	1:05	1:05
	Kodak CMS Open/Photoshop v 2.1 (RGB)	Mac	68040/40	4:50	4:40	4:44
	Kodak CMS Open/Photoshop v 2.1 (CMYK)[2]	Mac	68040/40	7:10	7:10	7:10
	Photo CD Acquire Module/Photoshop (RGB)	PC	Pentium/90	3:35	3:35	3:38
	Photo CD CMS Open/Photoshop (RGB)	PC	Pentium/90	4:45	4:45	4:35
Other	Human Software CD-Q (CMYK)[3]	Mac	68040/40	5:03	5:03	5:03
	Purup PhotoImpress software (CMYK)	Mac	68040/40	6:50	6:50	6:50
	Photo CD Open/PhotoStyler	PC	Pentium/66	1:14	1:14	1:14
	Kodak Photo CD Access Plus (CMYK)[4]	Mac	68040/25	7:03	7:03	7:05

*All timings are for Base*16 file (18 MB for RGB, 24MB for CMYK images).
In most cases faster CD-ROM speed does not translate into faster open times.
Faster processors and clock speeds deliver Photo CD images more quickly than slower processors and clock speeds.

Notes:
1. Version 2.2 takes advantage of Storm acceleration on machines with SuperMac, Storm, Radius and others that feature Storm Technologies' acceleration firmware. Version 2.2 is otherwise the same as 2.0.1.
2. This timing was done with the CMS SWOP standard CMYK profile for coated papers.
3. CD-Q runs considerably faster when Unsharp Masking is not active. This test uses no unsharp masking.
4. Photo CD Access Plus can use the CMS color profiles for converting its images into CMYK. For this test, the CMS SWOP coated paper color profile was used as the output profile.

330

APPENDIX IV
Software Resources

Adobe Systems
Incorporated
1585 Charleston Road
Mountain View, CA
94039
800-833-6687
Adobe ColorCentral
Adobe Dimensions
Adobe Illustrator
Adobe Photoshop 2.5
Adobe Photoshop 3.0
Adobe Premiere
Aldus PhotoStyler
Aldus PageMaker
Aldus Fetch
Aldus Freehand
Aldus Gallery Effects
Aldus Persuasion

Andromeda Software, Inc.
849 Old Farm Road
Thousand Oaks, CA
91360
800-547-0055
Andromeda Series I & II

Aladdin Systems, Inc.
165 Westridge Drive
Watsonville, CA 95076
Stuffit

Apple Computer, Inc.
20525 Mariani Avenue
Cupertino, CA 95014
408-996-1010
Apple Media Tool
Apple PhotoFlash
Apple QuickTime
AppleScript
MacTP

Archetype
100 5th Avenue
2nd Floor
Waltham, MA 02154
617-890-7544
Intercept
Design

Asymmetrix
110 110th Avenue NE
Bellevue, WA 98004
800-448-6543
Multimedia Toolbox

CANTO
800 Duboce Avenue
San Francisco, CA 94117
800-332-2686
Cumulus PowerPro 2.0
Cumulus PowerLite

Claris Corporation
5201 Patrick Henry Drive
Santa Clara, CA 95052-
8168
800-0325-2747
Claris XTND
Hypercard
MacDraw
MacPaint

Corel Corporation
1600 Carling Avenue
Ottawa, ONT K12 8R7
CANADA
800-836-3000
CorelDraw!
Corel Gallery
Corel Mosaic
Corel Presents
Corel Professional Photos

Daystar Digital, Inc.
5556 Atlanta Highway
Flowery Branch, GA
30542
800-532-7853
ColorMatch

DeltaPoint, Inc.
2 Harris Court Suite B-1
Monterey, CA 93940
408-648-4000
Graphic Tools

Deneba Software
3305 NW 74th Avenue
Miami, FL 33122
305-596-5644
Canvas

DIAMAR Interactive
Corporation
P.O. Box 4902
Seattle, WA 98104-0902
800-234-2627
Diamar Portfolios

Digidesign, Inc.
1360 Willow Road
Suite 101
Menlo Park, CA 94025
415-688-0600
ProTools
Sound Design II
SoundTools

Digital Collections, Inc.
1301 Marina Village
Parkway
Alameda, CA 94501
510-814-7200
Image AXS Software

Digital Stock Corporation
400 S. Sierra Avenue
Suite 100
Solana Beach, CA 92075
*Professional Series Photo
CDs*

DMMS Software
4617 Willow Lane
Dallas, TX 75244
214-404-9748
PhotoStep

Eastman Kodak Company
343 State Street
Rochester, New York
14650
800-242-2424 ext. 77
800-CD-KODAK (orders)
Create-It, Arrange-It, Build-It
Kodak Browser
Kodak Picture Exchange
Kodak's Precision Color
Kodak Shoebox
Management System
Photo Acquire Model
Photo CD Access
Photo CD Access Plus
PhotoEdge
Professional CD Library
QuickTopix

Eastman Kodak Company
CMS Division
164 Lexington Road
Billerica, MA 01821
800-75-KODAK
Kodak CMS Profiles
and Starter Pack

Equilibrium Technologies
475 Gate Five Road
Suite 225
Sausalito CA 94965
415-332-4343
DeBabelizer
DeBabelizer Lite

Electronics for Imaging
2855 Campus Drive
San Mateo, CA 94403
415-286-8600
EfiColor Profiles
EfiColor Xtension

Fractal Design
 Corporation
335 Spreckels Drive
Aptos, CA 95003
408-688-5300
Fractal Design Painter

Frame Technology
1010 Rincon Circle
San Jose, CA 95131
408-433-3311
FrameMaker

FSI Software
P.O. Box 748
Columbia, GA 31902-0748
706-324-6308
The Kolorist

Gazelle Technologies
7434 Trade Street
San Diego, CA 92121
619-536-9999
Professional Photo
Collections

Gold Disk, Inc.
P.O. Box 789 Streetsville
Mississauga, Ontario
CANADA L5M2C2
Astound

Helios Software AG
Lavesstrasse 80
W3000 Hannover 1
GERMANY
(49)511.36.81.093
(49)511.36.81.095 (fax)

HSC Software
6303 Carpenteria Avenue
Carpenteria, CA 93013
805-566-6200
Kai's Fractal Explorer
Kai's Gradient Designer
Kai's Power Tools
Kai's Texture Explorer

Human Software
14407 Big Basin Way
P.O. Box 2280
Saratoga, CA 95070-0280
408-741-5102 (fax)
CD-Q
Color Extreme

IBM Corporation
Personal Software
Products
11400 Burnet Road
Austin, TX 78758
512-836-7917
Linkway Line

Image Bank
Williams Square
 Suite 700
5221 N. O'Connor Blvd.
Irving, TX 75039
Photo CD Collections

Imspace Systems
Corporation
2665 Ariane Drive
Suite 207
San Diego, CA 92117
800-488-5836
Kudo CD Publisher
Kudo CD Manager

Interactive Media
Corporation
P.O. Box 0089
Los Altos, CA 94023-0089
415-948-0745
Media Cataloger

LEAD Technology
900 Baxter Street
Charlottesville, NC 28204
704-549-5532
LEADVIEW
LEADTOOLS

Lenel Systems, Inc.
290 Woodcliff Office Park
Fairport, NY 14450
716-248-9720
MacOrganizer
Media Organizer

Macromedia, Inc.
600 Townsend Avenue
San Francisco, CA 94103
415-252-2000
Action!
AuthorWare
Macromedia Director
SoundEdit Pro

Mark of the Unicorn, Inc.
222 Third Street
Cambridge, MA 02142
617-576-2760
Digital Waveboard

MacWorld CD Ventures
P.O. Box 105443
Atlanta GA 30348-5443
Tastemate Video Selection
System

Micrografix, Inc.
1303 E. Arapaho
Richardson, TX 75081
214-497-6431
Picture Publisher

332

Microsoft Corporation
One Microsoft Way
Redmond, WA 98052
800-426-9400
Microsoft Windows
Microsoft Word
PowerPoint

Multi-Ad Services, Inc.
1720 W. Detweiller Drive
Peoria, IL 61615
309-692-1530
Multi-Ad Search

The Multimedia Store
5347 Dietrich Road
San Antonio, TX 78219-2997
800-597-3686
Photo Factory for Windows

Nikon Electronic Imaging
1300 Walt Whiteman Road
Melville, NY 11747
516-547-4355
Image Access

Now Software, Inc.
921 SW Washington Street
Suite 500
Portland, OR 97205-2823
508-274-2800
Now Compress

Opcode Systems
3641 Have Drive
Suite A
Menlo Park, CA 94025
415-369-8131
Audioshop

O. Sage Consultants
7100 Regency Square Blvd.
Suite 136
Houston, TX 77036
713-785-5400
Sound Designer II

Panasonic Corporation
6550 Katella Avenue
Cypress, CA 90630
714-373-7200
3DO Interactive Multiplayer

Passport Designs
100 Stone Pine Road
Half Moon Bay, CA 94019
415-726-0280
Passport Producer Pro

Philips Interactive Media
111 Santa Monica Blvd.
Los Angeles, CA
310-444-6500
Philips CD-I Player

PhotoDisc, Inc.
2013 4th Avenue, Suite 200
Seattle, WA 98121
800-528-3472
Photography & Print Clip Media

Photone International
4108 Via Mirada
Sarasota, FL 34238
813-921-6741
Photone Prepress

Pinnacle Micro
19 Technology
Irvine, CA 92718
714-727-3300

Pixel Craft
P.O. Box 14467
Oakland, CA 94614
510-562-2480
Color Access

Prepress Technologies, Inc.
2443 Impala Drive
Carlsbad, CA 92008
619-931-2695
SpectreSeps Software
SpectrePrint Pro 4.0

Purup Pre-Press of America
1340 Mendota Heights Road
Mendota Heights, MN 55120
612-686-5600
PhotoImpress

Quark, Inc.
1800 Grant Street
Suite 200
Denver, CO 80203
303-894-8888
QuarkXPress
Quark Extensions

Radius, Inc./SuperMac Technology, Inc.
415 Moffett Park Drive
Sunnyvale, CA 94089
408-541-6100
SuperMac Accelerated Acquire Module
Thunderstorm Accelerator

Rasterops Truevision
7340 Shadeland Station
Indianapolis, IN 46256
317-841-0332
Bravado

Ray Dream, Inc.
1804 N. Shoreline Blvd.
Mountain View, CA 94043
800-846-0111
Ray Dream Designer
Ray Dream AddDepth

Software Publishing Corp.
3165 Kifer Road
Santa Clara, CA 95056-0983
408-988-7518
Harvard Graphics

Specular International
P.O. Box 888
Amherst, MA 01004
413-549-7600
Specular Collage

Strata, Inc.
2 West St. George Blvd., Suite 2100
St. George, UT 84770
801-628-5218
Stratavision 3D

333

Storm Technology
1861 Landings Drive
Mountain View, CA
94043
415-691-6000
Kids Studio

Symantec Corporation
10201 Torre Avenue
Cupertino, CA 95014
800-441-7234
DiskDoubler

SyQuest Technology
47071 Bayside Parkway
Fremont, CA 94538
800-245-2278
Removable hard drives

Tempra, Inc.
402 S. Kentucky Avenue
Suite 210
Lakeland, FL 33801
813-682-1128
Tempra Show

U-Lead Systems, Inc.
970 W. 190th Street
Suite 520
Torrance, CA 90502
310-523-9393
Image Pals2

Westlight
2223 South Carmelina
Avenue
Los Angeles, CA 90064
800-622-2028
QueStock

XAOS Tools, Inc.
600 Townsend Street,
270E
San Francisco, CA 94103
415-487-7000
Paint Alchemy

GLOSSARY

Access Plus A software package from Kodak that includes the basic Kodak Photo Access Software that allows the system to read Photo CD discs plus the Kodak Photo CD Player that lets the system act like a Photo CD player.

Acquire Module A Kodak add-on for the Adobe Photoshop program that lets that illustration package read in Photo CD images.

AIFF An abbreviation for Audio Interchange File Format, a common audio file format that can be imported by most multimedia authoring programs

antialiasing In video and graphics, efforts to smooth the appearance of jagged lines (jaggies) created by the limited resolution of a graphics system.

authoring system A program or programming environment designed to help users create multimedia programs. It usually requires a much more powerful computer system than needed for playback.

Base The Photo CD format that stores images as 768 pixels by 512 lines. This format is used both as the standard source for video display and as the starting component for resynthesizing the more detailed image formats.

Base/4 The Photo CD format that stores images as 384 pixels by 256 lines, or 1/4th the total number of pixels as the standard Base resolution format. It's intended primarily for previewing images on a video display.

Base/16 A Photo CD format that stores an image as 192 pixels by 128 lines, or 1/16th the total number of pixels as the standard Base resolution format. It's intended primarily for the thumbnail images printed on the disc jacket or for image retrieval.

bitmapped images Images made out of an array of dots rather than out of continuous lines or areas. Photo CD images are stored in bitmap format.

branching A feature available on Photo CD Portfolio discs that lets the user determine which sequence of images to see next by selecting from a menu of choices.

burn An informal term for the process of writing on to a recordable (write-once) CD.

calibration A procedure used to adjust a machine (such as a scanner, printer, or monitor) to a set of manufacturer's performance standards.

CD A trademarked abbreviation for Compact Disc, a series of optical discs that include the common CD audio disc, CD-ROM discs, and Photo CD discs.

CD-DA Short for compact disc–digital audio, audio in the standard format used for compact discs and players used for mass-market music applications. It uses 16-bit linear pulse coded modulation (PCM) sampled at 44.1 kHz, for an effective bandwidth of 20 kHz and a dynamic range of 98 dB.

CD-I Short for compact disc–interactive, a standard both for CDs containing combinations of sound, images, and computer instructions and also for players specially constructed for these discs. CD-I players can also present Photo CD discs.

CD-R Short for compact disc-recordable, a type of compact disc on which data can be written to by a special recorder. So far, all such discs in CD format are write-once, but read/write optical discs are available for other formats.

CD-ROM An acronym for compact disc–read-only memory, a type of optical data disc that uses the same basic technology as the popular CD audio discs. The standard CD-ROM drive can only read data (the data are permanently stamped on the disc during manufacturing or written using a write-once process). Each disc can hold about 600 MB of data.

CD-ROM XA An acronym for CD-ROM–extended architecture, a variation of the CD-ROM format that includes provisions for interleaved (alternating) blocks of compressed audio and other types of data. Photo CD discs are one type of CD-ROM XA disc.

CD writer A compact disc drive that uses a laser to record data onto suitable recordable CD discs.

chroma Short for chrominance, the color (hue) component of an image.

Chroma1 (C1) One of the two color signal components used to represent colors in the Photo YCC color method used for Photo CD images.

Chroma2 (C2) The second of the two color signal components used to represent colors in the Photo YCC color method used for Photo CD images.

clip art Images that are designed to be copied or moved into other layouts, and sold in collections as resources. Originally, clip art was physically clipped from books of images, but now is normally copied electronically or photographically.

clipping The loss of detail in highlight areas that can occur when original image data are lost during a scanning process.

CMYK A color model based on the cyan (C), magenta (M), yellow (Y), and black (K) inks used in color printing.

color balance The comparative brightnesses and densities of the various colors in a color image. Good color balance makes a scene appear lifelike, while poor color balance makes a scene appear to be shown through tinted glass.

color cast A tint or overemphasis of one color in a color image, particularly an unintended one.

color depth The number of colors available to represent each pixel (dot) in an image. It can be expressed in bits or in the number of colors. A 1-bit depth represents black-and-white, 8-bits is 256 colors, and 24 bits is approximately 16 million colors.

color encoding The method by which color values are represented in a particular color model or system. In the Photo YCC system used for Photo CD images, the color encoding system is a digital method based loosely on international television standards and a theoretical reference image-capturing device.

color gamut The range of colors that can be represented in a particular color model or encoding method.

color information In Kodak's terminology for the Photo CD system, a term used for data that includes both color (chroma) and brightness (luminance) information.

color management system Software that characterizes input, output, and display devices in terms of the way they reproduce color and modifies the presentation of color data on the monitor so that it will be an accurate predictor of what the final color output will look like.

color saturation The extent to which an object or image region shows a pure color rather than the color mixed with white or black. Sometimes referred to as the richness of the color.

color separation The process of dividing a colored image into a corresponding series of single-color images. Since color printing is done by printing three single-color images and black, color pictures and drawings must first be made into separate images for each of these colors.

compression The translation of data to a more compact form for storage or transmission (after which it can be restored to normal form). It is usually done by utilizing shorter codes to indicate repeating patterns and by dropping constant or unnecessary parts.

continuous tone Said of an image that has grays or shades of color. Continuous tone images cannot be reproduced in that form by most printing or digital display technologies, which either place ink or color at a given point or do not. Consequently, images with such tones must be broken up into small dark and light areas or series of different colored dots.

crop In both computer graphics and graphics arts in general, to select a part of an image by cutting off portions from the edges. Cropping is done to eliminate unwanted detail, allowing more attention to be focused on the remaining image.

Data Manager The software component of the Kodak PIW system for recording Photo CD discs that organizes the data received from the scanner and presents it for encoding into the Photo CD format.

device color profiles (DCPs) Description files used to characterize input sources and output destinations for purposes of precise color management. Kodak's Color Management Systems (KCMS) kits provide a variety of precision DCPs.

digitize To convert an analog signal (such as a signal from a camera or microphone) to the corresponding digital code values.

disc identification number A 12 or 16-digit number written in both barcode and regular numeric form near the hub of Photo CD discs, mainly intended for automatic disc identification and tracking.

dpi An abbreviation for dots per inch, a measure of the resolution of printers and other output devices.

dye sublimation A type of color printer that transfers the image to paper using a solid that vaporizes and is then deposited on or reacts chemically with a coating on the paper.

8-bit color Said of display systems that allocate 8 bits of memory to each pixel and therefore can show up to 256 different colors for each dot on the display. This is usually considered enough for program graphics but not enough for realistic photographic images.

electronic camera A camera that records an image directly in electronic form, either as digital data or as an analog signal. By contrast, most Photo CD images are first captured on film and later converted to electronic form.

EPS Short for encapsulated PostScript (EPS) or encapsulated PostScript Format (EPSF), a file format that contains PostScript coding for an image plus a bitmap representation of the result. Many Photo CD programs can work with EPSF images, and some can export Photo CD images to EPSF files.

Favorite Picture Selection (FPS) A feature on many Photo CD players that stores picture selections, view order, and any picture editing (such as zoom, crop, and rotation) for subsequent viewing sessions.

film scanner A device that reads a negative or slide and produces the corresponding digital data set. The standard Photo CD scanner has a resolution of 3072 pixels by 2048 lines, using 12 bits for each primary color.

filter   A software routine for altering images, packaged as a plug-in for a larger graphics program.

Form 1   As applied to CD-ROM data formats, a track format that uses the optional third layer of error detection and correction. All Photo CD discs are CD-ROM XA format Mode 2 Form 1.

4XBase   The Photo CD format that stores pictures as 1536 pixels by 1024 lines, or 4 times the total number of pixels as the standard Base resolution format. It's intended primarily for high-quality hardcopy output or for HDTV.

gamma   For photographic materials, cameras, and video image capture systems, an index number standing for the relation of illumination to response. Technically, it is the slope of the line that graphs that relation.

gold master   A disc created when data from are hard disk are written or "burned" to a compact disc, using a method called compact disc–recordable (CD-R).

Green Book   An informal name for the standard developed by Sony and Philips for CD-I discs and players. As with other CD standards, the name comes from the color of the cover of the standards document.

highlight   A bright part of an image, particularly one brighter than the diffuse (not mirrorlike) reflection from a flat nonfluorescent white object.

High Sierra   A system-independent format for CD-ROM data discs that has evolved into the ISO 9660 format. The High Sierra version was named after the hotel where the meeting that set up the format took place.

histogram   A chart showing the relative distribution of pixels or regions of each band of color or brightness in an image.

image pac   The multiple resolutions of each image the Photo CD system records on disc. The lower-resolution formats are recorded as complete images, while the higher-resolution image components are stored as residuals that must be combined with the lower-resolution components.

image pac extension (IPE)   A separate file added to each image in the Pro Photo CD format to carry the information needed to produce 64XBase high-resolution images.

index print   A sheet or card showing thumbnail renditions of the images store on a Photo CD disc.

Infoguard   A Kodak trademark for the special overcoat treatment applied to Kodak Writable CD discs

that makes them more resistant to scratching or other damage.

ISO 9660   A standard for CD-ROM discs intended for use with diverse computer systems. Because the Photo CD format is based on ISO 9660, most systems require any drivers needed to read an ISO 9660 disc in order to read a Photo CD disc.

jewelcase   A plastic case used to hold CD discs for sale or storage that features a transparent cover through which you can see the disc or a printed insert.

JPEG   An acronym (pronounced jay-pegg) for Joint Photographic Experts Group, but commonly used to refer to the lossey image compression method developed by that committee.

jukebox   A mechanism that holds from a few to hundreds of individual CD discs and presents them on command to a smaller number of playback or record stations.

keywords   The identifying parameters used a labels for storing and retrieving images in an image-management system.

Kodak Picture Exchange   A Kodak service designed to provide descriptions and electronic versions of stock photographs for graphic arts users, and then inform the photo supplier if the user wants to purchase the rights to reproduce the photo from a high-resolution format or from film.

Kodak Professional Image Library   A Kodak system for storing and retrieving Photo CD images, pictures in other graphics formats, and other types of multimedia data. It combines a PCD Jukebox 100 player with database and access software.

Kodak Writable CD   Kodak's term for the combination of the firm's Kodak PCD Writer, Kodak Writable CD Media, and Kodak CD Publishing Software. With these components and suitable source files, users can create CD-ROM, CD-ROM XA, CD-I, and CD-DA discs.

look-up tables (LUTs)   An ordered list of active colors for use in a graphic display, where each color in the list is selected from a much larger possible set (the palette). Because the look-up table is much smaller than the full color palette, it tales fewer bits to describe each color.

lpi   an abbreviation for lines per inch, a figure used to indicate the spacing of the dot patterns making up a halftone image.

luminance   The intensity, or brightness component, of an image. The luminance portion of an image is the gray, black, or white portion. It is combined with the chrominance (chroma) signal to create a color image.

337

Mode 1 The standard format for ordinary CD-ROM data discs. It provides 2,048 bytes of error-corrected data from each block on the disc and a single-speed transfer rate of 153.6 KB per second. Along with the data, it allocates 12 bytes for sync, 4 bytes for headers, and 288 bytes for error detection and correction.

Mode 2 The standard format for CD-ROM XA data discs and variations such as CD-I and Photo CD. The Form 1 version provides for a 4 byte head, an 8 byte subheader, 2,048 bytes of data and 280 bytes of error correction information in each block. The Form 2 version has the same 4 byte header and 8 byte subheader, but it makes 2,324 to 2,326 bytes available for data and 4 bytes for an optional error correction field.

multimedia The combination of still images, sound, and animation in a program for display on either the computer screen or a television set. Multimedia is often designed to be interactive, with input from the viewer affecting how the program proceeds.

multisession Said of CD discs that have been recorded in more than one sitting. The original CD specifications did not make any provision for such discs, so most early CD-ROM drives can only read single-session discs or the first session of a multisession disc.

NTSC Originally, an abbreviation for National Television Systems Committee, the industry group that formulated the standards for U.S. color television. Now used to denote the format recommended by that committee. NTSC signals use interlaced scans, 30 frames (full images) per second, and 525 horizontal lines per frame.

one-off An informal term for a write-once CD-ROM, especially one made as a sample.

Orange Book An informal name for the specification that describes the additions to the CD-ROM standards for multisession recordable CDs. As is the custom in CD standards, it is named after the color of the cover on the specification document. The Photo CD multisession specification is based on the Orange book.

palette The collection of colors or shades available to a graphics system or program. Also, the set of Photo CD images available for insertion into a Create-It presentation.

PCD Disc Transporter A CD-handling mechanism that can load and unload each of a sequence of up to 75 discs to a matching PCD Writer unit.

Photo CD A Kodak trademark for a set of technologies for storing and recalling images, particularly for taking images first captured on photographic film, digitizing them at multiple levels of resolution, and then storing them on CD-ROM discs. Images can be stored on a recordable disc by photofinishers for individual consumer or professional use, or included in a replicated (stamped) CD-ROM for mass distribution.

Photo CD Access Developer's Toolkit A relatively low-cost development package from Kodak that provides the routines developers need to include in their software to let it read Photo CD discs.

Photo CD Catalog A variation of the Kodak Photo CD format that stores up to 6,000 images recorded in only thumbnail and Base/4 resolutions rather than at the full set of resolutions available on standard Photo CD discs.

Photo CD Imaging Workstation (PIW) Kodak's name for a line of systems that include a scanner, computer, CD writer, accessory units, and the software needed to create Photo CD discs.

Photo CD Master The name for the original Photo CD format designed to store about 100 images per disc, with each image encoded in five different resolutions.

Photo CD Portfolio A variation of the Kodak Photo CD format that can include photographic images, graphics, text, stereo audio and a scriptlike program for accessing the material.

photofinisher A company that develops photographic film and produces photographic prints, either directly for customers or on behalf of businesses such as pharmacies. Kodak says it designed the Photo CD system particularly to fit the needs of "high-volume photofinishing operations."

PHOTOS folder In the view of a Photo CD disc provided by recent versions of the Macintosh Photo CD drivers, a group folder for each image holding individual folders for the image components (different resolution versions of the image).

Photo YCC The color model and encoding scheme used to represent Photo CD images. It converts each point in the image to a luminance (brightness) component and 2 chroma (color) components, then compresses the resulting data. Unlike most other color models, the Photo YCC model allows for highlights up to approximately twice as bright as the normal 100% white level.

Photo YCC to RGB video conversion A built-in operation in Photoshop that converts Photo CD images to the RGB format the program works with. While it performs an adequate job for most images, Kodak offers its own plug-in Photo CD Acquire Module with more parameters and adjustments.

PICT The standard file format used by Macintosh

applications to pass images back and forth and to store images on the Clipboard. Essentially, PICT files consist of the Macintosh QuickDraw routines needed to create the image.

polycarbonate   The material used for the substrate (base material) for CD discs.

precision transforms (PTs)   A color management system element that provides a means of precise color data translation between the various devices in a color desktop system.

press   To create replicates of a master CD disc by making plastic copies in molds. The process is also called *stamping*.

Print Photo CD   A variation on the basic Photo CD disc format for prepress work that also makes provision for raw data files from a variety of scanners and for both image and text data. It is supported by most major prepress equipment makers.

Pro Photo CD   A variation of the Kodak Photo CD format that adds a 64XBase high-resolution version of each image, but at the cost of holding fewer images per disc.

QuickTOPIX   A line of software programs from Optical Media International that can be used with a Kodak PCD Writer to record CD discs.

recordable CD   A compact disc on which data can be written individually in the field using a CD writer unit, rather than a stamped CD on which the data are molded into the surface during manufacture.

Red Book   An informal name for the standard developed by Sony and Philips for CD-DA (Compact Disc Digital Audio) discs and players. As with other CD standards, the name comes from the color of the cover of the standards document.

reference image-capturing device   A theoretical image-capturing device with defined chroma (color) and luminance characteristics used as the standard for the Photo CD system. Because actual film and digitizing devices have characteristics that are somewhat different than this ideal, a set of film terms is applied to each raw image as part of the transformation to Photo YCC encoded form.

residual   In the Photo CD system, a data set representing the extra information needed to produce a high-resolution image starting from a lower-resolution format.

resolution   For graphics output, a measure of how closely packed are the spots making up an image, often measured in dots or lines per inch.

RGB   A computer color display output signal and color encoding scheme comprised of separately controllable red, green, and blue elements.

rotation   A feature on most Photo CD players that

permits the user to turn the image to make any side the bottom. Most software programs that work with Photo CD images can also rotate the image by intermediate amounts as well.

safe area   The part of a presentation developed on a computer screen that is guaranteed not to be cut off by an output device, such as a television screen.

sample   As applied to the conversion of scenes and images to Photo CD files, the digital value reported for a point on the image.

scan   To convert an image from visible form to an electronic description. Most available systems turn the image into a corresponding series of dots but do not actually recognize shapes. However, some attempt to group the dots into their corresponding characters ("optical character recognition") or corresponding objects.

scanner   An input device that converts a drawing or illustration into a corresponding electronic bitmap image.

scene balance algorithm   An optional correction factor that can be applied during the creation of a Photo CD file to compensate for variations in the overall density and color balance of different images.

scene-space option   In scanning an image on a PIW, the option of turning off the universal film terms and referring to certain memory colors to produce a common rendition of the image.

script   A set of instructions produced by applications such as Arrange-It that can be used by the Build-It program to construct a Photo CD Portfolio disc.

session   A single continuous act of writing data and a table of contents (TOC) to a CD disc. The original CD format only allowed for a single session per disc, but Photo CD discs can contain multiple sessions.

short-run duplication   Producing few enough copies of a CD title that it is more practical to make them one at a time on a write-once system rather than making a master and stamping out copies.

single session   Said of CD discs that are pressed or recorded all at one time and have only one table of contents (TOC). This was the original format for all CDs, but Photo CD and some other formats now allow for multisession discs.

16XBase   The Photo CD format that stores pictures as 3072 pixels by 2048 lines, or 16 times the total number of pixels as the standard Base resolution format. It's intended primarily for high-quality printing.

stamped   Said of discs that are created by a molding process rather than recorded one at a time.

subsampling   In capturing or representing an image in digital form, the practice of representing the chroma (color) aspect of the image with fewer samples than the luminance (brightness part), making use of the human eye's lessened sensitivity to small color details. In the Photo YCC system used for Photo CD images, most image sizes allocate 1 sample of each color component to 4 samples of luminance.

substrate The polycarbonate plastic base material used as the structural core of a CD disc. The other layers, such as metalization, the dye recording layer, and the protective overcoat are layered over the substrate.

tele A feature on some Photo CD players and programs that lets the user zoom in (enlarge the image) to examine one portion in greater detail.

thumbnail A miniature copy of an image used for preview or as an icon (picture symbol) for the file containing the image.

TIFF Short for Tag Image File Format, a file format developed by Aldus and Microsoft to represent bitmap images, particularly those produced by scanners. It is actually an open-ended standard with several variants, so not all TIFF files are alike. Most Photo CD image editing programs can read and write TIFF files.

24-bit color Said of an image or system for working with an image that uses 24 bits to represent the color value of each pixel (spot on the image). Usually, the bits are allocated as 8 bits each for the three additive primary colors (red, green, and blue). That provides more than 16.7 million colors possibilities. This type of color is often called *true color* or *direct color* because the images look realistic and the values can be presented directly without using the information to look up further color values in a palette or color lookup table.

256-bit color Said of displays that can show each pixel as one of 256 different colors. Sometimes called 8-bit color for the number of memory bits needed to represent each pixel. This is usually considered the minimum acceptable color resolution for viewing Photo CD images, but it still produces quite a bit of color distortion such as banding and pixelation.

undercolor removal (UCR) In color printing, the full or partial replacement of overprinted dark colors by black ink during the making of separations or the printing plate. This process reduces the amount of ink required and helps prevent ink trapping.

universal film terms In the Photo CD system, a set of compensating factors applied to the raw data from a scanned image to make up for the difference between the characteristics of the film and the theoretical characteristics of the reference image-capturing device.

WORM For Write Once, Read Many, meaning disc technologies that allow data to be written or added to in the field and then read back as many times as desired. Current recordable CD methods are all a type of WORM technology.

writable CD media A disc or discs designed to allow data to be added later with a CD writer.

YCC A general abbreviation for color models that represent colors as a combination of luminance (abbreviated with "Y") and two color components (each abbreviated with "C"). This includes the Photo YCC model used for Photo CD images as well as in Betacam format used in video.

Y channel In the Photo YCC model used to represent colors in Photo CD images, the luminance (brightness) component.

Yellow Book An informal name for the standard developed by Sony and Philips for CD-ROM discs and players. As with other CD standards, the name comes from the color of the cover of the standards document.

zoom To change the size of the area of an image selected for viewing or display to provide either a more detailed view or more of an overview. Most Photo CD players provide one or more fixed zoom levels, while many software programs that work with Photo CD images allow the user to select any zoom factor within a specified range.

340

INDEX

341

Photo Credits

CUMULUS IMAGE & MULTIMEDIA DATABASE OFFER!

Cumulus PowerPro is Canto's extremely fast and powerful image and multimedia database solution based on a professional client/server network architecture.

Catalog any number of images or multimedia formats on the Apple Macintosh into any of several simultaneously open Cumulus databases.

Access with either the Cumulus•Client Software or directly from within other applications such as Quark XPress, Photoshop, PageMaker, FrameMaker, IsoDraw, RagTime or Cirrus.

Store a thumbnail representation of the image and all its descriptive information within the catalogs

Browse using search criteria such as keywords, status and full-text retrievable notes.

New features include full AppleScript support for automation, Hierarchical Keyword structure, and extensive Drag&Drop capabilities.

Drag & Drop of keywords onto selected images.

Drag & Drop between applications...even dragging of images into QuarkXPress.

Cumulus is OPI (Open Prepress Interface) aware. It works smoothly with e.g. Helios' OPI (Unix) or ColorCentral (Macintosh). Cumulus' unrivaled performance and professional feature set enable a complete "workflow control" of the imaging process—during creation, cataloging, editing, printing—and the retrieval and distribution (on-line, dial-in via Apple Remote Access or on CD-ROM) of the images or just the catalogs. Customizing services, CD-ROM-browser versions and site licensing are available.

❏ **Cumulus PowerPro 2.0 (client/server) - $100 off of $1,495.00 (5 user starter kit)**
❏ **Cumulus PowerLite 2.0 - $25 off of $199 (single user version)**

Mail this coupon with order to: **CANTO SOFTWARE, 800 Duboce Avenue, San Francisco, CA 94117, 415.431.6871, 415.861.6827(fax), applelink: CANTO.**

Enclosed is my ❏ check ❏ money order/Charge to my credit card ❏ VISA
❏ MC ❏ AMEX

No._____   Exp. Date _____

One per customer. Expires 9/1/95.

COREL PROFESSIONAL PHOTOS ON CD-ROM
BUY 3, GET 1 FREE!
THE WORLD'S LEADING PHOTO CD-ROM COLLECTION!

Save time and money on stock photography with the world's leading Photo CD-ROM collection. Each Corel Professional Photo CD-ROM contains 100 royalty-free photographs in the Kodak Photo CD format. For both Mac and PC. They are ideal for any visual communication including ads, brochures, presentations and multimedia. Each photo comes in five resolutions and can be exported in a variety of file formats. The Corel ArtView Screen Saver lets you turn any CD-ROM photograph into screen savers. Corel Mosaic Visual File Manager is included for quick and easy viewing, searching, and managing of photos, along with a printed reference guide.

Buy any 3 Corel Professional Photo titles, and get 1 for free!
Buy 6 get 2 for free, Buy 9 get 3 for free and so on! (shipping charges still apply)

Each title is only $24.95 U.S./$29.95 Cdn, plus $10 for shipping and handling for 1 - 5 titles, $15 for 6 - 11 titles, $20 for 12 - 24 titles. Check those you wish to order, plus your free title(s)!

❏ Sunrises and Sunset	❏ People	❏ WWII Planes	❏ Exotic Cars
❏ Patterns	❏ Wild Animals	❏ Mountains of America	❏ Food
❏ Indigenous People	❏ Action Sailing	❏ American National Parks	❏ Textures
❏ Aviation Photography	❏ Fighter Jets	❏ Landscapes	❏ People of the World
❏ Underwater Life	❏ Autumn	❏ New York City	❏ Winter Sports
❏ Nature Scenes	❏ Flowers	❏ Night Scenes	❏ Reflections

Corel Corporation
1600 Carling Avenue
Ottawa, Ontario CANADA K1Z 8R7
Telephone 1-800-772-6735
Telephone 1-613-728-3733
Fax   1-613-761-9176

Enclosed is my ❏ check ❏ money order/Charge to my credit card ❏ VISA ❏ MC ❏ AMEX

                    No._____   Exp. Date _____

On U.S. orders, no sales taxes apply. In Canada, please add 8 PST (Ontario residents only) and 7% GST to final order total. Offer expires September 1, 1995.

DIAMAR DIGITAL STOCK PHOTOGRAPHY
BUY ONE GET ONE FREE!

Professional-quality digital stock photography on CD-ROM, available in six volumes. File formats designed for every usage in the publishing and multimedia markets.

For high-quality 4-color printing: Kodak Photo CD and CMYK TIFF, pre-separated for printing directly from your publishing software.

For multimedia and on-screen presentations: 24-bit RGB TIFF, in 3 resolutions ideal for multimedia and indexed (256) color PICT optimized for Aldus Persuasion 2.x and 8-bit monitors.

For black-and-white printing: black-and-white TIFF files in two resolutions optimized for laser printing. Each volume includes 54 high-resolution images in 5 different file formats, and is compatible with both Macintosh and PC.

Use the photos royalty-free for most creative work, even with high-volume distribution. Includes full-color printed guide of photographs and 30-day money-back guarantee.

— —

DIAMAR Interactive Corporation - P.O. Box 4902 - Seattle, WA 98104-0902
206.340.5975 - 800.2DIAMAR (ORDERS) - E-MAIL DIAMAR @ HALCYON.COM
206.340.1432 FAX

Buy any volume of DIAMAR portfolios for the suggested retail price of $79.95 and get your choice of any other volume FREE. Offer valid with original coupon only, and via mail order only. Include $4.95 shipping and handling.

❏ **Backgrounds & Textures**   ❏ **Cities & Castles**   ❏ **Nature & Animals**
❏ **Landscapes & Scenery**   ❏ **Flowers**   ❏ **People & Lifestyles**

Mail your check, money order or credit information along with this coupon to: Diamar Interactive Corp. "Photo CD Handbook" Offer, P.O. Box 4902, Seattle, WA 98104-0902

Enclosed is my ❏ check ❏ money order/Charge to my credit card ❏ VISA ❏ MC
     No._____ Exp. Date _____

— —

EDUCORP PHOTO CD-ROM'S
$5.00 OFF!

PROFESSIONAL BACKGROUNDS - This best-selling CD lets you choose from 100 perfect backgrounds of marble, chrome, satin, special effects and more. These creative backgrounds are perfect for multimedia projects, ads, designs or digital art compositions. (Kodak Photo CD)

PROFESSIONAL PHOTOGRAPHY COLLECTION - Get 100 high-resolution photos covering a variety of topics including leisure, government, travel, scenic and food. Rated "5 Mice" by MacUser magazine! (Kodak Photo CD)

BEST OF SWIMSUIT VOLUME 1 - Enjoy 100 royalty-free high-resolution photos. Now you can take advantage of these images of beautiful women in the latest swimwear, photographed in exotic locations. Files available in 18MB resolutions! (Kodak Photo CD)

BEST OF PEOPLE IN BUSINESS - A collection of 100 photos, ranging from men and women in office settings, to office-related equipment and business graphics. (Kodak Photo CD)

EDUCORP   **PCD**
7434 Trade Street
San Diego, CA 92121-2410
800.843.9497 (orders)
619.536.9999
619.536.2345 fax

$5.00 Off Kodak Photo CDs! Order one of the CD's below and receive $5.00 off. Offer good for a limited time, so hurry. Get high quality, royalty-free stock photographs with unlimited reproduction rights for the best price!

EDUCORP is your premier source for CD-ROM titles, drives and bundles for the Macintosh and PC computers.

❑ Professional Backgrounds - $64.95   ❑ Best of Swimsuit - Volume 1 - $64.95
❑ Prof. Photography Collec. (HR) - $54.95   ❑ Best of People in Business - $69.95

Mail your check, money order or credit information along with this coupon to:
EDUCORP, 7434 Trade Street, San Diego, CA 92121-2410

Enclosed is my ❑ check ❑ money order/Charge to my credit card ❑ VISA ❑ MC ❑ AMEX

No._____   Exp. Date _____

TEST DRIVE THE FUTURE IMAGE REPORT

The Future Image Report is the information source decision makers turn to for timely unbiased information and cutting-edge analysis about the digital imaging revolution; from the top editorial team in the field, in a format designed for efficient reading. With this special offer you can "Test Drive" the publication leading analysts describe as "an essential reference for industry insiders" for six months, at 65% off the annual subscription price of $275.00. Get the information your business needs—industry news, business cases, technology previews—faster, more conveniently, and more intelligently. Put your company on the inside track in digital imaging.

— —

Yes, I want to find out what The Future Image Report can do for my business. Begin my six month "Test Drive" subscription now, at 65% off the normal annual price of $275.00.

Last Name _____ **First Name** _____

Title _____ **Dept./Division** _____

Company _____

Address _____

City _____ **State/Zip** _____

Phone _____ **Fax** _____

My special rate with this coupon is: ❑ **1/2 year:**   **$99.00/5 issues**
Additional shipping and handling:
Canada: **$8.00**
Europe/Australia/Asia/Latin America/Africa: **$20.00**

TOTAL   **$_____**

Enclosed is my ❑ **check** ❑ **money order/Charge to my credit card** ❑ **VISA** ❑ **MC** ❑**AMEX**

     No._____ **Exp. Date _____**

Signature_____

Please fax to 415.579.0566, or mail to: The Future Image Report, Attention: Circulation, 1020 Parrott Drive 1F, Burlingame, CA, 94010, USA. For information, call 415.579.0493.

— —

MAKE MAC & WINDOWS CD-ROM'S OF YOUR PHOTOS FAST!
CALL FOR SPECIAL OFFER!

Kudo CD Publisher is the FAST new way to organize and publish your photographs on Macintosh and Windows CD-ROM's. Use Kudo CD Publisher to create CD-ROM's for sale or to create digital archives of all your photpgraphs, film footage or graphic images. Kudo CD Publisher creates a visual interface for your photographs though the creation of a catalog of small "thumbnail" images. Find any image in a snap through keyword searches and more.

Step by Step Instructions: With the help of our step by step instructions you can easily create a great CD-ROM without having to be an expert. We'll guide you through each step in the development process. With the Kudo CD Toolkit many of the organizational tasks are automatically done for you.

Dual Platform: With one click of the mouse turn a Macintosh catalog into a Windows catalog.

No Royalty Payments: Create as many CD titles as you want for FREE.

Drag and Drop: Direct image placement from the catalog into your document. You don't need to find the original image, just drag the thumbnail to the open doument and Kudo does the rest.

Kudo CD Manager: Use this dual platform, image and multimedia database to keep track of thousands of images, sound and movie files, on large CD-ROM collections. Use Kudo CD Manager to catalog and annotate files. Use the Manager Toolkit to subdivide catalogs and move groups of images from place to place.

- ❏ Kudo CD Publisher v1.1 Macintosh & Windows - $500.00
- ❏ Kudo CD Manager v1.0 Macintosh & Windows - $129.00

Mail this coupon to: Imspace Systems Corporation, 2665 Ariane Dr., Suite 207, San Diego, CA, 92117, Phone: 800-488-5836, Fax 619 272-4292 All prices subject to change without notice. Offer expires 9/1/95.

Enclosed is my ❏ check ❏ money order/Charge to my credit card ❏ VISA ❏ MC ❏ AMEX

No._____ Exp. Date _____

MILLER IMAGING INTERNATIONAL, INC.
$50 WORTH OF PHOTO CD SCANNING
ABSOLUTELY FREE!!

Miller Imaging International, Inc. is a full-service Photo CD provider and one of the leaders in Photo CD technology, service, and quality. We also offer technical support along with instruction on acquiring Photo CD images properly.

Our Services Include: Image Archiving, Pro Photo CD, Portfolio Photo CD, Master Photo CD, Catalog CD,Writable CD, Image Scanning CLC 700 with Fiery 200i output, Technical Support, Customer Service, 24-Hour Turnaround Time, Open Late & Saturday, Mac & PC Support

Our Clients Include: Photographers, Advertising/Design, Architects, Talent/Modeling Agencies, Universities/Museums, Entertainment, Social Services, Real Estate, Government Services, Pre-Press, Multimedia

When it comes to scanning, processing, reproducing, or storing your images, come by and discover how **Miller Imaging International** offers state-of-the-art technology and equipment to bring it all together.

———————————————————————————————

This certificate is good for $50 worth of Photo CD scanning from Miller Imaging International, Inc. That's right, $50 absolutely free (does not include Photo CD disc). Offer expires January 1, 1996.

Mail your order to Miller Imaging International, Inc. 2718 Wilshire Boulevard, Santa Monica, CA, 90403, 310.264.4711.

———————————————————————————————

PHOTO FACTORY FOR WINDOWS ™
PHOTO CD IMAGING SOFTWARE
COMPLETE WITH 50 PHOTO CD IMAGES
&
50 ORIGINAL SONGS FOR ONLY $49.00!

Photo Factory for Windows™ makes working with Photo CD's simple and fun. Call up a contact sheet to see what's included on your Photo CD.

Crop, zoom, mirror and **flip** your images with a click of your mouse.

Adjust your images for color or contrast or batch convert images to any of seven popular image formats. Powerful features allow you to create electronic slide-shows and screensavers, complete with color backgrounds, music, text and voice-overs.

Use the Runtime Player that is included with your software to export your creation to be viewed by someone else.

— —

For more information about Photo Factory for Windows™ contact:

The Multimedia Store™
5347 Dietrich Road
San Antonio, TX 78219-2997
Orders: 1-800-597-3686
Information: 1-210-661-8398

Yes, I want to get Photo Factory for Windows™ on CD-ROM with 50 original Photo CD images and 50 original MIDI songs for only $49 plus $6 shipping and handling. To order, call 1-800-597-3686 with your credit card number or mail a check for $55 with your name, address and telephone numnber to The Multimedia Store, 5347 Dietrich Road, San Antonio, TX 78219-2997 (residents of Texas please add applicable sales tax.)

— —

YOUR FILM TO PHOTO CD IN 24 HOURS!

100 35MM SLIDES OR NEGS TO MASTER PHOTO CD
SPECIAL INTRODUCTORY OFFER - $99

Advanced Digital Imaging, Inc. is an international imaging bureau offering quick, quality services at competitive prices.

Our normal turnaround is 24 hours!

Call us for Master, Pro, Portfolio (for presentation or with Browser) and Writable Photo CDs, or Kodak digital cameras and printers.

We guarantee our work 100%—your complete satisfaction is our goal—we spare no effort to achieve it!

— —

YES, I would like 100 35mm slides or negatives made into a Master Photo CD for the low price of $99, a savings of $36.00, with return FedExpress Shipping included.

Enclosed is my ❏ check ❏ money order/Charge to my credit card ❏ VISA ❏ MC ❏ AMEX
Mail this coupon to:
Advanced Digital Imaging, Inc.
112 East Olive Street
Fort Collins, CO 80524
800-888-3686
303-482-0334 (fax)
CompuServe: 72702,2761
President: Jim Stouffer
General Manager: Kathy Bauer

— —

IMAGEPALS 2.0

THE INDISPENSABLE MANAGEMENT TOOL FOR GRAPHICS, PUBLISHING AND MULTIMEDIA USERS! ONLY $129!

ImagePals 2 is the indispensable management tool for users of image, graphic, animation, video and sound files.

Catalog your files, including Photo CDs, into visual thumbnail albums for quick and easy access.

Convert files among all popular file formats for compatibility with your favorite programs.

Drag and drop your files for seamless integration with your publishing, presentation and multimedia application.

See the complete library of image editing tools to help you create vivid, dramatic images every time.

Create exciting multimedia slide show presentations of your files complete with audio background and visual transition effects.

With **ImagePals 2,** your complete media management solution has arrived!

— —

— —

WESTLIGHT'S QUESTOCK
40% OFF THE REGULAR PRICE!

WESTLIGHT'S QUESTock... The first Photo CD Catalog Product designed to prompt visual creativity and conceptual thinking.

QUESTock Image Search and Comp System is a visual thesaurus containing thousands of professional low-resolution images from a selection of millions. The discs are an advanced interactive search system that converts ideas into visual solutions. QUESTock is the first comprehensive image language, representing 15 years of research into creative image through processes by a team of image, language and computer experts.

QUESTock has two versions. The CD-ROM version is compatible with both Macintosh and Windows systems. The Portfolio Version operates on either a Kodak Photo CD player or a CD-I machine. The disc operates using Kodak's new Browser software and is an excellent example for anybody setting up a digital image database.

— —

Special offer for Verbum readers — the two disc set is regularly $59.95, plus postage and handling (California residents add 8.25%). Send in the attached coupon along with your business card, the disc is yours for $39.95 - a savings of 40%. Offer expires September 30, 1995.

Satisfaction guarantee — if you are not completely satisfied with our discs, simply return them with the enclosed content within thirty (30) days for a complete refund.

Please indicate the version you prefer
❑ **Computer version**

Macintosh:	**IBM and PC Compatibles:**
Systems Software 6.0.7 or higher.	80386 or higher.
QuickTime version 1.5 or higher.	Windows version 3.1/enhanced mode.
24-bit or 32-bit color video display.	MS-DOS version 3.3 or higher.
8MB of RAM or higher.	8MB of RAM or higher.
Photo CD compatible CD-ROM XA drive.	CD-ROM XA Mode 2 Drive.

❑ **Portfolio version—requires either a Photo CD Player or a CD-I machine, and a television.**

❑ **YES! Please rush me my Pro Edition QUESTock Image Search and Comp System set for only $39.95 — a savings of 40% off the regular price of $59.95. Offer expires 9/30/95. Allow 4-6 weeks for delivery. $6.00 shipping and handling, 2-day rush $8.00. Mail your check, money order or credit information along with this coupon to: Westlight, 2223 S. Carmelina Avenue, LA, CA 90064, 800.622.2028.**

Enclosed is my ❑ **check** ❑ **money order/Charge to my credit card** ❑ **VISA** ❑ **MC** ❑ **AMEX**

No._____   Exp. Date _____

— —

SPECIAL OFFER FOR THE OFFICIAL PHOTO CD HANDBOOK
GET A $75 VALUE FOR ONLY $50!
WORKBOOK'S STOCK DISK 3
NOW ONLY $50!

Welcome to the Stock Workbook's Stock Disk 3, available in October 1994. This third disk produced by the Stock Workbook contains almost 8,000 images representing files from over 40 stock agencies.

Stock Disk 3 is available in CD-ROM format for both Macintosh and PC users equipped with a CD-ROM drive. Images are displayed in photo-realistic 24-bit color. Software provided on Stock Disk 3 allows you to access images by agency name, photographer or illustrator name, or by simply typing in specific subjects.

Stock Disk 3 is not a clip disk. it is a catalog representing the best photography and illustration from the best stock agencies in the U.S. These images are intended for viewing only. All usage must be purchased from the stock agency that holds the copyright.

— —

Fax your order to (213)856-4368 or phone (800)547-2688 or (213)856-0008.

Pay by VISA/Mastercard/American Express

Name_____ Company_____

Address_____

City_____ State_____ Zip_____

Phone _____ Fax_____

Credit Card No._____ Exp. _____

The Workbook
940 N. Highland Avenue
Los Angeles, CA 90038

— —

ZZYZX VISUAL SYSTEMS
20% OFF DIGITAL IMAGING SERVICES

ZZYZX Visual Systems, along with its parent company, A&I Color, is a full-service Digital and Photographic processing lab featuring Master & Pro Photo CD scanning, unparalleled photo composition and retouching, *plus* Kodak XL 7700 continuous tone prints and large-format Iris prints.

Our Services Include:
Image Archiving, Pro Photo CD, Master Photo CD, Writable CD, Image Scanning, Technical Support, Customer Service, 24-Hour Turnaround Time, Film Output, Large-Format Iris Printing, On-line Editorial Image Editing and Electronic Transfer, Multimedia Development and Consultation, Electronic Portfolios.

Our Clients Include:
The Walt Disney Company, 3-M Corporation, Applied Graphics Technologies, The Workbook, and many others.

— —

This offer is good for a 20% Discount on Master & Pro Photo CD Scans, a retouching or photo composite job 8.5 x 11 or 11 x 11 Kodak XL 7700 Prints, and Iris prints, any size.

ZZYZX Visual Systems/A&I Color Lab
949 N. Highland Avenue
Hollywood, CA 90038
Contact Kim Kapin
213.856.5260
Some restrictions may apply. Offer expires 9/1/95

— —

HI-REZ AUDIO ON CD-ROM
AUDIO CD-ROMS AT 40% OFF!

Hi Rez Audio is a collection of over 40 license-free music tracks and sound effects created by professional musicians with the needs of the multimedia producer in mind. If you want your projects to sound as good as they look, Hi Rez Audio invites you to listen.

An elegant interface allows you to browse through 40 minutes of Red Book Audio at the click of a mouse. For your convenience, digitized versions of 22KHZ and 11 KHZ AIFF, SoundEdit, and SoundEdit pro formats have been included.

"I can't be enthusiastic enough about the music!...Perfect for creating background moods!" - *Mac World Magazine*

"...delivers with a vengeance, A must for any multimedia producer!" - *Micro Publishing News*

"Excellent quality music...very accessible!" - *Bové and Rhodes Inside Report*

— —

Hi Rez Audio, Volumes One and Two are the ultimate sound sources for your multimedia productions and presentations. These discs retail for $149.00 each but with this discount coupon you can order each disc for the low price of $90.00 or both discs for $167.00. Simply fill out and mail in this coupon with your check payable to Hi Rez Audio, 4208 Belmont Park Terrace, Nashville, Tennessee, 37215. Be sure to include your telephone number and address. Requires Macintosh 6.07 or later.

Please check which discs and how many copies below. Allow one week for shipping and handling.

❑ **Hi Rez Audio, Volume 1**

❑ **Hi Rez Audio, Volume 2**

❑ **Both Volumes of Hi Rez Audio**

Offer expires September 1, 1995. Discount valid with coupon only.

— —

SIR SPEEDY

SIR SPEEDY PUTS THE POWER OF CD TECHNOLOGY AT YOUR FINGERTIPS! $20 OFF ON THE CREATION OF A KODAK PORTFOLIO CD! $2 OFF ON KODAK PHOTO CD PROCESSING!

Why publish and ship huge documents to far-flung places and constantly be in a bind for document storage?

Consolidate all your information on a small, portable Kodak Writable CD. And once you have these affordable CDs in hand, you can quickly and easily access your photographs, presentations and information. Just make us your total CD solution.

Why keep large files of transparencies and prints? Store and preserve all your photographs on a small, durable Kodak Photo CD.

Why be locked into old fashioned presentation, selling and training methods? Combine photos, text, graphics and sound on a small, interactive Kodak Portfolio CD.

$20 OFF on the creation of a Kodak Portfolio CD at any participating Sir Speedy or Copies Now location.

$2 OFF on Kodak Photo CD processing at any participating Sir Speedy or any Copies Now location.

Call 1-800-CD-Speedy for the location nearest you!

Offer expires September 1, 1995.

Z PUBLISHING, INC.

ALL 7 TITLES FROM BLUE RIBBON PHOTOGRAPHY SERIES
SPECIAL INTRODUCTORY OFFER - $259
SAVE $90!

The Blue Ribbon Photography Series is a growing collection of the best and most useful images from selected professional photographers. Included are a wide range of advertising, unusual and useful images for anyone using graphics—from corporate presentations to video game designers.

Each Blue Ribbon Photo CD Disk contains 100 images in five Kodak Photo CD resolutions up to 2048x3072.

The Blue Ribbon Photo CD's are compatible with both Mac and PC applications such as Photoshop, Painter, Picture Publisher and others.

Each package contains a license which gives the purchaser the right to use any image on the CD-ROM in any publication, multimedia products or video free of any royalties.

This offer includes the following CD-ROM titles: Photographs by Lee Hinton, Photographs by Barbara Sansone, Photographs by Andrew Hathaway, Photographs by Joe Belk and Craig Beaghler, Photographs by Richard Petersen, Photographs by Scott Lance, and 100 Images from the History of Art.

❑ **Please send the seven titles listed above from the Blue Ribbon Photography Series.**

Enclosed is my ❑ check /money order for $259 or charge to my credit card
❑ VISA ❑ MC   No._____   Exp. Date _____

Mail this coupon to:
Z Publishing
c/o California Mailing Services
2245 Paragon Drive
San Jose, CA 95131
or call 800.621.7174
or fax to 408.432.0483 (offer #180)

CMCD'S PHOTO CD LIBRARY!
30% OFF!
NO USAGE-FEE PHOTOGRAPHIC LIBRARY FOR MAC AND WINDOWS PCs!

Imagine a color-photographic library of images created and intended for computer aided-illustration, design, advertising, publishing, and presentation use. No hassles with royalties or usage contracts.

Each volume of the library contains more than 100 "reproduction-quality" images per disc. They are stored in the Kodak Photo CD format.

Please check out the sample images inside the bundled CD-ROM. Our Photo CD library is constantly expanding. Please call us toll-free for a current list.

— —

Each title is only $99.00 each, plus $9.95 for Shipping and applicable sales tax for California residents.

- ❑ Everyday Objects Vol. 1
- ❑ Everyday Objects Vol. 2
- ❑ Everyday Objects Vol. 3
- ❑ Just Tools
- ❑ Just Hands
- ❑ Sampler
- ❑ Metaphorically Speaking
- ❑ Just Documents
- ❑ ALL SEVEN DISCS ($499)

Call 800.664.2623 to order with your credit card or mail your check, money order or credit information along with this coupon to: CMCD, Inc., 600 Townsend Street, Penthouse, San Francisco, CA, 94103 - or fax 510.732.5182

Enclosed is my ❑ check ❑ money order/Charge to my credit card ❑ VISA ❑ MC

No._____   Exp. Date _____

Offer expires September 1, 1995.

— —

DEBABELIZER SPECIAL OFFER!

DeBabelizer Lite -
Special Photo CD Handbook Offer - $89
Save $40!
DeBabelizer Toolbox -
Special Photo CD Handbook Offer - $299
Save $100!

DeBabelizer Lite - the easy to use Graphics Translator.
- Translates over 55 bit mapped cross-platform graphics formats.
- Full support for AppleScript and Adobe and 3rd party Acquire, Filter and Export plug-ins.
- Translates single images or folders of images.

DeBabelizer Toolbox - Graphics Processing and Translation for Macintosh.
- Translates over 60 bit mapped cross platform graphics and animation formats.
- Contains many image processing, compositing, editing, palette manipulation and color reduction options.
- Batch processing and internal scripting automate production tasks.
- Full support for AppleScript and Adobe and 3rd party Acquire, Filter and Export plug-ins.
- Filter interpolation allows plug-in Filters to be used for animation effects.
- Much, much more.

- -

❑ **Please send DeBabelizer Lite for $89 plus shipping/handling.**
❑ **Please send DeBabelizer Toolbox for $299 plus shipping/handling.**

Enclosed is my ❑ check ❑ money order/Charge to my credit card ❑ VISA ❑ MC
No._____ Exp. Date _____

Mail this coupon to:
EQUILIBRIUM, Dept. VER
475 Gate Five Road #225
Sausalito, CA 94965
800-524-8651 and mention sales code VER. Offer expires September 1, 1995.

- -

10% OFF VERBUM BOOKS ON DIGITAL CREATIVITY!
ENJOY OTHER DESIGN PUBLICATIONS FROM VERBUM!

Multimedia Power Tools by Peter Jerram, Michael Gosney, and the editors of Verbum, contains 670 pages on how to do multimedia and 670 megabytes of animated, interactive tutorials on real-world projects by top producers—plus software from leading suppliers such as Macromedia, Strata, Apple, and Adobe. 8" x 9-1/4", 670 pp. with Mac CD-ROM, requires color Mac with 5 MB RAM, $50.00.

The Desktop Color Book, by Michael Gosney and Linnea Dayton, was produced with technical support from Eastman Kodak, Pantone and QMS. This concise, accurate, lushly-illustrated volume is the single most complete source of information on this complex topic. Completely updated, the expanded edition features a 50-page Verbum Gallery of exemplary color work from top digital artists. 10" x 8", 128 pp., full color, $19.95.

The Photo CD Book is a technically accurate, beautifully designed book that covers all aspects of Photo CD technology, products and services for use in photography, graphic design, presentations, publishing and multimedia. Developed by Verbum and the Eastman Kodak Photo CD team. 9" x 7", 64 pp., full color, $14.95.

The Gray Book, Second Edition, is a cornucopia of information and examples, showing how to achieve effective designs and illustrations with one color. The book contains over 250 computer-generated designs and illustrations by some of the top artists in the field, with tips on how the works were accomplished. 9.25" x 7.5", 224 pp. $22.95.

- -

❑ **Multimedia Power Tools - $45.00 (reg. $50.00)**
❑ **The Desktop Color Book - 2nd Edition - $17.95 (reg. $19.95)**
❑ **The Photo CD Book - $13.45 (reg. $14.95)**
❑ **The Gray Book - 2nd Edition - $20.65 (reg. $22.95)**

Enclosed is my ❑ check/money order or charge to my credit card
❑ VISA ❑ MC   No._____ Exp. Date_____
CA residents add 7.75% or applicable sales tax. $3.00 shipping/handling for first item, $1.50 each additional item.

Mail this coupon to:
VERBUM
P.O. Box 189
Cardiff-by-the-Sea, CA 92007
619.944.9977
619.944.9995 (fax)

- -